MINDFUL WORKBOOK FOR WOMEN

MW00947868

Second Edition

MINDFUL WORKBOOK FOR WOMEN

*Domestic Violence Group
Treatment Program*

Second Edition

Participant Workbook

WENDY W. COATES

All material in this book is protected by copyright. To reproduce or adapt it, in whole or in part, for any purpose whatsoever, by any means, including photocopying, reprinting, or any form of computer storage or programming, is a violation of copyright law.

Disclaimer: This workbook is intended as a general information resource. No technique is guaranteed to be safe and effective in all circumstances, and the author cannot guarantee any particular exercise's accuracy, efficacy, or appropriateness in every respect. All examples in this book are fictitious.

Copyright © 2018, 2019, 2023 Wendy W. Coates

Mindful Workbook for Women
Domestic Violence Group Treatment Program
Copyright © 2018 Wendy W. Coates

For more information on bulk purchase orders or program implementation, visit
https://www.facebook.com/treatment.program/

All Rights Reserved.

Library of Congress Control Number: 2016920546

ISBN: 978-1981992119

Material adapted from
Emotionally Intelligent Batterer Intervention
Acceptance-Based, Cognitive Behavioral Domestic Violence Group Treatment Manual
by Wendy W. Coates Copyright © 2017

PRINTED IN THE UNITED STATES OF AMERICA

Contents

Contents

Introduction

Mindful Workbook for Women is a domestic violence intervention participant workbook. Adapted for implementation efficacy, the *Second Edition* integrates ten years of participant feedback and utilization review. This is a trauma-informed, acceptance-based program.

Domestic abuse treatment is often the first counseling experience for many of our participants. Before attending your first meeting, you may experience a variety of emotions. Some people feel anxious or resentful, while others express interest and curiosity. Regardless of your feelings, you likely have questions about what to expect. Many people enter therapy with the false assumption that the therapist will fix their problems and tell them what to do, but it's helpful to think of a therapist as a guide or a coach. Imagine that you want to summit Mount Everest. You are an avid hiker, and it is your dream to achieve this goal. People who take on an expedition like this are capable but will not make the perilous journey alone. Instead, they will join a group led by an experienced guide. The guide cannot climb the mountain for you; each individual will do the hard work. The guide is simply there to share information, provide direction, and reduce high-risk mistakes along the way. <u>Whether you reach your goal is entirely up to you.</u>

The group facilitator will set the pace. Depending upon your program, you may watch the videos and complete the assignments together or be required to do them as homework. Regardless, you will get out of the program what you put into it. This manual is formatted for an open group, which allows participants to join at any stage. One of the many benefits of an open group is that the more advanced participants become resources for the newest members. Participation is essential; you are encouraged to share your thoughts and feelings. The group is a nonjudgmental environment that fosters attachment security. Much of your progress will occur outside the meetings, and the assignments will be written and experiential. To get the most benefit, think of yourself as a scientist experimenting with different formulas to find the successful combination to reach your goals. If you are happy with your life, then your formula is working for you. If you are not comfortable with your current reality or are running into trouble, it's time to consider changing. A successful scientist won't continue to combine the same compounds and expect a different result. During this program, allow yourself to be a curious observer, let go of judgment, and practice a new way of being.

STOP: <u>Before you attend your first meeting, turn to page 12 and complete the *Quick Note to Your Future Self.*</u> **During your introduction, you will share this note with the group**. On your graduation day, you will share your *Letter of Self-Compassion*.

What we think, we become.

Buddha

Chapter 1
Mindfulness Training

You have many habits that weaken you. The secret of change is to focus all your energy not on fighting the old, but on building the new.

~ Socrates

You cannot suffer the past or the future because they do not exist. What you are suffering is your memory and your imagination.

~ Sadhguru

Whatever is happening at this moment, that is your life. The future is not your life; it never arrives. What is actually here is always only this moment.

~ A. H. Almaas

You live most of your life inside your head. Make sure it's a nice place to be.

~ Unknown

For what you do to others, you do to yourself.

~ Eckhart Tolle

❖   Fact vs. Fiction

❖   Gaining Personal Agency

❖   Note to Your Future-Self

Mindfulness

Mindfulness is the ability to focus your attention on the present moment and observe thoughts and feelings as they come and go without judgment or resistance. Every time you have a feeling, there is a thought connected to it. When you pay attention to what you're thinking, you have control over your thoughts. If you don't pay attention to your thinking, you'll remain on autopilot. Most of us are unaware of the **thought** <———> **feeling** connection, and this lack of awareness leads to the inaccurate assumption that all of our experiences are reality-based. Each of us is *actively creating* our reality through the story we tell ourselves. Reality does not just happen to us; our thoughts create our reality. Feelings do not just happen; we actively produce feelings with our thinking.

Fact vs. Fiction

Fact vs. Fiction is a tool used to uncover your autopilot. Gaining awareness that thoughts produce emotions is personal agency. *Example*: A teacher is standing in front of her classroom, directing aggressive comments toward the entire class, rather than just one particular kid. She yells, "I've never dealt with such an awful group of kids! I can't wait until this year is over. They don't pay me enough to deal with this crap!"

There are thirty different students in this classroom who witness the same stressful event. Even though these students are all experiencing the same event (*fact*), their reality is independently created by the story they tell themselves (*fiction*). Each student's narrative leads directly to their emotional response. Read the thoughts below, and identify the feelings:

1. One student **thinks**, "Oh no, maybe I did something wrong. Maybe I'm the reason the teacher is so upset. It's all my fault." This student **feels**: _____

2. A second student **thinks**, "She has no right to treat us like this! It's not our fault she sucks at her job. She better get fired for this!" This student **feels**: _____

3. A third student **thinks**, "When people yell like this, they usually start throwing things. I'm too far from the door. How do I get out of here?" This student **feels**: _____

4. A fourth student **thinks**, "Look at this crazy teacher losing it! This is freaking awesome! Where's my phone? I want a video!" This student **feels**: _____

5. A fifth student **thinks**, "My teachers always hate me. I thought this year might be different, but nothing will ever change for me." This student **feels**: _____

6. A sixth student **feels** *empathy*; create a **thought** that leads to this feeling: _____

_____

7. A seventh student **feels** *gratitude*; create a **thought** that leads to this feeling: _____

_____

Each student in the class witnesses the same stressful event (*fact*), but each student has their own thoughts about it (*fiction*). **What they think about the event leads to how they feel**. The teacher can't *make* the students feel anything; their feelings come directly from their thinking. Gaining awareness of the **thought <——> feeling** connection is critical for emotional regulation and personal agency.

Feelings Follow Fiction*

You're at a friend's party, talking to someone you met for the first time. As you talk with her, you notice she avoids making eye contact with you (*fact*). Instead of making eye contact, she appears to be scanning the room. Your **thoughts** (*fiction*) about her behavior will lead to your **feelings**. Circle the feeling that follows each thought:

Fiction #1: "Maybe she's trying to get me to leave her alone; I hope I didn't offend her."
   Feeling: Angry   Anxious   Sad   Compassion

Fiction #2: "She's a snob! She thinks she's too good for me."
   Feeling: Angry   Anxious   Sad   Compassion

Fiction #3: "She must be really shy; maybe she struggles with social anxiety."
   Feeling: Angry   Anxious   Sad   Compassion

Fiction #4: "I bet she thinks I'm boring. Everyone thinks I'm boring; everyone avoids me."
   Feeling: Angry   Anxious   Sad   Compassion

Notice how other people don't have control over your feelings. Your feelings come directly from the story you tell yourself. To produce feelings of compassion, you must remove yourself from the equation using healthy boundaries: "She must be really shy; maybe she struggles with social anxiety." Personalizing produces anger and intolerance.

Video: Success Archive (2019). "Dr. Joe Dispenza: How Your Thoughts Are Connected To Your Future."
https://youtu.be/5reo3dXOicU **(13:34)**
Discussion: Dispenza states, "You think sixty to seventy thousand thoughts in one day, and ninety percent of those thoughts are the same as the day before. The same thoughts lead to the same choices, the same choices lead to the same behavior, the same behaviors create the same experiences, the same experiences produce the same emotions, and those same emotions drive the same thoughts. How you think, how you act and how you feel is called your personality, and your personality creates your personal reality. To create a new life, you would have to look at the emotions you live by every day and decide if they belong in your future. Nerve cells that fire together wire together. As you fire and wire the same circuits in the same way, they become more connected. By the time we're thirty-five years old, we become a set of memorized behaviors, unconscious habits, automatic emotional reactions, beliefs, perceptions, and attitudes that function just like a computer program… Don't respond to thoughts as if they are true."

1.) Identify some of the problem areas of your autopilot:

2.) Share an example of how your fiction is maintaining your problem pattern:

*Concept adapted from Greenberger and Padesky (2015).

Internal Dialogue Practice

Why do some of us have patterned thinking that produces chronic anger or anxiety while others have a baseline of contentment? We develop thought patterns during our younger years. The way our caregivers' process information becomes our way of thinking. The good news is that you can rewire your brain at any stage. Overriding patterned thinking is brain rewiring. Humans are habitual, and most of us think and act on autopilot. <u>Mindfulness is a state of awareness that defeats autopilot because it teaches you to allow thoughts and feelings to come and go.</u> Don't believe everything you think! Thoughts are just thoughts. <u>As you complete the exercises below, identify your internal dialogue and create a personal example:</u>

1.) Your child is having a loud tantrum in public. How you feel in this situation will uncover your internal dialogue:

Thought #1: "I'm failing as a parent." **You feel**: _____

Thought #2: "Everyone is looking at us. I can't believe he's doing this here." **You feel**: _____

Thought #3: "My kid is two years old; he's just being a two-year-old." **You feel**: _____

Thought #4: "He's such an entitled brat. We are raising a little monster." **You feel**: _____

Thought #5: "He must be exhausted. We've been going all day." **You feel**: _____

Thought #6: _____

_____ **You feel**: _____

2.) As you walk into a room full of people, you trip and fall on your face! Everyone turns to look. As you recover from the shock, the story you tell yourself will reveal your patterned thinking. Falling on your face is a stressful life event, but will your *fiction* take a bad situation and make it worse or better? When the *facts* of a situation are not changeable, your only control is your *fiction*. <u>Read the feelings below and create a thought that leads to each feeling.</u> <u>Then, create a personal example:</u>

Thought #1:_____
You feel: **embarrassed**

Thought #2:_____
You feel: **angry**

Thought #3:_____
You feel: **grateful**

Thought #4: _____

_____ **You feel**: _____

Present Moment

Our feelings provide clues to what we're thinking. Let's say you ask your friend, "How are you feeling today?" Your friend's emotional response will give you clues about their thoughts. If your friend's answer is, "I feel a little anxious." This response tells you that their thoughts are *future-focused*. Thoughts focusing on the future produce uncomfortable feelings such as worry, fear, anxiety, or dread. We have no control over the future, so when we think about what may or may not occur, we produce a fear response. In our classroom example, notice how the future-oriented thinker produced feelings of anxiety: "When people yell like this, they usually start throwing things. I'm too far from the door. How do I get out of here?" This student produced a fear response with their future-focused thoughts. People who struggle with chronic anxiety have future-focused thought patterns. **Anxious individuals spend very little time in the present moment**. As a society, we frequently encourage anxious thinking patterns in our children. *Example*: A young child slowly puts on his shoes while happily exploring the bright colors. The parent says, "Okay, let's get moving. Put your shoes on; let's go! We've got to run to the store and get back in time for your sister. The clock is ticking!" Without realizing it, we're teaching our children anxiety at a young age.

Share a **future-focused** (*"What if…"*) thought that produces anxiety, overwhelm, or dread:

Correct your future-focused thought by creating a **present-moment acceptance** thought:
> *Example*: "That's for my future self, not my today self. I'm going to wait and see."

Let's say that your friend's response is, "I feel a little down." This response tells you that your friend's thoughts focus on the *past*. Thoughts that focus our attention on the past produce uncomfortable feelings of sadness, regret, guilt, or shame. When we focus on the past, we place ourselves in a situation outside our control. In our classroom example, notice the emotional responses produced by the past-oriented thinkers: "Oh no, maybe I did something wrong; maybe I'm the reason the teacher is so upset. It's all my fault," and "My teachers always hate me. I thought this year might be different, but nothing will ever change for me." These students produced emotional responses of sadness, shame, or guilt. **Individuals who struggle with chronic depression spend much of their time thinking about the past**. Depression thoughts often sound like, "I shouldn't have done that. What's wrong with me? I've never been able to do anything right. Nothing will change." The thought processes of future-thinkers and past-thinkers focus on situations outside our control, and feelings of safety come from a sense of control.

Share a **past-focused** thought that produces regret, sadness, resentment, or shame (*"Should of," "Would of," "Could of"*):

Correct your past-focused thought by creating a **present-moment acceptance** thought:
> *Example*: "My past self was doing the best they could. I will not judge what I can't change."

Where does our control lie? What is the only time that exists? **The *present* moment is the only time that exists**. Five minutes ago is gone, and five minutes from now does not exist. One of the most effective ways to regulate emotions and produce feelings of peace and contentment is to focus your attention on the *facts* of the present moment. *Example*: When I'm feeling anxious about an upcoming meeting, bringing my focus to the *facts* of the present will reduce the anxiety. "What am I doing right now? Right now, I'm making coffee. I can handle making my coffee." When my thoughts focus on the future meeting, anxiety walks in the door and overwhelms me. When I return my thoughts to the present, I increase my sense of control and reduce anxiety. **Practice**: Bring your attention to the *now* by observing present sensations:

∼ Notice the contact between your feet and the floor…	∼ Notice the temperature of the air against your face…
∼ Notice the contact between your clothes and your skin…	∼ Notice how your lungs expand with your next inhale…

Video: TEDx (2012). "Shawn Achor: The Happy Secret to Better Work." https://youtu.be/fLJsdqxnZb0 **(12:20)**
Discussion: Achor states, "What we're finding is that it's not reality that shapes us, it's the lens through which your brain views the world that shapes your reality. And if we can change the lens, not only can we change our happiness, we can change every single educational and business outcome at the same time. It's assumed that our external world is predictive of our happiness level, but in reality, if I know everything about your external world, I can only predict ten percent of your long-term happiness. Ninety percent of your long-term happiness is predicted not by the external world, but by the way your brain processes the world. And if we change our formula for happiness and success, we can change the way we affect reality. We found that only twenty-five percent of job success is predicted by IQ, and seventy-five percent of job success is predicted by your optimism level, your social support, and your ability to see stress as a challenge instead of as a threat. We need to reverse the formula for happiness and success. We think we have to be successful to be happier, but our brains work in the opposite order. If we can find a way to become positive in the present, our brains work more successfully because dopamine floods into our system when we're positive. Dopamine has two functions, not only does it make you happier, it turns on all of the learning centers in your brain allowing you to adapt to the world in a different way. In just two-minutes a day for 21 days in a row, you can actually rewire your brain to become more positive:"
1.) Write down **three new things** you are **grateful** for each day. **2.) Journal** about **one positive experience** you've had during the past 24 hours. **3.) Exercise** teaches your brain that your behavior matters. **4.) Meditation** allows your brain to focus on the task at hand. **5.)** Random **acts of kindness**.
Practice: Follow the five-step formula each day this week and share your experience with the group.

Practice Brain Rewiring

Repeatedly practicing something new produces change. You can train your brain to focus on the present moment by intentionally redirecting your attention to the here and now. Simply ask yourself, "What am I doing right now? What am I thinking right now? What am I feeling right now? What are the sights, sounds, smells, and experiences surrounding me?" Practice bringing your attention to the present moment throughout each day. The more you practice, the easier it will become. Anytime you feel uncomfortable, ask yourself, "What am I thinking right now?" Focusing on the present is the first step of emotional regulation. **Changing your thinking leads to changes in your feelings**. You cannot snap your fingers and make a feeling disappear, but you can correct your thoughts to change your emotions. The biggest struggle for most of us is that we believe that the environment is creating our feelings. Read each scenario below. Use the feeling word as a guide and create a thought to produce each feeling.

---

1. Your son gets home from spending the weekend with your ex and says, "I had the best weekend ever!"

Thought #1: _____

You feel: **jealous**

Thought #2: _____

You feel: **worried**

Thought #3: _____

You feel: **relieved**

---

2. Your partner gets home from an AA meeting and says, "These meetings are changing my life!"

Thought #1: _____

You feel: **sad**

Thought #2: _____

You feel: **frustrated**

Thought #3: _____

You feel: **grateful**

---

3. Your partner tells you, "I'm ready to start a family, and if you can't commit, I'm moving on."

Thought #1: _____

You feel: **anxious**

Thought #2: _____

You feel: **angry**

Thought #3: _____

You feel: **excited**

---

4. Your partner tells you they want to try a temporary separation to help the marriage.

Thought #1: _____

You feel: **hurt**

Thought #2: _____

You feel: **betrayed**

Thought #3: _____

You feel: **relieved**

5. After months of working overtime, your boss tells you that you are underperforming compared to your peers.

Thought #1: _____

You feel: **resentful**

Thought #2: _____

You feel: **concerned**

Thought #3: _____

You feel: **motivated**

6. You confront your teen after you find alcohol in their backpack. Your teen repeatedly assures you it's not theirs; it belongs to their friends.

Thought #1: _____

You feel: **furious**

Thought #2: _____

You feel: **afraid**

Thought #3: _____

You feel: **thankful**

Mindful Practice Example

You have an important job interview, and you're feeling very nervous. Anytime you think about the interview, you're overwhelmed with anxiety. You know that you're qualified, yet you're filled with fear. On the morning of the interview, your heart is racing, and your breathing is rapid. You can't catch your breath, feeling like you might vomit. Then, you remember that feelings of safety come from focusing on the present moment. You actively bring your thoughts to the present by focusing on the minute details each step of the way: When taking a shower, you focus on the temperature of the water, the smell of the soap, and the water droplets running down the shower walls. When getting dressed, you focus on the texture of the material and the fresh smell of clean clothes. When driving your car, you focus on how the steering wheel feels in your hands and how your body feels sitting in the driver's seat. After you park, you allow yourself to notice your surroundings. You observe the colors of the leaves, the temperature of the air, the feeling of the light breeze, the architecture of the surrounding buildings, and the smell of the crisp fall morning. As you walk to the front door of the building, you focus on opening the door. What does the door handle feel like in your hands? **Staying in the present will keep you feeling calm and safe. Anxiety walks in the door as soon as your thoughts drift to the future**: "What if they don't like me? What if I say the wrong thing? What if I don't get this job? What if I mess up? How will I pay my bills?" The present moment is where your control lies. Intentionally focusing on the *facts* of the present leads to feelings of peace, contentment, and security.

Observer Stance - One of the best methods for managing uncomfortable emotions is to take the observer role. The observer is a nonreactive witness who gathers information without judgment or resistance. When you're emotionally flooded, the feeling pushes you to act, and acting while under the influence of emotions often leads to regret. To be a curious observer, follow these steps:

1. **Collect data with curiosity**: Stay with the *facts* rather than *fiction*. Don't judge, resist, or assume. *Example*: "My partner is yelling at me right now. They clearly have strong feelings because their voice is loud, and their face looks angry."

2. **Follow your feelings to your thinking**: If my body is in fight-or-flight mode, my thoughts are encouraging anger or fear. What am I thinking right now? *Example*: "I'm angry because I don't want them to yell. I want them to change."

3. **What is the emotion encouraging you to say or do**? While the feeling pushes you in a specific direction, you decide what you say and do. Don't let the emotion control you. *Example*: "The anger is pushing me to attack. Anger is telling me to make it stop."

4. **Stay in the present moment**: Notice the natural process of breathing. You'll ride emotional rollercoasters when you focus on the *future* or *past*. *Example*: "I'm focusing on the contact between my feet and the floor. I can feel my heart racing, and my breathing is rapid. I'm breathing into the physical discomfort. I will not let anger make decisions for me."

Homework - Choose a stressful situation over the next week and complete the steps:

1. **Collect data with curiosity**: _____

_____

_____

_____

2. **Follow your feelings to your thinking**: _____

_____

_____

3. **What is the emotion encouraging you to say or do**? _____

_____

_____

4. **Stay in the present moment**: _____

_____

_____

Note to Your Future Self - Write a note to your future self describing what you hope to gain from this program. Once you complete the program, look back at this note to see how far you've come.

Example: "Dear Future Me: I hope you can learn to slow down and stop overthinking. You've been resentful for a long time, and I want you to find peace in your life. I also hope you finally make a decision about your relationship. The back and forth is miserable for everyone, including your children, and you feel lost and stuck. I wish you clarity, strength, and peace."

Describe the recent struggles that led to your enrollment in this program:

_____

_____

_____

_____

_____

_____

Write a letter to your future self sharing your goals. Describe what you would like your life to look like when you complete this program. What specifically do you need to work on to achieve these goals?

_____

_____

_____

_____

_____

_____

_____

_____

_____

_____

_____

_____

_____

_____

_____

_____

_____

_____

Chapter 2
Deconstructing Abuse

Don't let the behavior of others destroy your inner peace.
~ *Dalai Lama*

No one is born hating another person because of the color of his skin, or his background, or his religion. People must learn to hate, and if they can learn to hate, they can be taught to love, for love comes more naturally to the human heart than its opposite.
~ *Nelson Mandela*

Darkness cannot drive out darkness; only light can do that.
Hate cannot drive out hate; only love can do that.
~ *Martin Luther King, Jr.*

People will forget what you said, people will forget what you did, but people will never forget how you made them feel.
~ *Maya Angelou*

Hurt people hurt people.
~ *Will Bowen*

❖ Abuse Thrives in Silence

❖ Hurt People Hurt People

❖ Types of Abuse

Self-Compassion

This chapter is often an eye-opener for many people as they discover that they have been *both* a victim and someone who has used abusive coping strategies. Many people engage in abuse because they don't know their behavior is abusive, and victims often don't realize they're being abused. This chapter can be challenging, and the emotions that arise can produce defensive coping strategies. If you find yourself feeling frustrated while reading this chapter, gently remind yourself to maintain a stance of curiosity and acceptance. Allow yourself to be a nonjudgmental observer and identify your history of abuse and victimization.

Video: TEDx (2018). "Chiara Lisowski: Survivor Domestic Abuse Speaks Up - I Left on a Tuesday." https://youtu.be/hWlN6Jf0WzQ (12:48)

Discussion: Lisowski states, "The abuser gradually chips away at the person's self-esteem, convincing them they are responsible for the abusive actions. They gradually isolate you from friends and family, making you believe that the only world that matters is the private world you share together. The good times are very high, and the bad times gradually get lower. I was absolutely convinced that the whole thing was my fault and that I needed to fix it. I was deeply ashamed, and I hid my reality from everyone and myself. My self-esteem had become so eroded that simple decisions became impossible. I became a sad shadow of my former self. I didn't even realize I was being abused… When you endure so much violence on a regular basis, and in such an unpredictable way, it makes you feel physically and mentally drained. To survive, you just try to hide the evidence and get through each day as normally as possible until you don't know what normal is anymore… I finally said the words out loud and broke my silence that I was being abused."

1.) Why does abuse thrive in silence?

Defining Abuse

There are five broad categories of abuse: physical, sexual, emotional, verbal, and financial. Within these categories, there are subgroups. In most unhealthy relationships, multiple forms are present. There are many warning signs indicating that you are in an abusive relationship. The most telling warning sign is **fear**. You are likely involved in an unhealthy relationship if you chronically feel like you're **walking on eggshells**. Other signs include a partner who belittles you or encourages feelings of self-loathing. **Healthy relationships add value to your life and make you feel comfortable and confident**. It's a significant warning sign if you do not feel good about yourself with your partner.

Many relationships are mutually abusive, and survivors are male and female. According to the National Institute of Health, domestic violence is the single greatest cause of injury to women. According to the Childhood Domestic Violence Association, children who grow up with domestic violence are six times more likely to commit suicide, fifty percent more likely to abuse drugs and alcohol, and 74 percent more likely to commit violent crimes (February 21, 2014).

Given the trauma history of our participants, many will naturally identify with the victim as we deconstruct these different forms of abuse. Healing our wounds comes from processing our trauma history. It's beneficial to allow yourself to identify your victimization and your controlling behaviors. Approaching this information with acceptance is critical because most individuals who use abusive coping strategies are individuals who are suffering. Judgment, denial, minimization, and blame will keep you stuck in unhealthy patterns.

Hurt people hurt people. ~ Will Bowen

1.) What does this quote mean to you? Think about the last time you hurt someone. How were you feeling at that time? Common emotions that trigger controlling behaviors include *fear, insecurity, shame,* and *rejection*. <u>What were vulnerable feelings present for you</u>?

2.) Most of us do not want to be alone with emotional pain. Abusive coping strategies are used to transfer one's discomfort to others. <u>Misery loves company</u>. To stop hurting others, we need to heal ourselves. <u>What is a statement of self-compassion you can use when you are hurting</u>?

3.) How does this quote increase your tolerance and insight? <u>How can you use the mantra, "Hurt people hurt people," when others display anger</u>?

Video: TEDx (2020). "Andrew Pain: Domestic Abuse: Not a Gender Issue." https://youtu.be/9HgPICMQLls (12:35)

Discussion: Pain states, "I honestly believed it was all my fault and that if I didn't keep provoking her, then she wouldn't keep getting mad at me, and the violence would stop. I could never find the magic answer for being that better husband who didn't provoke his wife. <u>Shame is a terrible thing; it is an effective silencer. Leaving is not as simple as it sounds because abusers rob you of your confidence, optimism, and support networks so that when you are in it, you can't see beyond it, and you're just surviving day by day</u>… Domestic abuse is not a man versus women issue; it is a human issue. If we are serious about tackling it, we must encourage women and men to come forward with their stories. I'm at peace about what happened because I've chosen to forgive. I trained myself over time to see every situation which involves my ex-wife not through the eyes of a bitter victim but through the eyes of a wise and external observer detached from the raw emotion. <u>If you're caught in an abusive relationship, the first step is to talk to someone you trust. Don't suffer in silence due to shame, pride, or fear</u>."

1.) <u>Think about a time when you have hidden a problem from others. Why did you stay silent?</u>

2.) <u>Did the silence keep the problem in place? Has silence extended an unhealthy relationship for you?</u>

Physical Abuse is using force against someone in any way that injures, endangers, or threatens that person. <u>Any unwanted touch can be considered physical abuse</u>. Violence is one of the most common forms, and the person who uses violence may suffer legal consequences.

Physical Abuse Example:
Shawna wanted to leave the room to avoid the conflict, but her partner wanted to continue the discussion. Her partner blocked the only exit and refused to move. Shawna couldn't take it anymore, so she pushed her way out, and her partner landed on the floor.

Share examples of **physical abuse**:

Intimidation is a subgroup of physical abuse that may not involve physical contact but can hold the same legal consequences. <u>Intimidation is any threat of harm that risks someone's safety or freedom</u>. Nonverbal posturing, facial expressions, or hostile gestures are abusive tactics to maintain control over others. Common intimidation tactics include: throwing objects, punching walls, standing over someone, pointing in someone's face, making violent gestures, displaying weapons, threatening suicide, or destroying property.

Intimidation Example:
While arguing with her partner at the kitchen table, Riley felt like she wasn't being heard. She became more and more frustrated as her partner interrupted her. When she reached her breaking point, she violently slammed her fist against the table to scare her partner into silence.

Share examples of **tactics of intimidation**:

Verbal Abuse is any degrading, threatening, devaluing, dominating, or verbally demeaning behavior. <u>Name-calling with a tone of disgust is a common form</u>. Victims of chronic verbal abuse can feel intense fear, anger, self-loathing, shame, depression, and hopelessness. Verbal abuse can damage a person's sense of self and lead to suicidal ideation.

Verbal Abuse Example:
Alicia feels like she is never good enough. If she's late, she's called 'unreliable.' If she's early, she's 'lazy.' If she plays with the children, she's 'immature.' If she doesn't, she's a 'negligent parent.' She's belittled if she shows emotion and a 'narcissist' if she doesn't. Her partner threatens to divorce her when she complains about the negative labels. She feels stuck, depressed, and hopeless in the marriage.

Share examples of **verbal abuse**:

Emotional/Psychological Abuse is any act used to control a person by diminishing their sense of identity or value. Emotional abuse erodes a person's sense of self until they feel lost in the relationship. The effects of emotional abuse are devastating and can be even more damaging than physical abuse. Emotional abuse aims to chip away at a person's self-worth, leading to insecure dependence on the partner. Victims may feel like there is no way out of the relationship or that they are nothing without their partner. More often than not, controlling partners endure emotional abuse as children, and as adults, they continue the cycle. The controlling partner tends to struggle with low self-esteem and an unrecognized dependence on the victim. Tactics used to gain control over a partner are attempts to reduce one's chronic fear. Tactics of emotional abuse encourage partners to distrust their view of reality and frequently blame themselves for the abuse they have suffered. Common forms include gaslighting, blaming, accusing, guilting, shaming, humiliating, manipulating, lying, and denying.

Gaslighting Example:
Liv mentioned she'd be home around five o'clock when leaving for work. When she arrived home around seven o'clock, her partner asked what had happened. Liv appeared confused, "What do you mean? I told you I'd be home late tonight. You don't listen to people, and that's why you have no friends." Liv's partner walks away from this conversation, feeling unsure, insecure, hurt, and ashamed.

Share examples of **emotional/psychological abuse**:

Share an example of **gaslighting**:

Sexual Abuse involves controlling the sexual relationship and coercing physical contact. Any sexually demeaning or humiliating behavior is abuse. Any situation in which a person is forced, intimidated, or manipulated into unwanted, unsafe, or degrading sexual activity is abuse. Victims who suffer both physical and sexual abuse are at a higher risk of being seriously injured or killed. When thinking of sexual abuse, people tend to think of rape and violence. More subtle forms include threatening infidelity, guilting, humiliation, degrading performance, or coercive shaming.

Sexual Abuse Example:
When around friends, Mia's partner criticizes her lack of sexual desire. When home alone, her partner threatens infidelity unless Mia submits to demands. After intimacy, her partner degrades her performance.

Share examples of **sexual abuse**, including subtle forms:

Animal Abuse is a subgroup of physical and emotional abuse. "Animal cruelty is linked directly or indirectly with every violent crime and even with most nonviolent crime" (Hovel, 2015). **Animal abuse is a crime in every state.** <u>According to the Humane Society of the United States, research studies show that pet abuse is one of four predictors of domestic violence and child abuse.</u> Animal cruelty is eleven times more likely in homes with domestic violence, and **witnessing animal cruelty in childhood is the greatest predictor of violence in adulthood** (Hovel, 2015). Partners who hurt animals are more likely to maliciously wound or kill their victims. When children witness violence in their homes, they are at increased risk of acting violently toward animals. Animals are abused to create an environment of fear, as tactics of control, and as displacement of anger. Abusing animals in the home creates a culture of normalized violence. Some common examples include chaining, abandonment, excessive crating, and starvation.

Animal Abuse Example:

When Zara was a child, her parents would threaten to give her dog away as a punishment. When that threat stopped working, they would harm the dog if Zara disobeyed. Zara lived with the constant fear that her compliance and submission were the only way to keep her dog safe.

Share examples of **tactics of control using children or animals**:

Financial Abuse is a common tactic used to gain control. This form of abuse may be subtle, but generally, it limits the partner's financial access and keeps them in a dependent position. <u>Research indicates that financial abuse is experienced in 99 percent of abusive relationships and is the leading cause of staying in or returning to the relationship</u> (NNEDV, 2015). Without assets, survivors often cannot provide for themselves and their children. As with all forms of abuse, financial abuse may progress over time. Subtle forms include providing an allowance, hiding assets, denying access to funds, shutting off credit cards, checking receipts, or manipulating partners into staying home full-time.

Financial Abuse Example:

Lila is not allowed access to the bank account because her partner says she is not good with money. She must seek permission before making a purchase, and if her partner disapproves, she's forced to make returns. If she wants to go out with friends, her cards are shut off to keep her home. She is guilted, harassed, and manipulated into quitting her job because childcare is too expensive.

Share examples of **financial abuse**:

Chapter 3
Cycle of Abuse

You are not stuck. You are just committed to certain patterns of behavior because they've helped you in the past. Now, those behaviors have become more harmful than helpful. The reason why you can't move forward is because you keep applying an old formula to a new level in your life. Change the formula to get a different result.

~ Emily Maroutian

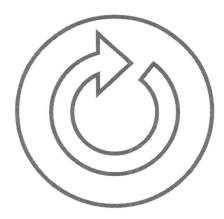

❖ Signs of Emotional Abuse

❖ Cycle Core: Denial, Blame, Fear, and Hope

❖ Catch/Correct Mantras

Acceptance

Individuals often struggle with abusive coping strategies because they are unaware that their behavior is abusive. This chapter focuses on identifying the cycle of abuse, and most who participate in this program find this cycle to be familiar. <u>Adults who use abusive coping strategies are overwhelmingly likely to have been abused as children, and the cycle of violence repeats</u> (Hovel, 2015). <u>According to the US Department of Justice, Bureau of Justice Statistics (2015), over eighty percent of men who abuse their partners grew up in violent homes.</u>

Video 1: Psych2go (2020): "14 Signs of Emotional Abuse in Relationships." https://youtu.be/rFHWnAn9ULk (4:13)

Video 2: Gibbons (2020): "Mark'd Award Winning Emotional Abuse Short Film." https://youtu.be/EavMqZ_6UvQ (6:45)

Video 3: Made by Mortals (2023): "Eggshells: A Short Film About Domestic Abuse." https://youtu.be/YlHxhmOsrHo (5:16)

Discussion: Emotional abuse is often **invisible** because it does not leave marks. Video 1 outlines 14 signs, and Videos 2 and 3 creatively display the hidden wounds caused by emotional abuse. Share personal examples of each, and while watching, identify examples from the videos.

1.) Identify examples of **blame**:

2.) Identify examples of **walking on eggshells**:

3.) Identify examples of **pretending to be supportive**:

4.) Identify examples of **changing plans** to maintain control:

5.) Identify examples of **shifting from emotionally available to distant**:

6.) Identify examples of **saying hurtful things and playing it off as a joke**:

7.) Identify examples of **making the partner guess**:

8.) Identify examples of **ignoring feelings**:

9.) Identify examples of **gaslighting**:

10.) Identify examples of **acting differently around others**:

11.) Identify examples of **using conditional love to manipulate**:

12.) Identify examples of **ignoring accomplishments**:

13.) Identify examples of **saying they are not being helpful**:

14.) Identify examples of **needing to know where the partner is at all times**:

Cycle Theory of Abuse

"Domestic violence is the single most important factor that creates violent individuals and perpetuates the cycle of abuse" (Hovel, 2015, p. 5). Domestic abuse typically follows a pattern, adapted from Lenore Walker (1979), consisting of three phases repeated in an abusive relationship. The cycle of violence applies to an abusive relationship regardless of gender.

Tension Stage

The cycle of abuse begins with the *tension stage*. This stage is marked by chronic hypervigilance on the part of the victim. The controlling partner is becoming more irritable, moody, and impatient while the victim feels like they are walking on eggshells. Some of the behaviors in the tension stage include: arguing, degrading, criticizing, intimidating, nitpicking, provoking, silent treatment, sarcasm, and hostility. Victims often feel the controlling partner is attempting to bait them into conflict. When the controlling partner successfully elicits a response, they use it to turn the tables and play the victim. The duration of the tension stage is unpredictable; it can be brief, or it can last for months. Rather than holding the partner accountable, the victim may blame outside factors or themselves. The victim's fear may lead to accommodating behaviors to prevent violence, but the controlling partner holds all the power and rapidly changes the relationship rules. **Most survivors are unaware that they are not responsible for the abuse and hold false hope that they can somehow prevent it**. With blame, the survivor is more likely to remain in the relationship. While the violence may be relatively minor during this stage, this is a high-risk time for the victim because the tension stage is the road leading to the explosion.

Provide examples of your experience in the **tension stage**:

Explosion Stage

An increase in the severity of abuse characterizes the *explosion stage*. This acute stage can last anywhere from a few minutes to a few days. The end of the explosion stage can be unpredictable, and it can abruptly end if someone needs medical care, if the victim escapes, or if the controlling partner walks away. After the explosion, the survivor often shows signs of trauma. The survivor may be unresponsive and silent or very angry and vocal. Common emotions the survivor feels at different recovery times include fear, anger, depression, and hopelessness. According to the National Domestic Violence Hotline, many survivors think about leaving. However, in most cases, it takes the survivor an average of seven cycles before they leave the relationship.

Provide examples of your experience in the **explosion stage**:

Post-Explosion Stage

The *post-explosion stage* is a time of reconnection. During this stage, the controlling partner often becomes loving and apologetic, shows remorse, begs forgiveness, and promises it will never happen again. The controlling partner may also try to make the survivor feel guilty for wanting to leave. <u>The survivor often fails to recognize that the purpose of this stage is to manipulate them into remaining in the relationship</u>. <u>According to the National Domestic Violence Hotline, leaving an abusive relationship is dangerous for the survivor. Approximately seventy-five percent of people killed by intimate partners are murdered when they attempt to leave or have left the relationship</u>. In most abusive relationships, the survivor does not have the means to leave. Isolation, economic control, and chronic devaluing manipulate the victim into a state of dependence. Victim blaming makes the survivor feel responsible for the violence. This stage ends when the tension stage slowly builds, and the cycle endlessly repeats.

> Provide examples of your experience in the **post-explosion stage**:

Three Common Characteristics of the Cycle*

1. The more times this cycle completes, the **shorter the cycle length**. *Example*: Early in the relationship, it may have taken a year to run through the cycle, but now it takes only a few weeks. Over time, the cycle will rapidly increase in frequency.
2. Each time the cycle repeats, the **severity of the violence increases**. *Example*: Early in the relationship, the violence included pushing, throwing objects, and threatening. Later, the violence includes punching, using weapons, restraining, and strangulation.
3. Each time the cycle repeats, the **length of the post-explosion stage shortens**. *Example*: Early in the relationship, the partner was remorseful, apologetic, and loving. Now, the controlling partner blames the victim for the violence, and the tension phase quickly returns.

> In what ways can you relate this cycle to your adult relationships or your childhood home?

Cycle Core

Denial, **blame**, **fear**, and **hope** are at the center of the abuse cycle. For the cycle to repeat, these four factors are usually present. The controlling partner will *deny* the abusive behaviors, while the victim will often do the same. Many survivors remain in the relationship because they do not know they are suffering abuse. Partners will deny the abuse due to feelings

---

* D. Sonkin and M. Durphy (1997).

of shame. <u>With denial on board, no change will occur, and the cycle will repeat.</u> *Blame* is another powerful distortion that keeps the abuse cycle spinning. <u>The controlling partner will blame the victim and outside factors, such as work, family, or financial stress.</u> The dominant partner often struggles with chronic *fear* and attachment insecurities, and they cope by gaining control of their partner. The ultimate fear is losing the victim, which is why the end of the relationship holds the highest fatality risk. The victim often copes with feelings of fear by accommodating, avoiding, or being defensive. *Hope* is the emotion that surfaces during the post-explosion stage. <u>The controlling partner may manipulate the survivor into blind hope through guilt, coercion, or religious moralizing.</u> Hope encourages the survivor to look for signs that the love will last.

Video: WPSU (2010): "Telling Amy's Story." https://youtu.be/TsFv4DiPKFg (15:09)

Discussion: This documentary portrays pervasive control and chronic fear found in some abusive relationships. While watching, identify your experience with insecurity and control, and look for examples of the **cycle core**. <u>Share examples from the video and personal examples</u>:

Denial: _____

Video Example: _____

Blame: _____

Video Example: _____

Fear: _____

Video Example: _____

Hope: _____

Video Example: _____

Mantra Homework

Take a curious stance this week. Step back from your interactions with others, and watch your thoughts and feelings as they come and go. Rather than acting on a thought, take a moment to ask yourself, "Is this helping me or hurting me?" <u>Don't believe everything you think; thoughts are just thoughts!</u> Apply *Catch/Correct*: catch the problem thought and correct it.

<u>Beliefs are formed through exposure.</u> Core beliefs develop from repeatedly thinking or receiving messages. Once a message is internalized, we act as if it is true. Consider some of the critical feedback you have received from others. *Example*: If you have received feedback that you are controlling, you may want to create a healthy boundary mantra, such as: "I decide for me, and you decide for you." Read the example mantras, and create your own. Consider your problem areas when creating your mantras. Repeat your mantra at least five times each day. <u>Read the example guiding mantras and create your own</u>:

Example Mantras

We are all of equal value.

I only have control over myself.

Every storm comes to an end.

It's okay not to be okay.

Comparison is the thief of joy.

Expectations lead to disappointment.

Sometimes not getting what we want is the gift.

That's for my future self, not my today self.

We are only given what we can handle.

My past self was doing the best they could.

Do I want to be right, or do I want to be happy?

We all take turns suffering; it's my turn.

Practice: Create three **mantras** that you will repeat to yourself at least <u>five times a day</u>:

1. _____

2. _____

3. _____

Homework - Catch/Correct is a tool used to rewire patterned thinking. Allowing a harmful thought to go uncorrected strengthens that pathway in your brain and increases the chance it will repeat. When you notice a problem thought, catch it and correct it.

Example Catch ————————————————> **Example Correct**

1. "No one ever appreciates me." ————> "I only have control over myself. Do I appreciate me?"

2. "I would never treat anyone like that." ————> "Comparison is the thief of joy. Stay in your lane."

3. "They should respect me." ————> "Expectations lead to disappointment. Let go of control."

Practice: Catch problem thoughts and practice correcting them:

Catch: _____

Correct: _____

Catch: _____

Correct: _____

Catch: _____

Correct: _____

Chapter 4
Identifying Warning Signs

The way out of our cage begins with accepting absolutely
everything about ourselves and our lives.
~ *Tara Brach*

It's not what you say to others that determines your life, it's what
you whisper to yourself that has the most power.
~ *Robert Kiyosaki*

When I ignore red flags, I might believe I'm giving the other person a chance,
but I'm actually ignoring my intuition.
~ *Yasmine Cheyenne*

Each morning we are born again, what we do today is what matters most.
~ *Buddha*

❖　　Identifying Red Flags

❖　　BELIEVE Model

❖　　Self-Care Practice

Red Flags

Red flags tell us that we are driving down the road leading to a high-risk situation. Knowing your cues is critical in ending the cycle of abuse. Suppose you know that some of your signs include a pounding heart, revenge thoughts, tunnel vision, rumination, and clenched fists. In that case, you will have the opportunity to intervene and initiate your de-escalation plan.

Gabby's Story Example

Read the story below and identify Gabby's **BELIEVE Model warning signs**. Underline any of Gabby's cues, red flags, triggers, and abusive behaviors.

He does this all the time; I'm not sure why I would expect it to be any different. I never get a break. I just want a partner, but instead, I have another child. All men think that everyone has to cater to them. As usual, I get home from running the kids everywhere, and he's sitting on the couch. He knows that I worked all day, he knows that I'm tired, and he knows that I will be home late. I do not understand why he would not think about starting dinner! Who sits on the couch doing nothing while their wife runs around doing everything? It's unbelievable! Most of the time, I just ignore him, and eventually, he realizes something is wrong. I don't know what happened that night, but I just couldn't stand it for another second. My stomach was turning, and I felt like I couldn't catch my breath. He's always on his phone, and I know something is happening. Either he's addicted to his stupid games or cheating because no one spends that much time on their phone. So I told the kids to go do their homework while I started dinner. But I couldn't do it; I could not cook dinner again while he just sat there. I could feel my heart pounding, and my face was getting hot. That's when I started shutting the cabinets as loud as possible. I wanted him to notice that I was upset. I expected him to check on me and maybe even offer to help, but instead, he just yelled at me to quiet down! That was my breaking point. I walked over to him, and he was still on his phone. I could see that he was texting someone, so I tried to grab it. I just wanted to see what he was doing. I have a right to know if something is going on. I was so angry! I just kept thinking I would never treat anyone the way he treated me. When I tried to grab the phone, he pulled his arm away. So I slapped him, but not hard. I just wanted him to give me the phone. His face got really angry, and I could tell he was trying to hide something. I grabbed the remote off the coffee table and threw it as hard as possible at him. That's when he stood up and just started walking away from me. He said I was crazy and he wouldn't put up with me anymore. He had no right to walk away from me, so I just started hitting him. If he would've given me the phone, I would've stopped. I just wanted to see what he was hiding from me. That's when he went to the garage to hide. He spends every second in his cave; I'm so sick of it! I followed him out, and he kept telling me to leave him alone. He loves his car more than anything, so I grabbed my son's baseball bat and took my anger out on his car. He's lucky I hit the car instead of him, but he still flipped out and called the cops. It's ridiculous that I get blamed for all this when I wasn't the one who started it. This would never have happened if he didn't push me to my limit.

BELIEVE Model is used to identify early warning signs that you may be in an unhealthy or abusive relationship. These are harmful coping strategies used to gain control over others.

Belittling/**B**oundaryViolations: Dictating, providing unsolicited advice, evaluating others, devaluing, degrading, stepping on someone's toes, falling in love very quickly, providing approval, exclusivity, intensity, and talking over someone are typical examples of poor boundaries and belittling.
Identify a personal example and an example from Gabby's Story:

Entitlement/**E**xcuses: Believing you have the right to make demands, hold expectations, or force views onto others is entitlement. Excuses follow entitled behavior, which leads to victim uncertainty and self-doubt. The controlling partner sets the relationship rules, forcing the partner to live within the system. Rules do not apply equally, and they are frequently changed. Excuses keep the cycle spinning. To reveal your entitlement, complete the sentence: "My partner should…" "I have the right to …"
Identify a personal example and an example from Gabby's Story:

Lies/**M**anipulation: Gaslighting, denial, blame, guilting, and shaming are common tactics in abuse. These tools maintain control and dominance in the relationship.
Identify a personal example and an example from Gabby's Story:

Isolation/**I**ntimidation/**I**ntensity: Harassing, coercing, love bombing, and threatening are common in abuse. These tactics produce dependency by removing any competition or threat.
Identify a personal example and an example from Gabby's Story:

Extreme Jealousy: Victims often misread jealousy as love or passion, but it is a dangerous sign of toxic insecurity and control. Healthy relationships provide mutual independence, trust, and freedom.
Identify a personal example and an example from Gabby's Story:

Volatility/**V**ictim Stance: Controlling partners will display intense, erratic behaviors followed by a victim stance. Rather than showing accountability or remorse, they blame others and play the victim.
Identify a personal example and an example from Gabby's Story:

Eggshells: Fear is present if you frequently feel like you are walking on eggshells. Fear destroys relationships, exists in every abusive partnership, and is not present in healthy relationships.
Identify a personal example and an example from Gabby's Story:

Video: Small Voice Films (2016). "Caged In (Extended Version) - Award Winning Domestic Violence Short Film." https://youtu.be/iiF9ays47EI (14:20)

Discussion: While watching the video, identify examples of the **BELIEVE Model**:

Belittling/**B**oundary Violation:

Entitlement/**E**xcuses:

Lies/Manipulation:

Isolation/**I**ntimidation/**I**ntensity:

Extreme Jealousy:

Volatility/**V**ictim Stance:

Eggshells:

Video: Psych2Go (2020): "6 Differences Between Healthy and Unhealthy Love." https://youtu.be/4c5dFcC4LNY (8:11)
Discussion: While watching the video, note the differences between unhealthy and healthy love. Share personal examples for each, and identify which you struggle with most often:

1.) Intensity vs. Stability: _____
_____

2.) Isolation vs. Independence: _____
_____

3.) Jealousy vs. Concern: _____
_____

4.) Belittling vs. Teasing: _____
_____

5.) Manipulation vs. Generosity: _____
_____

6.) Volatility vs. Honesty: _____
_____

Red Flag Physical Cues: Think of a time when you were really angry. What were your automatic physical cues during this fight-or-flight response? Some natural body changes include rapid heart rate, shallow breathing, muscle tension, sweating, and hand tremors.

In **Gabby's** story, what are **Gabby's physical cues**?

List your **physical cues** indicating that you are under the influence of anger:

Red Flag Feeling Cues: Vulnerable emotions often precede destructive or abusive behaviors. Frequently, we think we are just angry, but remember that anger is a secondary emotion, and there is a more vulnerable emotion under anger. For many, vulnerable emotions under anger include insecurity, hurt, fear, rejection, sadness, and shame.

What are **Gabby's feeling cues**?

List some of your common **feeling cues**:

Red Flag Behaviors: When under the influence of anger, we exhibit familiar behavioral cues. Some cues include a clenched jaw, pacing, sarcasm, cursing, and posturing.

What are **Gabby's red flag behaviors**?

List three of your **red flag behaviors**:

1. _____

2. _____

3. _____

Red Flag Thoughts: Keep in mind that our thoughts drive our emotions. What are some examples of relationship beliefs or thoughts that strengthen anger and encourage aggression? Some high-risk thoughts include: "You always do this to me!" "Who do you think you are?" "You're trying to piss me off!" "You should respect me." "I would never treat you that way."

What are **Gabby's red flag thoughts**?

List three of your **red flag thoughts**:

1. _____

2. _____

3. _____

Catch/Correct Practice - Create a corrective thought for each of your **red flag thoughts above**:

Correction 1:

Correction 2:

Correction 3:

Red Flag Setups: When we fail at self-care, we dramatically decrease our tolerance and increase our reactivity. What are your self-care needs? Some basic self-care needs include: eating regularly, getting enough sleep, setting limits, going to the gym, alone time, and socializing.

What are some of the ways **Gabby** failed at meeting her **self-care** needs?

Think about the last time you did something you regretted. What were some of the ways you set yourself up by failing to meet your own **self-care** needs:

Daily Self-Care

Self-care is the practice of taking an active role in protecting our well-being. Engaging in self-care releases feel-good chemicals, and we can boost our levels of these happiness hormones with simple lifestyle changes. The following are examples of daily self-care activities that release these critical hormones:

Dopamine *the reward chemical*	**Serotonin** *the mood stabilizer*	**Oxytocin** *the love hormone*	**Endorphin** *the pain killer*
• complete a task • eat protein • celebrate a win • favorite hobbies • get enough sleep • meditate • exercise • listen to music	• high-protein food • lift weights • sun exposure • ride a bike • swim • meditate • exercise • massage therapy	• pet a dog/cat • hug or cuddle • play music • time with friends • be kind to others • meditate • exercise/yoga • intimacy	• laugh • watch a comedy • dark chocolate • dance • essential oils • meditate • exercise • ice cream

Share your favorite self-care activities:

Daily:

Weekly:

Monthly:

Homework 1: Identify personal examples of the **BELIEVE Model**:

Belittling/**B**oundary Violation:

Entitlement/**E**xcuses:

Lies/Manipulation:

Isolation/**I**ntimidation/**I**ntensity:

Extreme Jealousy:

Volatility/**V**ictim Stance:

Eggshells:

Homework 2: Practice daily self-care this week, and share examples:

1.) Identify one of your **dopamine**-releasing self-care activities: _____

2.) Identify one of your **oxytocin**-releasing activities: _____

3.) Identify one of your **serotonin**-releasing activities: _____

4.) Identify one of your **endorphin**-releasing activities: _____

Video Homework: TEDx (2018). "Katrina Blom: You Don't Find Happiness, You Create It." https://youtu.be/9DtcSCFwDdw (15:32)

Discussion: Blom states, "Your brain is not always on your side when it comes to creating happiness. To counter this is going to take more than positive thinking; it takes positive action. Happiness is a skill we can all work on. Have you ever found yourself in a situation where you were really worried about something, and you kept worrying even though you knew that worrying would not change the situation or help in any way? Nevertheless, you just kept worrying. If I ask you to keep your focus on your breath and not think about anything else for five minutes, I doubt anyone in this room would be able to do that. If I ask you to raise your hand for five minutes, we all would be better able to achieve this. It's difficult to control our thoughts, and we have a better chance at controlling our actions. Well-being is built by positive action. What do you think your brain prioritizes: all the things you do well or the ones you should improve? The negative effects of a setback are more than twice as strong as the positive effects of a success. We feel worse about losing money than we feel about gaining the same amount. If you receive a compliment from a co-worker and then a complaint from another, these two comments don't neutralize each other. The complaint would leave a stronger emotional mark. Why do we carry this emotional asymmetry? Happiness is not something you find outside of yourself, and it's not something you have; it's a skill we can all work on. Dedicating yourself to caring for your relationships might be one of the most powerful actions you can take when it comes to happiness."

Practice: The Dalai Lama said, "If you want others to be happy, practice compassion. If you want to be happy, practice compassion." When we are compassionate toward others, our brain releases Oxytocin, which elevates our happiness level. Share an example of using compassion as part of your daily self-care:

Chapter 5
Coping with Anger

Whatever is begun in anger ends in shame.
~ *Benjamin Franklin*

Holding onto anger is like drinking poison and
expecting the other person to die.
~ *Buddha*

I sat with my anger long enough, until she told me her real name was grief.
~ *C.S. Lewis*

Anger is an acid that can do more harm to the vessel in which it is stored
than to anything on which it is poured.
~ *Mark Twain*

❖   Key Concepts for Anger Regulation

❖   **STAR** - Building the Anger Fire

❖   Vulnerable Emotions Under Anger

❖   Three Steps to Regulate Emotions

Short Story

"A monk decides to meditate alone, away from his monastery. He takes a boat and goes to the middle of the lake. He closes his eyes and begins to meditate. After a few hours of unperturbed silence, he suddenly feels the blow of another boat hitting his. With his eyes still closed, he feels his anger rising. When he opens his eyes, he is ready to shout at the boatman who dared to disturb his meditation. But, when he opened his eyes, he saw that it was an empty boat floating in the middle of the lake… At that moment, the monk achieved self-realization and understood that anger is within him; it simply needs to hit an external object to provoke it. After that, whenever he meets someone who irritates or provokes his anger, he remembers the other person is just an empty boat. Anger is within."   ~ *Thich Nhat Hanh*

Story Discussion: What happened to the monk's anger in the story? Apply *fact* vs. *fiction*:

Justified Anger

People frequently ask, "Aren't we allowed to be angry? Isn't anger justified?" Benjamin Franklin answered this best when he said, "Anger is never without reason, but seldom a good one." Anger is a natural part of being human, but while it can be easily justified, we must ask ourselves if it is helpful in each situation. Anger is an emotion that negatively impacts your quality of life. After decades of imprisonment for rising against apartheid, Nelson Mandela said, "As I walked out the door toward the gate that would lead to my freedom, I knew if I didn't leave my bitterness and hatred behind, I'd still be in prison."

Most people come to therapy in search of happiness. Anger is an emotion that blocks happiness. Why is anger so uncomfortable? Like fear, anger is a survival emotion that initiates the fight-or-flight response. If anger is not uncomfortable, we might fail to pay attention to it or act upon it. What type of behavior does anger encourage? Anger is looking for someone to blame for your pain. Anger wants a fight, and anger encourages thoughts of revenge. Anger thrives on judgment, criticism, and shame. We hold onto anger and resentment for others because we want them to suffer the way we are: misery loves company. The problem with carrying grudges is that, ultimately, the one you are hurting is yourself. Buddha said, "Holding onto anger is like drinking poison and expecting the other person to die."

People who struggle with chronic anger tend to attempt to exert control over others. Control is a coping strategy used to reduce fear, but it is a setup for disappointment because you only have control over yourself. Eliminating anger requires holding yourself accountable. With accountability, you feel grounded and empowered. Many ask, "How can I hold myself accountable when other people cause the problem?" Each individual subjectively creates reality, and blame gives your power away.

Next time you are involved in a conflict, notice your thoughts. You will likely judge, condemn, and blame the other person. This is a critical time to learn how to shift your focus back to yourself. Accountability sounds like: "I'm feeling disappointed because I held an expectation. Expectations lead to disappointment." Studies show that happy people are happy because of their thinking, not because of their life circumstances. Holding ourselves accountable sounds like this:

"I'm feeling angry right now because of my thoughts. How else can I view this situation?" The goal is to walk away from this program feeling like a weight has been lifted off your shoulders. It's important to know that you are the only one who can remove that weight, and you will remove it by changing your thoughts.

Discussion: Think about the last time you felt angry. How did you justify the anger? Did you judge, criticize, or condemn? Did you blame, negative label, or view yourself as a victim? <u>Share your anger justification</u>:

Key Concepts for Anger Regulation

1. Anger does not exist without judgment or criticism.

2. Acceptance and compassion extinguish anger.

3. Anger needs an enemy to exist; anger thrives on blame. Accountability weakens anger.

4. Acting while under the influence of anger leads to regret.

5. Shifting to an observer stance eliminates acting while under the influence of anger.

6. Anger covers vulnerable emotions like fear, hurt, sadness, rejection, and shame.

7. Anger goes away more quickly when we identify and soothe the underlying emotions.

8. Anger is produced by our thoughts about events, not the actual events themselves.

Discussion: Which of the above concepts for anger regulation do you find most helpful and why?

Anger Meter

Like most emotions, anger ranges in intensity. Low-level anger is described as irritable, annoyed, or frustrated. A mid-level of anger is mad, hostile, or angry. The highest levels of anger may be described as pissed, furious, or enraged. <u>It is helpful to view the anger meter as a road.</u> <u>The moment you turn your car onto the anger meter, you are driving down the road leading to</u> <u>rage.</u> The longer you drive your car down this path, the faster your car goes. *Example*: A stressor occurs, and you feel annoyed. You have just turned your car onto the anger meter. At mile markers one through three, your car cruises at a comfortable speed, and taking an exit ramp is relatively easy. However, as you continue driving, your car accelerates quickly. Once you reach mile marker five (*hostile*), your car is driving fast, and taking an exit ramp becomes more difficult. When you hit mile marker ten (*enraged*), your car is speeding out of control. The best time to take the exit ramp off the road leading to rage is during lower levels.

Anger Meter

1   2   3   4   5   6   7   8   9   10

Annoyed ~ Irritated ~ Frustrated ~ Hostile ~ Mad ~ Angry ~ Pissed ~ Furious ~ Enraged

---

Video: TEDx (2015): "Russell Kolts: Anger, Compassion, and What It Means to Be Strong." https://youtu.be/QG4Z185MBJE (13:01)

1.) Kolts talks about how we hold onto anger because it helps us feel strong, powerful, and in control. Essentially, we use anger to avoid vulnerability, avoidance is a fear-based coping strategy, and compassion is the courage to turn toward and embrace discomfort. We use anger to escape more vulnerable feelings of fear, hurt, and shame. What are common vulnerable emotions under anger for you?

2.) Identify vulnerable emotions under the anger in the short story at the beginning of this chapter:

3.) Identify vulnerable emotions under Kolts' anger in the video:

4.) Kolts shared a few anger management tools: 1.) Instead of denying, avoiding, or blaming, try turning toward the vulnerable emotions and acknowledge your struggle. 2.) Instead of listening to anger, try slowing down your body. Slowing down the body slows down the mind. 3.) Take a moment to shift perspective and ask yourself, "What does this situation look like for others? How does it make sense to them?" Which of these tools do you find most helpful? Share a personal example using one of the tools:

How it Works: STAR

STAR is an acronym used to gain self-awareness and produce positive change. You can plug any uncomfortable situation into the formula to understand your problem thinking. The **S** in **STAR** stands for the *stressor*. A stressor is any uncomfortable situation. You will experience daily stressors, many of which are outside your control. People who live happy lives do not experience fewer stressors; they simply have a different way of processing information that leads to their contentment. The **T** in **STAR** stands for *thoughts*. Your thoughts become your reality. *Example*: If it's raining outside and I think, "The rain is so beautiful," I will feel peaceful and happy. On the other hand, if I think, "I hate the rain; today is ruined," I will feel angry and disappointed. The rain didn't produce my feelings; my thoughts produced my feelings. The **A** in **STAR** stands for *affect*. Affect is your emotional response. Every thought you have produces a feeling, and feelings motivate your behavior. The **R** in **STAR** reflects your behavioral *response*.

(S) Stressor: It's raining

(T) Thought: "I hate the rain; today is ruined."

(A) Affect: Angry and disappointed

(R) Response: Cancel my plans, sulk, turn on the TV

Building the Anger Fire*

To understand the anger response, imagine building a fire. To build a fire, you need fuel and a spark. Think of stressors as fuel and thoughts as the spark. The formula to build an anger fire is: **Stressor *(fuel)* + Thoughts *(spark)* = Anger *(fire)***

Stressor *(fuel)* - Anger starts with a compromised state, which is anything that places you in a vulnerable position. Compromised states often occur when you fail at self-care or have unmet expectations. *Examples*: skipping meals, not getting enough sleep, overextending, poor boundaries, caffeine, and passivity.

Thoughts *(spark)* - Anger thoughts fall into the three general categories. Read the examples below:

1. **Victim/Unfair/Stuck**: blame, catastrophize, poor me: "No one appreciates me. Nothing goes my way."

2. **Judgment/Criticism**: negative labels, overgeneralize: "That's stupid. You're so selfish. That's disrespectful. You're lazy. You're too sensitive. That's insane. You're crazy."

3. **Right/Wrong**: comparing, religious moralizing, shaming, demanding: "I would never…You're supposed to… I shouldn't have… I have the right to expect…Who would do that?"

Anger Fire Example

Imagine you arrive home from work feeling hungry and exhausted (*fuel*). Soon after you walk in the door, your family complains that dinner is ruined because you're late (*fuel*). Their complaints, combined with your exhaustion, are difficult to tolerate, but without a *spark*, there is no fire. The spark comes with your *victim* thought: "They're so ungrateful! I work two jobs, and this is the thanks I get." Now you have someone to blame for your pain, you view yourself as a victim, and the situation seems unfair. Once the anger *spark* ignites into a fire, your response is hostile. It's a simple formula for putting the *fuel* and the *spark* together.

Practice - Read the **STAR** examples, and correct the thoughts to change the response:

Stressor: You feel stressed, hungry, and exhausted. Your family is complaining. (*fuel*)

Thought: "They're so ungrateful! I work two jobs, and this is the thanks I get." (*spark*)

Affect: Anger (*fire*)

Response: "You're so selfish and ungrateful! This is why I don't want to come home." (*fire*)

Revised STAR: Create a thought of **compassion** or **gratitude** to neutralize the anger.

Stressor: You feel stressed, hungry, and exhausted. Your family is complaining. (*fuel*)

Thought:

Affect:

Response:

---

* Concept adapted from M. McKay and P. Rogers (2000).

Stressor: You're told you have to take a pay cut if you want to keep your job. (*fuel*)

Thought: "The rich get richer. I do all the work, and they make all the money." (*spark*)

Affect: Anger (*fire*)

Response: You walk out on the job. (*fire*)

Revised STAR: Create a thought of **compassion** or **gratitude** to neutralize the anger.

Stressor: You're told you have to take a pay cut if you want to keep your job. (*fuel*)

Thought:

Affect:

Response:

Video: TED (2019): "Ryan Martin: Why We Get Mad and Why it's Healthy." https://youtu.be/0rAngiiXBAc (13:06)

1.) Martin discusses how it's not the event that makes us angry because we don't all get mad at the same things. Anger requires a pre-anger state (*fuel*) and an anger appraisal (*spark*). Martin discusses how angry people tend to catastrophize, blame, overgeneralize, demand, and negative label. <u>What anger thought patterns do you struggle with the most?</u> <u>Please share an example</u>:

2.) Martin discusses how anger, like any emotion, is energy. The energy that comes from anger can be channeled into something productive. <u>Share an example of channeling anger energy in a helpful way</u>:

Underlying Emotion

      Why is it essential to search for the underlying emotion when we experience anger? Identifying vulnerable emotions will pave the way to emotional regulation. **People who struggle with anger are people in pain**. Anger is a secondary emotion, which means there is a more vulnerable emotion under anger, such as hurt, shame, and fear. With chronic anger, fear tends to be the most common underlying emotion. Fear quickly turns to anger because it helps us feel powerful, strong, and in control. <u>Fear is a survival threat, and anger is a protective shield.</u> Essentially, we use anger to avoid feeling vulnerable. Avoiding vulnerability means the underlying emotion remains unprocessed, which blocks healing, and we stay angry. Anger encourages us to focus on the enemy and destroy the threat. Aggression may be valuable in some circumstances, but most of the time, the aggressive response is not in our best interest and often leads to regret.

Three Steps to Regulate Emotions

1. **Identify**: Identify the <u>vulnerable emotions</u> under the anger: "Right now, I'm feeling hurt."

2. **Validate**: Remind yourself that it's <u>normal to feel</u>: "It's okay that I'm upset. It's natural to feel hurt in a situation like this."

3. **Admire**: <u>Our emotions are messengers; they tell us something valuable about ourselves.</u> <u>Find the beauty in the emotion</u>: "I'm feeling hurt because this person is important to me. My hurt is a reminder that I have the courage to care."

Emotional Regulation Practice - Read the examples and practice the steps:

Example: After repeatedly asking your teen to clean up after himself, you come home from a long day to find the sink filled with dishes. Your anger comes from the thought, "I would never disrespect my parents this way. How many times do I have to repeat myself to get him to listen?"

1. **Identify**: "I'm feeling disappointment, worried, and hurt."

2. **Validate**: "It's normal that I'm feeling this way. Sometimes parenting is really challenging."

3. **Admire**: "The disappointment, worry, and hurt are reminders that my child is very important to me. I would not feel upset if I didn't care, and I'm thankful I'm a devoted parent."

Practice 1: You return home excited to share great news with your partner. You expect to be met with enthusiasm, but instead, your partner criticizes you. You feel angry.

1. **Identify**: _____

2. **Validate**: _____

    _____

3. **Admire**: _____

    _____

Practice 2: You have been sacrificing many late nights at work with the hope of a promotion, but it was given to someone else who did not put in the extra hours. You feel angry.

1. **Identify**: _____

2. **Validate**: _____

    _____

3. **Admire**: _____

    _____

I sat with my anger long enough, until she told me her real name was grief. ~ C.S. Lewis

Practice 3: You're driving on the highway, and someone suddenly cuts you off. You quickly slam on the brakes to avoid crashing. Your children are in the car, and you feel angry.

1. **Identify**: _____

2. **Validate**: _____

    _____

3. **Admire**: _____

    _____

Practice 4: Your partner asks you to come home early to spend quality time together. You make the sacrifice, but your partner is not there when you get home. You feel angry.

1. **Identify**: _____

2. **Validate**: _____

    _____

3. **Admire**: _____

    _____

Chapter 5 Overview Questions

1. Please review the **Key Concepts for Anger Regulation**. Which of these do you find most helpful? How will you apply it to regulate anger?

2. Which of the **Anger Thought Categories** (*victim/unfair/stuck, judgment/criticism, right/wrong*) do you struggle with most?   Share a personal example:

3. Why is it essential to identify the **vulnerable emotions** under anger? How does **compassion extinguish anger**? Share an example of using compassion to neutralize an angry thought:

Chapter 6
Creating Safety Plans

If you hate a person, then you're defeated by them.
~ *Confucius*

As I walked out the door toward the gate that would lead to my freedom, I knew
if I didn't leave my bitterness and hatred behind, I'd still be in prison.
~ *Nelson Mandela*

Any person capable of angering you becomes your master; he can anger you
only when you permit yourself to be disturbed by him.
~ *Epictetus*

If you are patient in one moment of anger, you will escape
a hundred days of sorrow.
~ *Chinese Proverb*

Where there is anger, there is always pain underneath
~ *Eckhart Tolle*

❖   Stages of Anger

❖   Anger Control Plan / Healthy Coping Strategies

❖   Kick Anger to the Curb: De-Escalation Plan

1	**2**	**3**	**4**	**5**	**6**	**7**	**8**	**9**	**10**

Annoyed ~ Irritated ~ Frustrated ~ Hostile ~ Mad ~ Angry ~ Pissed ~ Furious ~Enraged

Stages of Anger

Imagine that you are in your car, happily cruising down the road. Without the influence of anger, you're listening to music and feeling content. Suddenly, you find yourself stuck in traffic. You're at a dead stop, and you're beginning to realize that you're not going to make it to your destination on time. You experience a fleeting moment of disappointment, and then you hear the back door open and close. Anger has just jumped into the backseat of your car! At first, anger remains in the backseat, telling you things like, "You're never going to make it to work. Nothing ever goes your way." While anger is sitting in the backseat, you are experiencing low levels of anger (*annoyed, irritated, frustrated*). Anger at a low level is a backseat driver who is bugging you, and you're feeling irritated. As anger continues to poke at you, it becomes more difficult to tolerate. As things escalate, you begin to lose your ability to tolerate anger's provocation.

Next, anger climbs up front and sits in the passenger seat next to you. When anger climbs into the passenger seat, you are experiencing mid-levels of anger (*hostile, mad, angry*). As anger moves closer to you, it now has more influence over you. While sitting next to you, anger's comments escalate. Passenger-seat anger is trying to piss you off by saying things like, "This is unbelievable! You'll probably lose your crappy job; your worthless boss is just looking for a reason." Passenger-seat anger is trying to wear you down for what comes next.

Passenger-seat anger's goal is to weaken you because anger ultimately wants to drive your car. When anger notices that you're losing your cool, that's when anger reaches for the steering wheel. When anger grabs control of the steering wheel, you are entering the highest levels of anger (*pissed, furious, enraged*). If you continue driving with anger steering the car, you are making a very high-risk decision. With anger in control, you are likely going to crash because anger is a terrible driver. When you crash your car, you are responsible for the damage because it was you who continued to press the gas pedal. The only safe decision that will protect you and others from serious harm is to stop your car immediately. Once you stop the car, you now have the time you need to figure out how to kick anger to the curb. **Don't let anger carjack you!**

Three Steps to Regulate Emotions - Please apply the three steps to the example above:

1. **Identify**: Identify the vulnerable emotions under the anger.

2. **Validate**: Remind yourself that it is normal to feel.

3. **Admire**: Find the beauty in the emotion.

1. **Identify**: _____

2. **Validate**: _____

3. **Admire**: _____

Video: TEDx (2019): "Juna Mustad: Anger is Your Ally: A Mindful Approach to Anger." https://youtu.be/sbVBsrNnBy8 (17:21)

1.) Mustad asks, "Are you an anger stuffer or an erupter?" Both of these coping strategies create significant relationship problems. <u>Describe your experience managing anger</u>:

2.) Acting under the influence of anger leads to regret because our prefrontal cortex (*cognitive control*) goes offline when emotionally flooded, and we fall back into old habits. Mindfulness practices rewire the brain to prevent the prefrontal cortex from going offline. Mustad discusses these mindfulness practices: "Breathe, name it, do it differently, and inquire." <u>Share a personal example using one of those tools</u>:

3.) Mustad discusses some of the benefits of anger: "Anger reveals our boundaries, anger heals trauma, and anger inspires action." <u>Share a personal example of anger as an ally</u>:

Anger Control Plan

What should you do when you feel angry? Do not do or say anything! **Acting while under the influence of anger leads to regret**. When anger is in the driver's seat, anger wants you to act immediately because anger wants control. If you choose to pause, you will defeat anger. <u>Fast strengthens anger; slow strengthens you</u>. To slow down, use any of the following tools: *Mindful Minute, Underlying Emotion, STAR, Catch/Correct,* and *Pause.*

Mindful Minute
Slowly inhale and silently count from one to five until your lungs are filled with air. As you exhale, slowly and silently count from five back down to one. Repeat this process six times for a mindful minute. With each exhale, you weaken anger and strengthen yourself.

Underlying Emotion
Anytime you feel angry, there are vulnerable emotions under the anger. Anger pushes you to act immediately because anger wants control. Before you say or do anything, search for the underlying emotions. Once you identify the emotions, validate and create a statement of self-admiration. "I'm feeling hurt and worried right now. It's okay that I'm feeling this way. These feelings mean I care, and I like that about me."

STAR
When you begin to feel frustrated, take a moment to plug your experience into the **STAR** outline. Identifying anger thoughts allows you to correct your thinking.

Catch/Correct
Once you identify your anger thoughts, use self-compassion, gratitude, acceptance, self-admiration, normalizing, and accountability corrections.

> *If you are patient in one moment of anger, you will escape a hundred days of sorrow.*
> ~ Chinese Proverb

Pause to Strengthen You

When under the influence of strong emotions, a *pause* is our first line of defense. During times of intense anger or fear, our prefrontal cortex shuts down, which is the part of our brain responsible for decision-making and good judgment. Losing access to the prefrontal cortex explains why we regret our decisions while angry.

People often say, "I was not thinking; I just reacted," or "I go from zero to one hundred in a split second." These are reminders that slowing down is essential to a prevention plan. When anger is in the driver's seat, anger steers you toward thoughts and behaviors that strengthen anger. What strengthens anger? Anger is looking for a fight, and anger wants to prove others wrong. Anger loves to convince you that you've been victimized or mistreated. The problem is that anger distorts reality. *Example*: Have you ever written an aggressive email while angry? The next day, you regret sending it. Under the influence of anger, the email sounded appropriate, and it felt good to click send because anger distorted your view and encouraged aggression.

Remember that when you experience a lower level of anger (frustrated, annoyed), it's a sign that you are driving on the road leading to rage. Monitoring your lower levels of anger is essential because they are the early warning signs. An individual who says, "I go from zero to one hundred in a split second," is often an individual who isn't aware of the lower levels of anger. When driving down the road leading to rage, it's much easier to put on the brakes when feeling frustrated than when feeling furious. By the time you feel enraged, anger has taken control of the steering wheel, and your car is recklessly driving at very high speeds. The longer you stay on the road leading to rage, the more out of control you become.

How Does the Pause Work? **Follow these Five Steps**:

1. **Accountability**: Even if you think your partner is the one escalating, use an "I" statement rather than a "you" statement when calling a pause. Good boundaries lead to healthy relationships. Do not tell your partner what to do; simply share what you will do. **Accountability reminder: I am my problem, and I am my solution**.

2. **Assert**: Set the limit and provide a brief plan.

3. **Reassure**: Tell your partner when you will return. Either partner can call a pause at any time, and it must be honored. The pause is used to protect the relationship.

4. **Disengage**: Whether your partner responds or not, leave without further discussion. Do not wait for permission, and do not debate the pause.

5. **De-Escalate**: Use the healthy coping tools in your de-escalation plan.

> *As I walked out the door toward the gate that would lead to my freedom, I knew if I didn't leave my bitterness and hatred behind, I'd still be in prison.* ~ Nelson Mandela

Pause Example

1. **Accountability**: "I'm starting to feel upset, so I need to pause." <u>Be sure to talk about *your* feelings, not your partner's feelings</u>. Problematic statement: "I can tell you are freaking out, so we should probably take a break."

2. **Assert**: "I'm going to the gym." <u>Do not pick a trigger location</u>. If your partner doesn't like your best friend, you may want to choose a different location. Exercise is an effective way to reduce stress.

3. **Reassure**: "I'll be back in about an hour." <u>Give yourself enough time to calm down</u>.

4. **Disengage**: <u>Turn and leave silently</u>. Remember that any unwanted touch can be an assault. If your partner blocks your path, keep your hands to yourself and find another exit. If there isn't another exit, you may want to become a statue until they disengage. After the pause is initiated, it is essential to disengage physically, emotionally, and verbally.

5. **De-Escalate**: <u>Use healthy coping strategies</u>. No alcohol or drug use. Use your favorite de-escalation tools and self-care to regulate your emotions.

Pause Practice - Discuss the pause when you and your partner are calm. It's important to feel that you are working as a team to create a safe environment. <u>If your goal is to remain in the relationship, the pause will be the most crucial tool in your toolbox. Practice and share your experience with the group</u>:

1. **Accountability**:

2. **Assert**:

3. **Reassure**:

4. **Disengage**:

5. **De-Escalate**:

Video: TEDx (2019): "Lucy Hone: The Three Secrets of Resilient People." https://youtu.be/NWH8N-BvhAw (16:20)

Discussion: Hone shares her traumatic loss and the three strategies of highly resilient people: **1.)** Resilient people <u>normalize suffering</u> because they know it is a natural part of life. We all take turns suffering, and acceptance increases tolerance. Resilient people do not view themselves as victims. Instead of asking, "Why me?" resilient people ask, "<u>Why not me?</u>" **2.)** Resilient people are highly skilled at <u>hunting gratitude</u> and focus effectively on <u>what they can change</u> rather than what they cannot. **3.)** Resilient people are high in <u>accountability</u> and frequently ask themselves, "<u>Is what I'm doing helping me or hurting me?</u>" **Practice:** <u>Think of a personal stressor, and practice using each of these resilience strategies.</u>

Normalize Suffering: (Why not me?)

Hunt Gratitude: (I'm grateful that…)

Accountability: (Is this helping me or hurting me?)

De-Escalation Plan: Kick Anger to the Curb

Anger thrives on judgment, aggressive images, negative labels, poor me thinking, revenge thoughts, and thoughts of injustice. Engaging in thoughts that feed anger is the same as throwing fuel on a fire until it rages out of control. If you want a fire to die down, do not add fuel to it. In order to remove anger from your car before it grabs the steering wheel, you need to use anger-weakening tactics. <u>Practice the following anger-weakening tactics:</u>

1. **Catch/Correct:** Pay attention to your thoughts and correct those that strengthen anger.

2. **Compassion is a fire extinguisher:** To create self-compassion, ask yourself what you would say to your best friend. In the anger visualization, compassion may sound like: "I'm feeling worried because my job is important, and I have an outstanding work ethic."

3. **Use the warm half-smile:** Smiling releases feel-good chemicals, sending calm messages.

4. **Relax your jaw:** A clenched jaw strengthens anger.

5. **Take a slow, deep breath into your stomach:** Be sure to feel your stomach expand with your breath. Diaphragmatic breathing sends a message of calm to the brain.

6. **Lower your voice and slow down:** Slowing your body slows down your mind. You can weaken anger by lowering your volume or softening your tone of voice.

7. **Disengage by removing yourself from the stressor:** Anger loves a fight! When you are under anger's influence, do not continue to interact with someone who is provoking you.

8. **Change your focus:** If you're standing, sit down. If you're sitting, lay down. Hold an ice cube in your hand until it melts. Drink a glass of cold water. If you're inside, go outside.

9. **Self-Admiration:** A person experiencing anger is a person in pain. Self-admiration is a validation statement: "I really admire how resilient I am."

Soothing Self-Talk

Use coping mantras to weaken anger and strengthen you. **Practice** - Circle your three favorite coping statements below, and create three of your own:

1. "No amount of regret changes the past."
2. "You live most of your life inside your head. Make sure it is a nice place to be."
3. "Feelings are temporary; this too shall pass."
4. "We are only given what we can handle."
5. "Don't judge yourself by your past. You don't live there anymore."
6. "Sometimes things don't go our way, and that's okay."
7. "I can't control others, but I can control myself."
8. "If I am easily offended, I am easily manipulated."
9. "People can try to make me angry, but I get to decide what I feel."
10. "Be kind to past versions of yourself who didn't know the things you know now."
11. "Life is unfair; we all take turns suffering."
12. "Blame gives away my power; accountability is strength."
13. "We are all far from perfect."
14. "Emotional pain means I am alive."
15. "Everything happens for a reason."
16. "Expectations lead to disappointment."
17. "Comparing leads to resentment."

Mantras: Create one that empowers, one that normalizes, and one that encourages healthy boundaries.

1. _____

2. _____

3. _____

Stressor: You loan a friend money, and they do not pay you back.

Anger Thought: "They're taking advantage of me. They think I'm a fool."

Acceptance Thought: "Sometimes_____

Accountability Thought: "I chose_____

Self-Admiration Thought: "I like that I_____

Gratitude Thought: "I'm thankful_____

De-Escalation Example - I had to work late, and I asked my partner if they'd make dinner. I arrived home, but my family wasn't there. Later, I discovered they went out to dinner without me.

1. **Identify/Validate**: Lean into the vulnerable emotions under the anger: "I **feel** rejected, disappointed, and hurt. It's **natural** to feel upset in a situation like this."

2. **Present Moment**: Remind yourself that the discomfort is temporary. DO NOT add permanence with words like *always* or *never*: "**Right now**, I'm tired, and I'm looking for someone to blame."

3. **Accountability**: "*Is this helping or hurting me?*" Anger needs an enemy; remove the target. Place yourself in a position of power and remove victim stance: "I **chose** to work a long day and come home late. I feel rejected coming home to an empty house, and they feel rejected when I work late."

4. **Acceptance**: "*Why not me?*" Normalize your experience to increase tolerance and weaken anger: "**Sometimes** we get what we want, and sometimes we don't. Feelings of hurt and rejection are a **normal** part of relationships. Emotional pain means I'm alive. It's my turn to be rejected."

5. **Self-Admiration**: Identify the beauty of the emotion: "The rejection is a **reminder** that my family is important to me. I would not have felt hurt and abandoned if I didn't love them so much."

6. **Gratitude**: Resilient people *hunt the gratitude* to overcome hardship and eliminate resentments: "I'm **grateful** I'm managing these feelings before I take them out on my family."

7. **Compassion**: Take a moment to put yourself in their shoes and see it from their perspective: "My partner is overwhelmed with the kids, so it's easy to forget. I know I've disappointed them, too."

Homework - Choose a stressor and use the de-escalation plan below to fill in the details.

1. **Identify/Validate**: "It's normal to feel…"

2. **Present Moment**: "Right now…"

3. **Accountability**: "Is this helping me or hurting me? I'm choosing…"

4. **Acceptance**: "Why not me? Sometimes…"

5. **Self-Admiration**: "This feeling reminds me that I…"

6. **Gratitude**: "I'm thankful that…"

7. **Compassion**: "From their perspective…"

Chapter 7
Problem Patterns

Unless you learn to face your own shadows, you will continue
to see them in others, because the world outside you is
only a reflection of the world inside you.
~ Carl Jung

Avoiding your triggers isn't healing. Healing happens when you're triggered
and you are able to move through the pain, the pattern, and the story,
and walk your way to a different ending.
~ Vienna Pharaon

You are the problem. And you are the solution.
~ Buddha

When someone tries to trigger you by insulting you or by doing or saying
something that irritates you, take a deep breath and switch off your ego.
If you are easily offended, you are easily manipulated.
~ Unknown

❖   Trigger-Behavior-Reward Autopilot

❖   Harmful Coping Strategies

❖   Fact - Fiction - Feeling

❖   De-Escalation Plan

TED Talk - Judson Brewer: A Simple Way to Break a Bad Habit (9:24)

"This reward-based learning process is called positive and negative reinforcement, and basically goes like this...<u>See food, eat food, feel good, repeat. Trigger, behavior, reward</u>...Well, after a while, our creative brains say, 'You know what? You can use this for more than just remembering where food is. You know, next time you feel bad, why don't you try eating something good so you'll feel better?' Same process, just a different trigger...<u>See cool, smoke to be cool, feel good, repeat. Trigger, behavior, reward</u>. And each time we do this, we learn to repeat the process, and it becomes a habit. <u>So later, feeling stressed out triggers that urge to smoke a cigarette or to eat something sweet</u>. Now, the prefrontal cortex, the youngest part of our brain from an evolutionary perspective, understands on an intellectual level that we shouldn't smoke. And it tries its hardest to help us change our behavior...We call this cognitive control. <u>Unfortunately, this is also the first part of the brain that goes offline when we get stressed out</u>. Now, we can all relate to this in our own experience. We're much more likely to do things like yell at our spouse or kids when we're stressed out or tired, even though we know it's not going to be helpful. <u>When the prefrontal cortex goes offline, we fall back into our old habits. The paradox here is that mindfulness is just about being really interested in getting up close and personal with what's actually happening in our bodies and minds from moment to moment</u>. And this willingness to turn toward our experiences is supported by curiosity, which is naturally rewarding. What does curiosity feel like? It feels good. And what happens when we get curious? <u>We start to notice that cravings are simply made up of body sensations—and these body sensations come and go</u>. We become this inner scientist eagerly awaiting the next data point. Now, this might sound too simplistic to affect behavior. But in one study, we found that mindfulness training was twice as good as gold-standard therapy at helping people quit smoking... So if you don't smoke or stress eat, maybe the next time you feel this urge to check your email when you're bored or trying to distract yourself from work, or maybe to compulsively respond to that text message when you're driving, see if you can tap into this natural capacity: <u>just be curiously aware of what's happening in your body and mind in that moment</u>. Instead of seeing the text message, compulsively text back, feel a little bit better—notice the urge, get curious, feel the joy of letting go and repeat." J. Brewer (February 2016). Adapted from "Judson Brewer: A Simple Way to Break a Bad Habit." TED Talks. www.ted.com.

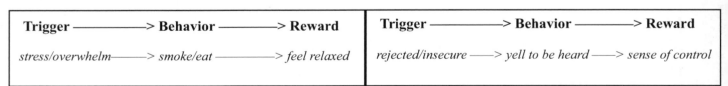

Trigger ————————> Behavior ————————> Reward	Trigger ————————> Behavior ————————> Reward
stress/overwhelm————> *smoke/eat* ————————> *feel relaxed*	*rejected/insecure* ——————> *yell to be heard* ——————> *sense of control*

Autopilot

People who live on autopilot are heavily influenced by their emotions, and they often react to stressful situations using unhealthy coping strategies, such as *avoidance* and *control*. Accountability and mindfulness are tools used to defeat unhealthy problem patterns. In his TED Talk, Judson Brewer discusses the reward-based learning process. Our context-dependent memory system forms harmful habits: *trigger-behavior-reward*. We can apply this formula to learn more about our problem relationship patterns.

❖ **Trigger**: A trigger is any **uncomfortable emotion**. Uncomfortable emotions are responses to stressors. Conflicts at work or home are common *external* stressors. Everyday *internal* stressors include exhaustion, hunger, fatigue, or upsetting thoughts. When identifying triggers, look for anything that places you in a **compromised state**. Compromised states occur when you lack self-care, have poor boundaries, struggle with passivity, avoid vulnerable emotions, lack self-awareness, or fail to heal old wounds.

❖ **Behavior**: Once you experience a trigger emotion, the coping process begins. The behavior is the **coping strategy**. Common harmful coping strategies include *avoidance* and *control*.

❖ **Reward**: The reward is simply a **temporary break** from the trigger emotion.

Autopilot Example: The *Round 1* example below shows how an *avoidant* coping strategy reinforces the trigger emotion. In *Round 2,* the problem pattern escalates with a *control* coping strategy.

Round 1

❖ **Trigger**: Relationship conflict leads to feelings of **failure** and **insecurity**. These feelings remind me of times in my childhood when I felt like nothing I did was good enough for my parents.

❖ **Behavior**: I use an **avoidant coping strategy** of going to the bar after work instead of going home.

❖ **Reward**: I use alcohol to **avoid** my feelings and my partner.

Round 2

❖ **Trigger**: When I arrive home late, my partner complains and accuses me of having an alcohol problem. The conflict leaves me feeling even more **insecure**, **inadequate**, **ashamed**, and **anxious**.

❖ **Behavior**: I respond using a **control coping strategy**: I *blame* my partner, "You're the reason I don't want to come home. You endlessly nag. Being married to you would make anyone want to drink."

❖ **Reward**: Blaming my partner gives me a **temporary break** from feeling responsible for our problems. It also pushes my partner away and ends the current conflict.

Video: TEDx (2018): "Lauren Weinstein: Don't believe everything you think." https://youtu.be/Xdhmgp4IUL0 (21:55)

Discussion: Weinstein talks about how our beliefs hold us back like invisible ropes. The first step toward change is becoming aware of our ropes, and the second step is actively pulling against them. Weinstein asks and answers, "How do you break the ropes that tie you down? Don't believe everything you think."

1.) Our invisible ropes become our triggers. Identify one of your invisible ropes:

2.) What impact does the invisible rope have on your relationships?

3.) Share the tools you will use to break free from the destructive belief:

Taylor's Story Example

Taylor had a very stressful day at work. While driving home, she was overwhelmed. She noticed the awful traffic and thought about how no one ever appreciated all of her hard work. While driving, her frustration escalated until she yelled at the other cars and pounded on the steering wheel. When she finally arrived home, she walked straight past her partner, Jeff, without acknowledging him. Taylor thinks, "I'm too tired to do anything for anyone else. Everyone always wants something from me; no one understands how hard my life is." Jeff thinks, "I'm here waiting for her, and she doesn't even notice me. She obviously doesn't care about me anymore. Well, I don't care about her, either. I'm sick of this!" *Practice*: Complete the Fact vs. Fiction outlines below. Then, create healthy responses in the scenario.

Taylor's Fact vs. Fiction Outline

Fact: Work problems and traffic

Fiction: "I'm too tired to do anything for anyone else. Everyone always wants something from me; no one understands how hard my life is."

Feelings: _____

Coping Response: _____

Jeff's Fact vs. Fiction Outline

Fact: Taylor ignored him

Fiction: "I'm here waiting for her, and she doesn't even notice me. She obviously doesn't care about me anymore. Well, I don't care about her, either. I'm sick of this!"

Feelings: _____

Coping Response: _____

Healthy Fiction for Taylor - Keep the *facts* the same, and correct the *fiction* to change the response:

Fiction: _____

Feelings: _____

Coping Response: _____

Healthy Fiction for Jeff - Keep the *facts* the same, and correct the *fiction* to change the response:

Fiction: _____

Feelings: _____

Coping Response: _____

Taylor's Problem Pattern

* **Trigger**: Work stress leads to Taylor's *insecurity*, *fear*, and *self-doubt*. In her childhood home, Taylor learned to hide these vulnerable emotions. Taylor's father would cover up his feelings by using *avoidance*. With emotional discomfort, Taylor's father would withdraw and turn to alcohol. When his family complained, he would use a *control* coping strategy of anger to keep them away.

* **Behavior**: Taylor's childhood experiences taught her to cope using *avoidance* and *control*. Instead of healthy self-care, Taylor learned to use a protective shield of isolation, anger, and victim stance.

* **Reward**: Taylor's reward is a *temporary reduction* of her emotional discomfort. Jeff's response to the rejection allows Taylor to justify her anger. Anger and resentment are more comfortable for Taylor than fear and insecurity.

Jeff's Problem Pattern

* **Trigger**: Taylor's rejection leads to Jeff's emotional *pain*. Jeff feels *afraid* when his attempts to connect are rejected. Jeff grew up feeling invisible in his home. Jeff's mother emotionally abandoned him using anger or silence. The silence was unbearable, so he preferred his mother's anger. Anytime Taylor turns away from him, Jeff begins to feel afraid of abandonment, and he aggressively pursues connection.

* **Behavior**: Jeff uses a *control* coping strategy when he aggressively pursues Taylor. He is desperate to connect, but his aggressive behavior only pushes her away.

* **Reward**: Jeff's reward is connection which *temporarily reduces* his fear. When Jeff aggressively pursues Taylor, she matches his aggression. Her angry response reduces his fear of abandonment.

Your Problem Pattern: Take a closer look at your relationship patterns. Pick a familiar conflict, and complete the problem pattern below. When uncovering your trigger-behavior-reward, look for childhood family dynamics that influence your current emotional triggers and coping responses.

* **Trigger**: (emotions/baggage)

* **Behavior**: (avoidant/control coping strategy)

* **Reward**: (temporary break)

Unless you learn to face your own shadows, you will continue to see them in others, because the world outside you is only a reflection of the world inside you.
~ Carl Jung

Taylor's De-Escalation Plan

Let's rewrite Taylor's Story. This time, Taylor implements a de-escalation plan *before* she arrives home. When Taylor notices that she is pounding on the steering wheel and yelling at the other cars, she realizes she is in a compromised state. She decides to take control of the situation rather than allow her emotions to remain in the driver's seat:

1. **Identify/Validate Your Feelings**: Taylor takes a deep breath, "Okay, what is going on with me? I'm **feeling** furious, anxious, and overwhelmed. Today was rough, and it's **normal** to feel this way." This is where Taylor begins the process of regulating her emotions. Taylor identifies and validates her feelings, so her feelings don't make the decisions for her.

2. **Present Moment**: Taylor thinks, "**Right now**, this is really uncomfortable. Sometimes we struggle, and that's okay." Taylor uses words like *right now* and *sometimes* to remind herself that the uncomfortable situation is temporary.

3. **Accountability**: *Is this helping or hurting me?* After Taylor validates her feelings, she can begin to put things in a new perspective. She takes a few deep breaths: "Sometimes work is stressful, but I **choose** to work because I want to pay my bills. Getting angry doesn't reduce the stress." Taylor uses the power words *I choose* to put herself in a position of control. Accountability leads to stability.

4. **Acceptance**: *Why not me?* Taylor thinks, "**Sometimes** we get what we want, and sometimes we don't. We all take turns struggling, and I guess it's my turn." Taylor switches from resistance to acceptance.

5. **Self-Admiration**: Taylor continues, "The overwhelming feelings **remind** me that I work really hard, and sometimes I push myself past my limit. I **admire** my work ethic, endurance, and grit." Self-admiration is one of the best tools for regulating uncomfortable emotions.

6. **Gratitude**: Taylor sighs, "I'm so **grateful** I have not given up." Gratitude brings feelings of peace.

7. **Compassion**: Taylor thinks, "My boss was doing her job; it is nothing personal. I'm very proud of myself today. It could have been a disaster, but I made it." Compassion for self and others aids in healing.

Avoiding your triggers isn't healing. Healing happens when you're triggered and you are able to move through the pain, the pattern, and the story - and walk your way to a different ending. ~ Vienna Pharaon

Your Problem Pattern: Pick a familiar conflict and complete the problem pattern below.

❖ **Trigger**: (emotions/baggage)

❖ **Behavior**: (avoidant/control coping strategy)

❖ **Reward**: (temporary break)

De-Escalation Plan Practice: Use your problem pattern example above to create your own plan:

1.) Identify/Validate Your Feelings: "It's normal to feel…"

2.) Present Moment: "Right now…"

3.) Accountability: "Is this helping me or hurting me? I'm choosing…"

4.) Acceptance: "Why not me? Sometimes…"

5.) Self-Admiration: "This feeling reminds me that I…"

6.) Gratitude: "I'm thankful…"

7.) Compassion: "From their perspective…"

You are the problem. And you are the solution. ~ Buddha

Video Homework: TEDx (2019): "Peter Sage: How to be Your Best When Life Gives You It's Worst." https://youtu.be/I4svF7J6MWg (16:15)

1.) Sage shares the toolset he used to thrive in prison. The first tool discussed is the **power of acceptance**. Sage states, "If you are complaining about something that has already happened, you are wasting your time. As soon as I walked into the prison, I implemented a zero-tolerance policy on any thoughts that started with "What if" or "Why" because you can't go back and change anything. You can choose to sit there and feel sorry for yourself, or you can unhook the energy of resistance and use that energy toward your next move." Share a personal example of using acceptance to free up the energy of resistance:

2.) The second tool he shares is **contrast frames**. Sage states, "Most of what we give meaning to is based on what we compare it to. The trick with contrast frames is to contrast where you are with something that makes you feel empowered. Freedom is a state of mind, and no one can take that away from you. I was freer in my little prison cell than many of the officers who were coming in, hating their jobs. The strongest trees don't grow in the best soil; they grow in the strongest winds." Contrast frames teach us to focus on what we *have* rather than what we do not have. *Example*: While dreading a sink full of dishes, you remind yourself, "The dishes mean we got to eat today. I'd much rather wash dishes than go hungry." Share a personal example of using contrast frames to increase your resilience during adversity:

Chapter 7 Overview Questions

1. What are your common trigger emotions?

2. What problem-coping strategy do you use most often? What is the impact of that strategy?

3. What did you learn about your problem pattern? What keeps the pattern in place?

4. What is your favorite step in the de-escalation plan? Share an example:

Chapter 8
Protective Shield

Our own worst enemy cannot harm us as much as our unwise thoughts.
No one can help us as much as our own compassionate thoughts.
~ *Buddha*

Don't believe everything you think. Thoughts are just that – thoughts.
~ *Allan Lokos*

It's not what you look at that matters, it's what you see.
~ *Henry David Thoreau*

Imperfection is not our personal problem—it is a natural part of existing.
~ *Tara Brach*

To contact the deeper truth of who we are, we must engage in some activity or
practice that questions what we assume to be true about ourselves.
~ *A. H. Almaas*

❖   Harmful Coping Strategies

❖   Deconstructing Distortions and Defenses

❖   Problem Autopilot

It's not what you look at that matters, it's what you see. ~ Henry David Thoreau

Harmful Coping Strategies

Coping strategies are behaviors we use to regulate emotion. If you are self-aware, you will use healthy coping strategies such as exercise or self-care. If you lack self-awareness, you often react to emotional triggers with a destructive protective shield of *avoidance* or *control*.

Harmful Coping Example: Your toddler jumps on the bed after being told to stop. He falls off, hurts himself, and begins to scream. When you hear the cry, your *fear* instantly turns to *anger*. Your response is aggressive, "This is why I told you NOT to jump on the bed!" In this example, the parent uses a *control* coping strategy of *blame*.

Healthy Coping Example: Using the scenario above, a self-aware person does not need a protective shield. When you hear the cry, you allow yourself to feel afraid. Because you can regulate fear, you can respond with compassion, "Are you okay, buddy? Show me where it hurts."

Video: RSA (2015): "Brene Brown on Blame." https://youtu.be/RZWf2_2L2v8 (3:28)

Discussion: Brown discusses the research on blame, "When something bad happens, the first thing we want to know is, 'Who's fault is it?' I'd rather it be my fault than no one's fault. Why? Because it gives us some semblance of control. But, here's what we know from the research: blame is simply the discharge of discomfort and pain, and blaming is very coercive in relationships."

1.) Blame is a control coping strategy that takes a bad situation and makes it worse by adding anger to the equation. *Video Example:* **Fact**: Coffee spilled everywhere. **Fiction**: "The coffee spilled because my husband *made* me stay up late." Using *blame* adds anger, and anger encourages aggression. Blame took a bad situation (*coffee mess*) and worsened it (*relationship mess*). As you go through the harmful coping strategies in this chapter, notice how each strategy takes a bad situation and makes it worse. What if the person in the video did not use blame? Create an alternate blame-free story for the video:

Deconstructing Distortions and Defenses

Gaining awareness is the first step toward defeating harmful coping strategies. To become self-aware, you need to familiarize yourself with your protective shield. Your protective shield is comprised of cognitive distortions and defense mechanisms (*harmful fiction*). Distortions and defenses are harmful coping strategies when feeling vulnerable, unstable, or insecure. While everyone has used all of these, you will notice that some are more familiar to you than others. **Practice**: Please read the following list, and take note of the ones that seem most familiar. Share a personal example for each distortion and defense in the space provided.

> *Our own worst enemy cannot harm us as much as our unwise thoughts.*
> *No one can help us as much as our own compassionate thoughts. ~ Buddha*

1. Personalizing is the process of making everything about yourself. You will see events as directly related to you rather than considering other possibilities. In "Taylor's Story" from chapter 7, Jeff personalizes when he assumes that Taylor ignored him. Another example is assuming the driver in front of you is driving extra slow because they are trying to make you mad.
Fact: My partner is angry.
Fiction: "My partner is angry because I did something wrong."
Corrective Mantra: *It's not about me.*

2. Assuming is a distortion that is similar to mind reading. You will assume you know people's thoughts and feelings without allowing them to speak for themselves, which is why this distortion causes many relationship conflicts. In "Taylor's Story," Jeff assumed that Taylor didn't care about him.
Fact: As soon as I walk into the room, my partner closes their laptop.
Fiction: "My partner is hiding something from me."
Corrective Mantra: *When we assume we are wrong more than right.*

3. Blaming is a distortion where you hold other people responsible for your feelings or problems. Blaming others diminishes your power. *Examples*: "You're making me feel bad about myself" or "You know how to push my buttons; you're making me angry." In reality, you control your thoughts, feelings, and behaviors. No one can *make* you feel any particular way. Most of your feelings come from your thoughts, *not* your circumstances.
Fact: My partner called the police after a conflict.
Fiction: "If my partner didn't call the police, I would not have been arrested."
Corrective Mantra: *Stay in your lane; don't give your power away with blame.*

4. Catastrophizing is taking things to a negative extreme, ruminating about a parade of horribles, and forecasting worst-case scenarios. *Examples:* "My child did not wash their hands before eating, so we're all going to get sick" or "I've had a headache all day, and it's probably a brain tumor."
Fact: I did not pay the rent on time.
Fiction: "We will be evicted and homeless for the rest of our lives."
Corrective Mantra: *Step off the emotional rollercoaster.*

5. Should is a shaming word that produces anger. It is important to accept life as it is, not as it *should* be. In "Taylor's Story," Jeff uses a *should* when he thinks Taylor *should* not ignore him.
Fact: My child talks back to me.
Fiction: "My child should respect me. They should not treat me like that."
Corrective Mantra: *Change should to "wish," "want," or "would like."*

6. Overgeneralizing is a distortion where you make general conclusions about life from a single incident. You will know you are overgeneralizing when you hear yourself using words like *always, never, no one,* or *everyone.* Overgeneralizing distorts reality by adding permanence.
Fact: I wasn't invited.
Fiction: "I'm never included in anything. No one likes me."
Corrective Mantra: *Use words like "right now" or "sometimes" to increase tolerance.*

7. Polarized Thinking is the all-or-nothing thinking pattern. You use this type of thinking when you place people or situations in "either/or" categories, ignoring the middle ground. *Examples*: "Either I'm promoted or a failure." "If it doesn't happen now, it never will." "My house is a mess; I'm a slob."
Fact: My partner didn't text me back.
Fiction: "If they don't respond, they don't love me."
Corrective Mantra: *Find the middle ground.*

8. Negative Filtering removes all the positive information and focuses only on the negative.
Fact: I've consistently delivered all my projects on time, but I missed a deadline today.
Fiction: "Missing a deadline is unprofessional. I'm incompetent, and I should be fired."
Corrective Mantra: *Hunt the positive to balance your perspective.*

9. Displacement is used when you cannot directly confront someone who has hurt you. Instead of asserting yourself, you pick a safe target to attack. *Example*: "My boss yelled at me today, and I felt embarrassed. When I got home from work, I yelled at my children for leaving their toys everywhere."
Fact: I'm at dinner with friends, but I'm thinking about my job stress.
Fiction: "My friends are so annoying tonight. I can't stand being around them."
Corrective Mantra: *If you are looking for a punching bag, go to the gym.*

10. Projection is typically used when you unconsciously reject something about yourself. You don't want to own the unacceptable trait, so you place it on someone else. *Examples*: A dishonest person accuses others of being dishonest. I'm cheating on my spouse, but I accuse my spouse of cheating on me.
Fact: I secretly despise my mother-in-law.
Fiction: "I can tell that my mother-in-law hates me by how she looks at me."
Corrective Mantra: *Imperfections mean I'm human. Don't project — accept.*

11. Compartmentalizing suppresses uncomfortable thoughts and feelings when you do not want to change. This defense prevents you from connecting the dots, so you fail to see the relationship between different problems. *Example*: I don't identify that my drinking is causing my marital problems.
Fact: The school called complaining that my son was bullying others.
Fiction: "My son is very well-behaved at home. People are too sensitive these days."
Corrective Mantra: *Connect the dots.*

12. Entitlement convinces you that you're *owed,* which leads to poor boundaries. *Example*: If you hold a door open for a stranger, you are not owed a thank-you. You decide if you hold the door open, and the stranger decides if they acknowledge you. If you expect a thank-you, you set yourself up for anger.
Fact: I worked a ten-hour day while my partner was home.
Fiction: "After such a long day, dinner should be ready when I get home."
Corrective Mantra: *We are not owed anything. Expectations lead to disappointment.*

13. Denial can be a helpful coping strategy when you've received traumatic or shocking information. Temporarily denying reality can provide the time needed to adapt and cope. Denial becomes a problem when used chronically. *Example*: A parent who denies that their child has a drug problem.
Fact: My partner moved out and filed for divorce.
Fiction: "Everything's fine; we just need a chance to talk."
Corrective Mantra: *Lying to myself does not change the truth. Denial keeps me in the dark.*

14. Rationalization is used to justify inappropriate behaviors to avoid feelings of guilt or shame. *Example*: "I would not cheat on my taxes if the government actually put my money to good use."
Fact: I yelled at my child, and I called them names.
Fiction: "There's only so much a person can take before they lose it. My child pushed me to my limit."
Corrective Mantra: *Don't avoid the truth. Own Your Own Stuff!*

Homework - <u>Create a Trigger-Behavior-Reward outline using your problem distortions/defenses</u>.

Trigger: I was feeling overwhelmed and alone. I thought, "If my partner loved me, I would not feel this way (*polarized thinking/blame*)." My father would *blame* my mother when he was unhappy, too.

Behavior: I *blamed* my partner because I felt they *should* do more to help. I thought I *shouldn't* have to ask for help; they *should* just know what I need (*entitlement/should*). I said, "You are *never* there for me. This marriage has been a total joke, and it's *always* going to be like this because you're *never* going to change." (*negative filtering/catastrophizing/generalizing*)

Reward: The anger I felt toward my partner gave me a false sense of control, which *reduced* my feelings of insecurity. My partner responded to my aggression with remorse, which made me feel less alone.

Trigger: (emotions/baggage)

Behavior: (distortions/defenses)

Reward: (temporary break)

Homework - Watch the videos below and answer the discussion questions.

Video: Fearless Soul (2018): "Joe Dispenza: Learn How to Control Your Mind." https://youtu.be/v7KQsS2kLM4 (17:03)

Discussion: Dispenza discusses the body as the unconscious mind, pulling us toward the familiar, even if the familiar is not in our best interest. Meditation/visualization creates new neural pathways in the brain and helps you achieve your goals. *Example*: You usually yell at your children to stop fighting; therefore, your brain has a pathway that encourages you to yell when they fight. A brain association means: <u>They fight —> you yell</u>. *Visualization:* Imagine a desired response to the same stressor, and visualize yourself responding successfully: <u>They fight —> you slow down and use positive parenting tools</u>. Repeat the corrective visualization to create a new neural pathway in your brain.

1.) <u>Choose a common stressor that you would like to manage better</u>:

2.) <u>Share your corrective visualization</u>:

Video: TED (2016): "Isaac Lindsky: What Reality are You Creating for Yourself?" https://youtu.be/cmpu58yv8-g (11:46)

Discussion: Lindsky discusses, "What you see is not objective reality; what you see is a personal reality created by your brain. You create your own reality, and you believe it. How do you live your life with eyes wide open? -- Hold yourself accountable for every moment, every thought, and every detail. See beyond your fears, and recognize your <u>assumptions</u>. Harness your internal strength, and silence your internal critic. Accept your strengths and weaknesses, and understand the difference. Your fears, critics, villains, heroes -- they are your <u>excuses</u>, <u>rationalizations</u>, <u>shortcuts</u>, <u>justifications</u>; they are your surrender. <u>They are fictions you perceive as your reality</u>."

1.) Lindsky discusses how your personal narrative creates your reality, and these stories are harmful fiction. Review the distortions and defenses discussed in this chapter, and identify the ones you struggle with most. <u>What impact does your fiction have on your reality</u>? <u>Describe how your distortions and defenses take bad situations and make them worse</u>:

Chapter 9
Family History Exercise

A dysfunctional family is any family with more than one person in it.
~ *Mary Karr*

Trauma is a fact of life. It does not, however, have to be a life sentence.
~ *Peter A. Levine*

There are three solutions to every problem: *accept it*, *change it*, or *leave it*. If
you can't accept it, change it. If you can't change it, leave it.
~ *Buddha*

Happiness is a choice, not a result. Nothing will make you happy until you
choose to be happy. No person will make you happy unless you decide to
be happy. Your happiness will not come to you. It can only come from you.
~ *Ralph Marston*

Every storm runs out of rain.
~ *Maya Angelou*

❖   Internal Dialogue

❖   Childhood Experiences

❖   Family Drawing Exercise

Video: TEDx (2013): "Shirzad Chamine: Know Your Inner Saboteurs." https://youtu.be/-zdJ1ubvoXs (20:32)

Discussion: Chamine shares his childhood experiences, "My father was scary, angry, and unpredictably violent. My mother was always running around, terrified. I didn't get much love. Since my life was in my parents' hands, it would have been absolutely terrifying to admit they were flawed. So, instead, a voice started forming in my head, saying that my parents were perfect, and the reason they didn't love me was because I was unworthy of their love. I now call this voice the "Judge." Of course, once the Judge started judging me, it also had to start judging everybody else around me. The Judge character in my head was constantly and brutally beating down not only others, but myself. It was the invisible lens in my head that distorted my reality. **I later discovered that in addition to the Judge, there are nine other saboteurs**… Even in a perfectly happy childhood, you still develop a couple of these saboteurs as coping mechanisms as a vulnerable kid. For example, you might develop Controller tendencies to feel safer in a chaotic environment or become the Victim to get more attention. These saboteurs pretend they are you, but they aren't you. A war is constantly raging inside your head between your saboteurs and your original true self, whom I call your Sage."

Example: Chamine discusses weakening the inner saboteurs by exposing and labeling them. Once you identify a saboteur, you can replace it with your Sage perspective, your positive intelligence brain. The Sage will take every circumstance and turn it into an opportunity. Read the ten saboteur examples below and notice which ones seem most familiar. Then, share three of your own.

1. **Judge**: "My Judge voice tells me that my partner is disrespectful."

2. **Controller**: "My Controller voice tells me I need to get my children to do as I say."

3. **Stickler**: "My Stickler voice tells me that there is a right way and a wrong way."

4. **Victim**: "My Victim voice tells me that no one appreciates me."

5. **Avoider**: "My Avoider voice tells me that I cannot deal with this right now."

6. **Restless**: "My Restless voice tells me to distract myself and stay busy."

7. **Hypervigilant**: "My Hypervigilant voice tells me I can't let my guard down or trust anyone."

8. **Pleaser**: "My Pleaser voice tells me that I need to make sure everyone is happy."

9. **Hyper-Achiever**: "My Hyper-Achiever voice tells me that I'm worthless if I don't succeed."

10. **Hyper-Rational**: "My Hyper-Rational voice tells me I need to stick with what I know."

Practice: Chamine states that regardless of our childhood experiences, we all have the Judge and at least one additional saboteur. Identify which saboteurs you experience most, and share personal examples:

1.) _____

2.) _____

3.) _____

A dysfunctional family is any family with more than one person in it. ~ Mary Karr

History Exercise: Your internal dialogue is an adaptation to your early experiences. <u>Complete the sentences below</u>:

The most challenging part of my childhood was _____

_____

_____

The thoughts and feelings related to this are _____

_____

_____

The long-term impact of this struggle is _____

_____

_____

The best part of my childhood was _____

_____

_____

The thoughts and feelings related to this are _____

_____

_____

The long-term impact of this is _____

_____

_____

Looking back on my early experiences, the messages I received about myself include _____

_____

Superpower Family Drawing - Create a drawing of your childhood family in the space provided below. Assign each member superpowers representing their character traits and role. Each member can have multiple powers; be sure to include yourself as a superhero.

Example Drawing: "My mother is the storm, raging out of control. My father is the boat sailing out to sea, leaving us alone in the storm. My brother has the power of invisibility, and I am the umbrella of protection, keeping my brother safe from the storm."

Drawing Discussion

1. In his TED Talk, Chamine stated, "Even in a perfectly happy childhood, you still develop a couple of these saboteurs as coping mechanisms as a vulnerable kid." Review your drawing, and describe the connection between your saboteurs and your childhood experiences:

2. Share an example of a childhood theme in your adult relationships: *Example*: "I never felt good enough as a child, and I don't feel good enough in my marriage."

3. Do you feel like you've gravitated toward the familiar when you look at your adult relationships? Do you notice similarities between your childhood family and your adult family? Explain:

Chapter 10
Trauma Recovery

Helplessness and isolation are the core experiences of psychological trauma.
Empowerment and reconnection are the core experiences of recovery.
~ *Judith Herman*

As traumatized children, we always dreamed that someone would come and
save us. We never dreamed that it would, in fact, be ourselves, as adults.
~ *Alice Little*

Unexpressed emotions will never die. They are buried alive,
and they will come forth later in uglier ways.
~ *Freud*

We are not what happened to us. We are what we are holding onto.
~ *Nansia Movidi*

Don't judge yourself by your past. You don't live there anymore.
~ *Ifeanyi Enoch Onuoha*

❖   Unresolved Trauma

❖   Three-Stage Trauma Recovery - *Face It, Feel It, Heal It*

❖   Quicksand Escape Steps

Video: Daniel Beaty (2010): "Knock, Knock on Def Jam Poetry." https://youtu.be/RTZrPVqR0D8 (2:35)

Discussion: Beaty states, "I write these words for the little boy in me who still awaits his papa's knock… Twenty-five years later, a little boy cries. So, I write these words, and I try to heal. I try to father myself, and I dream of a father who says the words my father did not…" Beaty uses poetry to process his childhood trauma. How do you relate to this video? What could have helped him heal during his childhood without changing his traumatic loss? Share your thoughts:

Memory

The brain pairs experience with emotion. Generally, if your early caregivers are loving and attentive, your brain will associate intimate relationships with feelings of safety and comfort. As a result, you will likely seek intimacy and feel secure in close relationships. On the other hand, let's say that your early caregivers are abusive or rejecting. In this scenario, your brain associates relationships with feelings of fear, ambivalence, pain, or anger. An insecure attachment can lead to chaos and conflict within relationships.

Unresolved Trauma

When past trauma goes unresolved, you carry it through life. The harmful baggage influences the way you think, feel, and behave. To let go of the weight, you'll need to *face it*, *feel it*, and *heal it*. Read the example below, and complete the unresolved trauma exercise.

Trauma: abandonment in childhood

Message: "If I need others, they will hurt me. I'm not lovable."

Baggage: "I either avoid close relationships or I am desperate for connection. When I'm in a committed relationship, my partner feels suffocated. I will do anything to keep a relationship going, even if it's toxic."

Trauma: betrayal trauma/trust violations

Message: _____

Baggage: _____

Trauma: physical/emotional abuse

Message: _____

Baggage: _____

Three-Stage Trauma Recovery

1. **FACE IT**:   process the trauma - *develop a sense of control*
2. **FEEL IT**:   acceptance and compassion - *lean into the emotional pain*
3. **HEAL IT**:   re-story to find the gift from the suffering - *answer, survival, message*

Stage 1: Face It

Judith Herman said, "Helplessness and isolation are the core experiences of psychological trauma. Empowerment and reconnection are the core experiences of recovery." What is trauma? Can an experience be traumatic for one person but not for another? Two elements are required for trauma: *a lack of control* and *emotional suffering*. "To restore its equilibrium, the brain tries to quiet our sensitized trauma-related memories by pushing us to have repetitive small 'doses' of recall…Our brains are naturally pulled to make sense of trauma in a way that allows us to become tolerant to it, to mentally shift the traumatic experience from one in which we are completely helpless to one in which we have some mastery" (Perry & Szalavitz, 2006, pp.53–54). Research shows that rushing people to talk about their traumatic experiences can sometimes be counterproductive. It's essential to follow the lead of each individual.

The first recovery step usually occurs naturally following a "socially acceptable" traumatic experience. *Example*: Imagine you're driving, and another car crashes into you. The accident is devastating, and the other driver is killed. After you recover from the shock, you begin telling the detailed events to anyone who will listen. This is the first step of trauma recovery. By retelling the story, you are *facing it*. Now, let's change the circumstances: Imagine you caused the accident because you were texting while driving. With the addition of *shame* to the equation, you cannot process the trauma. The human response to shame is to go into hiding, which is one of the reasons why childhood abuse can lead to lifelong suffering. Children tend to blame themselves for the abuse, which blocks the first step of trauma recovery.

Stage 2: Feel It

Ifeanyi Enoch Onuoha said, "Don't judge yourself by your past. You don't live there anymore." The second step of recovery requires embracing uncomfortable emotions with acceptance. *Example*: Imagine getting a piercing or tattoo. You know that it will be painful, but you breathe deeply and lean into the pain. Leaning into the pain with acceptance allows you to reach your goal. Similarly, trauma recovery requires leaning into emotional pain. When processing trauma, turning toward yourself with a loving heart is critical. Research shows that compassion produces change, and shame produces stagnation. "Recovery happens when you can name the truth and receive the validation, compassion, and understanding that is needed. Keeping secrets deadens a part of us and stops the healing of our emotions and spirit. Telling the truth brings the heart back to life" (Casarjian, 1995, p.39).

Stage 3: Heal It

Nansia Movidi said, "We are not what happened to us. We are what we are holding onto." People under the influence of depression have selective memories and recall things that are consistent with their depressed mood. This is a self-sustaining pattern: a depressed mood leads to negative memory recall, which leads to a continued depressed mood. Individuals who suffered abuse, neglect, or abandonment in childhood can distort new events in a negative light.

To heal, you must change your brain by intentionally re-storying your history (Amen, 2015). The final stage of recovery is creating a re-story to move beyond the trauma. During recovery, people often become stuck with "why" questions. "Why did that happen?" "Why did I do that?" "Why didn't they love me?" "Why did they abuse me?" The "why" questions are like quicksand; they hold you back while slowly pulling you deeper. To escape the quicksand, re-story your history to change your relationship with the past.

Quicksand Escape Steps:
1.) Provide a fact-based *answer* to the "why" questions
2.) Focus on how **you** *survived* the trauma
3.) Find the *message* and *gift* from the emotion

Example 1: "Why didn't my mom love me? Why did she reject me?"
1.) *Answer*: My mom lacked the ability to love. She rejected me because of her inadequacies.
2.) *Survival*: I grew up feeling insignificant, but I stayed focused on my future. I was amazingly resilient.
3.) *Message*: The hurt reminds me that family is important to me and makes me a loving, devoted parent.

Practice - Share a personal "why" question, and use the *Quicksand Escape Steps* to become unstuck:

"Why_____

1.) *Answer*:

2.) *Survival*:

3.) *Message/Gift*:

Three-Stage Trauma Recovery: "Why did I text and drive? Why did I cause a fatal car accident?"

Face It: "I never imagined destroying so many lives in seconds, but I did. I used to think I was invincible, but I had poor judgment. It was a human moment with devastating consequences."

Feel It: "The emotional pain is so intense that I lose touch with reality. Sometimes, I feel like I'm not in my body; it's a terrifying, hollow, empty feeling. When I think about the pain I've caused, my sorrow turns to self-hatred. I would do anything to change positions with the person I killed, and the regret is unbearable."

Heal It: *Answer*: "At that moment, I had extremely poor judgment." *Survival*: "I cannot change my fatal decision, but I am grateful that I've responded with accountability and remorse." *Message/Gift:* "The regret reminds me that I'm a good person who is empathic. This tragedy has given me the gift of humility."

Video: TED (2018): "Azim Khamisa, Ples Felix: What Comes After Tragedy? Forgiveness." https://youtu.be/85hbMtegrLc (13:06)
Discussion: They both suffered traumatic losses. What tools or mindset did they use to heal? How did they use accountability and normalizing to forgive? Apply the Three-Stage Trauma Recovery to their story:

Face It:

Feel It:

Heal It:

Video: TEDx (2019): "Matt Brown: The Barbershop Where Men Go to Heal." https://youtu.be/4UhP3OZ9ZCEw (25:25)

Discussion: Brown shares his own story of childhood abuse. He states, "I grew up my whole life wearing masks. If we can't take our mask off and be real, then all we have left is anger. We wear socially acceptable masks of pride and anger, but inside we are just hurt little boys. I help men take their masks off one haircut at a time… Shared pain feels less traumatic. Your childhood wasn't your fault, but your healing is now your responsibility. I chose to forgive my father. Forgiveness doesn't condone his actions, but it releases me."

1.) Brown states, "The mask protected me, but if we want to heal, we need to be seen. You are only loved as much as you are known, but will you have the courage to be known?" Bessel van der Kolk said, "As long as you keep secrets and suppress information, you are fundamentally at war with yourself." Share how avoiding painful memories has affected your life:

2.) Nansia Movidi said, "We are not what happened to us. We are what we are holding onto." Share an example of choosing forgiveness or acceptance in order to let go of painful baggage:

Healing Visualization

Alice Little said, "As traumatized children, we always dreamed that someone would come and save us. We never dreamed that it would, in fact, be ourselves, as adults." Corrective visualizations are one of the most effective tools during the final healing stage. "Healing your inner child is a process of letting him or her know that now there is someone with whom their pain and innocence can be safely shared. This someone is the healthy adult within you" (Casarjian, 1995, p.49).

Visualization Example: Get comfortable in your chair, and close your eyes. Take three slow, deep breaths: As you inhale, breathe in *peace*. As you exhale, let go of *tension*. As you inhale, breathe in *love*. As you exhale, let go of *resentment*. As you inhale, breathe in *warmth*. As you exhale, let go of *insecurity*. As you continue to breathe in deeply, allow your breathing to keep you relaxed and peaceful. Now, imagine yourself during a time when you were feeling afraid and alone; a time when you were suffering and no one was there for you. Notice how old you were. See what you looked like back then. Now, imagine your adult self interacting with your younger self. Look deep into the eyes of your younger self, and ask them to share their painful experiences, feelings, and unmet needs. Allow yourself to respond to your inner child with compassion. Tell your younger self they are worthy of love and reassure them that they will never be alone again. Continue to visualize sitting with your younger self until you feel safe and peaceful. Imagine both of you experiencing a new bond founded on love and forgiveness.

Example Trauma: I was texting while driving, and I caused a fatal car accident.

Example Healing Visualization: "I visualize my current self returning to the accident scene. I look deep into the eyes of my younger self, and I see feelings of pain, shock, and despair. It was a time when I felt alone and terrified. I could see the pain wash over my younger self at the moment of recognition that I'd made a fatal mistake. At that moment, my younger self needed to hear that the mistake would not define me as a human being. The suffering ahead was beyond imaginable, but the path would lead me to who I am today. In the depths of despair, I would ultimately find my best self. The future gift of the suffering is my generosity, humility, and compassion for others."

Three-Stage Trauma Recovery Example

Face It: I felt like my father never liked me, and one day, he just left. My mom was stressed, and she'd blame me. She'd tell me it was my fault he left. She used to say that her life would have been better without me. I was raised in a home with people who were incapable of love. I grew up feeling unwanted, and I hated myself. I did a lot of drinking, drugs, and fighting. As an adult, I always hear myself say, "No one cares about me." This theme is from my childhood. I was raised by people who were incapable of caring for me.

Feel It: I was a kid who just wanted to be loved. I grew up feeling worthless, and I did not allow myself to care about anything. I was always angry, and it was the only thing that kept me going. Beneath the anger was deep pain, but I was terrified of the depths of my despair, so I didn't go there. Anger saved me.

Heal It: *Answer*: I was worthy of love, but they lacked the ability to love. *Survival*: I survived by creating deep connections with my friends as a kid. I had the strength to create a family for myself. *Message/Gift*: My childhood suffering has given me the gift of being a devoted parent and partner. *Visualization*: I close my eyes and focus on my breath. I take in five slow, deep breaths. I remind myself that I am safe. I visualize my adult self connecting with my inner child. I look deep into the eyes of my younger self, and I see the pain and despair. I imagine sitting with my younger self, and my heart is filled with love for this child. I allow my younger self to share their experiences with me. My adult self is the loving parent that my younger self always needed. I take time to comfort my younger self. I imagine holding the child in my arms, and the anger decreases. I tell my younger self that they will never be alone again. I focus my attention on my breathing. I take five slow, deep breaths. When I'm ready, I open my eyes.

Video: TEDx (2020): "Debi Silber: Do You Have Post Betrayal Syndrome?" https://youtu.be/iyqOR69dHiU (11:33)

Discussion: Silber states, "Healing from betrayal is different than any other life crises. With betrayal, your whole self has to be rebuilt… Ninety percent of people who have suffered betrayal trauma want to move forward, but they don't know how. Betrayal affects every area of life. In relationships, if we don't learn the profound lesson that betrayal is trying to teach, we have repeat betrayals or we put that big wall up and don't let anyone get close. We can't undo betrayal, but we can decide how long it affects our lives. If you are willing to use the trauma as an opportunity to learn and grow, the gift of betrayal is transformation. There's a difference between resilience and transformation. Resilience means your house needs a new paint job, so you paint it. Transformation means a tornado has leveled your house. You have every right to stand there and mourn the loss of your house until your last breath. You don't have to do anything, but if you choose to rebuild, that's transformation…When you heal from betrayal, you'll see a version of yourself emerge that never would have shown up if that experience didn't happen."

1.) Silber uses the analogy of rebuilding a house to describe healing. Share a personal example of transformation:

2.) Silber discusses the gift of betrayal and states, "We can't undo betrayal, but we can decide how long it affects our lives." Share an example of choosing to rebuild. What tools did you use to let go? What version of yourself emerged from the suffering?

Practice 1: Use the example provided to practice the stages of healing.

FACE IT: In my home, my younger brother was the target. My parents always picked on him. I was their favorite, and I never got in trouble. When my brother was really young, he would cry to me and ask for help, but I never did anything to help him. It's hard to admit, but I picked on him, too. It ruined my brother's life. As an adult, he's a mess. I wish I could go back and protect him; I have so much regret.

FEEL IT: (acceptance and compassion - lean into the emotional pain without resistance)

HEAL IT: (re-story to find the gift from the suffering - *answer, survival, message/gift*)

Practice 2: Use the example provided to practice the stages of healing.

FACE IT: I grew up in a family feeling loved, but I always felt a little different. When I was young, I remember asking my mom if I was adopted, but she laughed it off. My younger siblings seemed so close, and I never really fit in. As an adult, I discovered the truth when my son had medical issues. I asked my mom about our medical history, and she finally confessed. They didn't want me to feel different because I was their only adopted child. At that moment, my whole life changed in an instant. I didn't know who I was, and everything I thought I had known for thirty years was a lie. It felt as if I'd lost my identity.

FEEL IT: (acceptance and compassion - *lean into the emotional pain*)

HEAL IT: (re-story to find the gift from the suffering - *answer, survival, message/gift*)

Homework: Practice applying the stages of trauma recovery to heal and let go of past baggage.

FACE IT: (process the trauma - *develop a sense of control*)

FEEL IT: (acceptance and compassion - *lean into the emotional pain*)

HEAL IT: (re-story to find the gift from the suffering - *answer, survival, message/gift*)

Visualization: (heal your inner child)

Chapter 11
Substance Use and Shame

Truth is like a surgery, it hurts but cures. Lie is like a painkiller,
it gives instant relief but has side effects forever.

~ Krishna Kumar

Shame dies when stories are told in safe places.

~ Ann Voskamp

Nothing ever goes away until it has taught us what we need to know.

~ Pema Chodron

If all you can do is crawl, start crawling.

~ Rumi

Be kind to past versions of yourself who didn't know what you know now.

~ Unknown

❖   Problem Coping Strategies

❖   Identify Your Cage

Problem Coping Strategies

The World Health Organization (August 2022) estimates that alcohol use is involved in roughly fifty-five percent of domestic violence incidents. Substance use is an *avoidant* coping strategy and is highly correlated with shame. As we discuss addiction, the "substance" can be anything we turn toward to avoid emotional discomfort, such as alcohol, electronics, work, love, food, drugs, pornography, gambling, sex, spending, exercise, etc.

TED Talk - Brene Brown: Listening to Shame (20:38)

"Shame is a focus on self; guilt is a focus on behavior. Shame is, 'I *am* bad.' Guilt is, 'I *did* something bad.' Guilt: 'I'm sorry; I *made* a mistake.' Shame: 'I'm sorry; I *am* a mistake.' There's a huge difference between shame and guilt, and here's what you need to know: Shame is highly correlated with addiction, depression, violence, aggression, bullying, suicide, and eating disorders. And here's what you need to know even more: guilt is inversely correlated with those things. The ability to hold something we've done or failed to do up against who we want to be is incredibly adaptive. It's uncomfortable, but it's adaptive. Shame is an epidemic in our culture… Very quickly, some research by Mahalik at Boston College. He asked, 'What do women need to do to conform to female norms?' The top answers in this country: nice, thin, modest, and use all available resources for appearance. 'What do men in this country need to do to conform with male norms?' The answers were always: show emotional control, work is first, pursue status and violence…We have to understand and know empathy because empathy is the antidote to shame. If you put shame in a Petri dish, it needs three things to grow exponentially: secrecy, silence, and judgment. If you put shame in a Petri dish and douse it with empathy, it can't survive." B. Brown (March 2012). Adapted from "Brene Brown: Listening to Shame." TED Talks. https://youtu.be/psN1DORYYV0

1.) Brown stated, "Shame is highly correlated with addiction, depression, violence, aggression, bullying, suicide, and eating disorders." Why do you think shame is so destructive? Share messages of shame you have carried:

2.) Unlike shame, guilt is highly adaptive and requires vulnerability. Vulnerability is the courage to allow yourself to be seen. In order to feel guilt, you must be honest with yourself and hold yourself accountable. Guilt is a sign of courage. Please share an experience when you felt guilty:

3.) Brown discussed the research that shame grows in "secrecy, silence, and judgment." The antidote to shame is empathy. Practice correcting your messages of shame with empathy:

Video: TEDx (2020): "Sue Bryce: Changing Perspective from Shame to Self-Worth" https://youtu.be/5_Tq5A0m7_U (15:32)

Discussion: Bryce states, "Shame is the guiding light to your self-worth. <u>Your pain simply comes from resistance and not accepting yourself.</u> The only person who can decide if you are worthy of anything is you. The worst and best part of this work is you are the poison, and you are the antidote. How do you rewrite your story? Go back to the moment right when you feel fear before you take action. Question everything fear tells you. Observe your thoughts in this moment, and you will see yourself searching for your old story. **Whatever you do in this moment, do not numb the pain.** <u>Don't eat it, don't drink it, don't shop it.</u> **We've become a numbing culture. Instead of numbing, just feel and observe.** When we disable our avoidance, we start evolving, and this is where you create a new story. **You will become as successful as the amount of pain you are willing to endure.** <u>It's very important to stay present because if you go back to the past, you will bring in resentment. If you go into the future, you will bring in fear.</u> Observe yourself until you have complete control over how you respond. I want you to master the focus of self-acceptance, self-awareness, and pure self-love because this is where you challenge your old identity. There is more power in emotional mastery than in any skill you can learn. I suffered deep shame for being uneducated, and ironically, I built an education company. **I embraced my greatest shame**, **and it became my superpower.** It's never too late to rewrite your story."

1.) Bryce states, "You will be as successful as the amount of pain you are willing to endure." Learning to tolerate uncomfortable emotions eliminates problem coping strategies. *Example*: If I can tolerate fear, I do not need to use *avoidance* (substance abuse) or *control* (domestic abuse). <u>Practice embracing an uncomfortable feeling with the three steps of emotional regulation:</u>

Identify: (name the vulnerable emotion)

Validate: ("It's okay that I feel…")

Admire: ("This emotion reminds me that I…")

2.) Bryce discusses *defeating resistance* by turning shame into your superpower. <u>Think about a message of shame you have carried, and reframe it into one of your strengths:</u>

TED Talk - Johann Hari: Everything You Think You Know about Addiction Is Wrong (14:42)

"Why do we carry on with this approach that doesn't seem to be working? The thing I realized that really blew my mind is almost everything we think we know about addiction is wrong. I met a man called Bruce Alexander. He's a professor of psychology in Vancouver who carried out an incredible experiment I think really helps us to understand this issue. Professor Alexander built a cage that he called 'Rat Park,' which is basically heaven for rats. They've got both the water bottles, the normal water, and the drugged water. But here's the fascinating thing: In Rat Park, they don't like the drug water. They almost never use it. None of them ever use it compulsively. None of them ever overdose. <u>You go from almost one hundred percent overdose when they're isolated to zero percent overdose when they have happy, connected lives</u>... There was a human experiment into the exact same principle happening at the exact same time. It was called the Vietnam War. In Vietnam, twenty percent of all American troops were using loads of heroin...they didn't go into withdrawal. Ninety-five percent of them just stopped... Professor Alexander began to think there might be a different story about addiction. He said what if addiction isn't about your chemical hooks? <u>What if addiction is about your cage? What if addiction is an adaptation to your environment</u>? There was another professor called Peter Cohen in the Netherlands who said maybe we shouldn't call it addiction; maybe we should call it bonding. <u>Human beings have a natural and innate need to bond, and when we're happy and healthy, we'll bond and connect with each other, but if you can't do that because you're traumatized or isolated or beaten down by life, you will bond with something that will give you some sense of relief. Now, that might be gambling, that might be pornography, that might be cocaine, that might be cannabis, but you will bond and connect with something because that's our nature</u>...The opposite of addiction is connection." J. Hari. (June 2015). Adapted from "Johann Hari: Everything You Think You Know about Addiction Is Wrong." https://youtu.be/PY9DcIMGxMs

Video Discussion:

1.) Hari discusses the theory that addiction is an adaptation to our environment and a form of bonding. The cage analogy highlights the connection between substance use and our headspace. Think about your headspace/lifestyle when you had an addiction mindset of numbing or avoiding the pain. <u>Share examples of your cage</u>:

2.) Similar to the *control* coping strategy of domestic abuse, distorted thoughts of minimization, denial, and blame feed the *avoidant* coping strategy of substance use. <u>Choose one of your avoidant coping behaviors, and provide an example for each cognitive distortion below</u>:

Minimization: ("It was just a few drinks.")

Denial: ("I don't have a problem.")

Blame: ("I was overserved.")

Chapter 12
Understanding Emotional Intelligence

All changes, even the most longed for, have their melancholy,
for what we leave behind us is a part of ourselves; we must
die to one life before we can enter into another.
~ Anatole France

Pain is inevitable. Suffering is optional.
~ Buddha

Suffering usually relates to wanting things to be different than they are.
~ Allan Lokos

❖   Core Factors of Emotional Intelligence

❖   Catch/Correct

❖   High EQ Characteristics

❖   Riding Emotional Waves

Emotional Intelligence

Studies show that emotional intelligence (EQ) is the most significant predictor of performance in the workplace and the strongest driver of personal excellence (Bradberry & Greaves, 2009). Your EQ level impacts almost everything you do and say each day. Studies find that when emotional intelligence is factored into the equation, it is the missing link that explains why people with average IQs outperform people with the highest IQs 70 percent of the time (Bradberry, 2015). Research shows that 90 percent of top performers have high emotional intelligence (Bradberry, 2015). EQ is a flexible set of skills that can be improved, and by the time you complete this program, you will have elevated your level!

Some families naturally model emotional intelligence, while others teach children to deny emotions. Freud said, "Unexpressed emotions will never die. They are buried alive, and they will come forth later in uglier ways." Rejecting or denying an emotion does not make it disappear; the emotion remains unprocessed and heavily distorts your reality. This process creates relationship problems by encouraging *avoidant* or *control* coping strategies.

EQ Example

A little boy falls and begins to cry. What is a typical adult response in this situation? "Shake it off, kid! You're okay. Be a man; men don't cry." On the other hand, a little girl falls and begins to cry. What is a typical adult response? The adult may scoop her up, cuddle, nurture her, and allow her to express feelings of hurt, pain, and fear. The message to the little girl is that her feelings are normal, natural, and acceptable (high EQ). The message to the little boy is that it is not okay to feel vulnerable emotions such as hurt, fear, sadness, or pain (low EQ). What emotion is left for the little boy? *Anger.* Anger is an emotion that blocks healing and gives you a false sense of control. So instead of feeling vulnerable, you will just feel angry.

The most effective way to manage emotions is through acceptance. If you are taught to resist emotions, you will automatically fail to regulate them. What is the impact on the individual who is trained to reject feelings? Usually, the result is to use *avoidant* or *control* coping strategies. Anger is a harmful strategy used to *avoid* vulnerable emotions and *control* others. The problem with anger is that it heavily distorts reality, encourages aggression, and engages your natural fight/flight/freeze survival response.

Discussion Questions:

1.) How did your childhood family respond to your emotional needs?

2.) What were acceptable emotions in your home? How did you know they were approved?

3.) Which emotions were rejected, dismissed, or avoided? How did you know they were unacceptable?

Video: TEDx (2015): "Amy Morin: The Secret of Becoming Mentally Strong." https://youtu.be/TFbv757kup4 (15:01)

Discussion: Morin states, "Three kinds of destructive beliefs rob us of our mental strength."

~ Unhealthy beliefs about **ourselves**: The pity party keeps us stuck and focused on the problem.

~ Unhealthy beliefs about **others**: We give our power away when we blame or think, "I *have to…*"

~ Unhealthy beliefs about the **world**: Entitlement doesn't change reality; it just makes you resentful.

Catch/Correct Practice - share an example of correcting the **three destructive beliefs** below:

1.) SELF: "Why do these things *always* happen to me? *Nothing* goes my way."

Correct:

2.) OTHERS: "My boss *always makes* me stay late. I *have* to work endlessly."

Correct:

3.) WORLD: "It *should* be my turn to catch a break. I've put in my time."

Correct:

Three Core Factors of Emotional Intelligence

1. **Awareness**: Your ability to accurately **identify** and **accept** your emotions. A low-EQ individual is likelier to say, "I feel *fine*" or "I feel *good*." A high-EQ individual has a healthy emotional vocabulary and will share a more detailed description, such as "I feel *happy*," "I feel *anxious*," or "I feel *hurt*." *Example*: "I am feeling frustrated right now." The opposite of self-awareness is **reactivity**. The reactive individual lacks self-control and uses blame to avoid emotional accountability. *Example*: "You're pushing my buttons. You're pissing me off." **Practice** emotional awareness: "I'm feeling _____

2. **Self-Regulation**: Your ability to stay **flexible** and move in a positive direction. *Example*: "I'm really disappointed I didn't get the promotion, but this is probably the wake-up call I needed." The opposite of flexibility is **rigid** thinking. *Example*: "I didn't get the promotion because nothing good ever happens to me. Hardworking people never get ahead." **Practice**: <u>Share an example of when you were able to manage disappointment effectively</u>: _____
_____

3. **Compassionate Curiosity**: This is your ability to look beneath surface behavior and approach others with **curiosity**. *Example*: "My son was quiet during dinner. When asked, he said he was 'fine.' Then, he casually mentioned that he had a big test the next day. That's when I realized he felt worried." The opposite of curiosity is **judgment** and **assumption**. *Example*: "What's wrong with you? We spent a long time cooking dinner, and you're ruining it for everyone." **Practice**: <u>Share an example of looking beneath the surface and approaching others with compassion</u>: _____
_____

High EQ Characteristics

What are the common characteristics of an emotionally intelligent individual? In the June 2015 *Forbes* article "Are You Emotionally Intelligent? Here's How to Know For Sure," Travis Bradberry shares research on the hallmark high EQ characteristics. **Practice**: As we highlight a few, mark "Yes" if the characteristic describes you and "No" if you need to work on it.

1. **Curious Stance**: A curious individual gathers information with acceptance because they are aware that *all human behavior makes sense within context.* They avoid judging, comparing, and shaming. Judgment sounds like "*Why* would you say that?" Curiosity sounds like, "What were your thoughts?" Shaming sounds like, "You *should* listen to me." Acceptance sounds like, "I would like you to listen."

❏ Yes

❏ No

> Share an example of responding with **curiosity**:

2. **Own Your Strengths/Weaknesses**: The high-EQ individual can readily accept compliments and tolerate criticism. <u>When you own a weakness, you remove its power over you.</u> *Example*: As you arrive at the office, your boss angrily states, "You're late." A defensive response is, "The traffic was awful, and I couldn't find parking." This response is an anxious running-away response that weakens you. Owning your error sounds like, "Yes, I'm late. I apologize. I will work through lunch today." With accountability, you feel confident.

❏ Yes

❏ No

> My **strength**:
>
> My **weakness**:

3. **Don't Hold Grudges**: Very often people think they're making others suffer when they hold onto grudges, but the reality is that the only one who suffers is you. Condemning, judging, and revenge thoughts produce chronic discomfort.

❏ Yes

❏ No

> Share an example of **letting go of a grudge**:

4. **Set Limits**: Failing to set limits frequently leads to feeling overextended, devalued, or used. People who struggle to say no endure chronic resentment and fatigue as they feel trapped by the need to please others. Often people will attempt to say no, but they leave themselves open to manipulation. *Example*: Your boss asks you to stay late, but you want to go home. An individual who struggles with limits may respond with, "I don't know if I can stay late tonight." Notice how the ambivalence in this statement invites manipulation. An individual comfortable setting clear limits may say, "I wish I could help you out, but unfortunately, I can't tonight." With this response, the individual closes the door to being manipulated. It may be time to look in the mirror if you feel you're being mistreated.

❏ Yes

❏ No

> Share an example of **saying no**:

5. **Accept Your Mistakes**: Similar to embracing your weaknesses, accepting your mistakes is an agent of strength and change. Running from mistakes interferes with your ability to stay grounded, feel confident, and feel comfortable in your skin. Poor judgment is an aspect of being human. Often people deny or distance themselves from their mistakes because they lack self-acceptance. Use your errors as a guide rather than a negative label.

❒ **Yes**

❒ **No**

Practice acceptance by sharing a **mistake**: "I had poor judgment when I…"

6. **Reject Perfectionism**: People often set perfection as a goal because they believe it is a motivator, but the reality is that it's a form of self-sabotage. Equating perfection with success is a setup for chronic failure because perfection doesn't exist. Buddha said, "Pain is inevitable. Suffering is optional." Perfectionism produces unnecessary suffering.

❒ **Yes**

❒ **No**

Share an example of **rejecting perfectionism**:

7. **Gratitude**: Research shows that thoughts of gratitude improve your mood due to the reduction of the stress hormone cortisol (Bradberry, 2015). Buddha said, "Happiness does not depend on what you have or who you are. It solely relies on what you think."

❒ **Yes**

❒ **No**

Share a **gratitude statement**: "One thing about myself I'm grateful for is…"

Video: TEDx (2016): "Joan Rosenberg: Emotional Mastery: The Gifted Wisdom of Unpleasant Feelings." https://youtu.be/EKy19WzkPxE (15:17)

Discussion: Rosenberg states, "More than anything else, what holds people back is their challenges with unpleasant feelings…If you can move through and experience eight unpleasant feelings, you can pursue anything you want in life. It's a simple formula: **1.) One choice: stay present**. It's about awareness, not avoidance. **2.) Eight Unpleasant Feelings**: sadness, shame, helplessness, anger, vulnerability, embarrassment, disappointment, and frustration. When an emotion gets triggered, chemicals are released by our brain that flush through our bloodstream, and they activate bodily sensations. What we feel emotionally is felt in the body first as a physical sensation. It doesn't feel good, and that's what we want to get away from… **3.) Ninety Seconds**: **ride the emotional wave**. The biochemical rush is a wave that lasts roughly sixty to ninety seconds. Feelings are temporary."

Practice: Use mindfulness tools to stay present during your next emotional wave. Do not distract, avoid, deny, or control. Practice and share an example using the simple formula above:

Homework - Choose a feeling from each continuum below to practice the **Three Steps** from **Chapter 5**:

Anger Continuum

1	2	3	4	5	6	7	8	9	10

Annoyed~Irritated~Frustrated~Hostile~Mad~Angry~Pissed~Furious~Enraged

Anger is a survival emotion that initiates the fight/flight/freeze response. "With *anger*, blood flows to the hands, making it easier to grasp a weapon or strike at a foe; heart rate increases and a rush of hormones such as adrenaline generates a pulse of energy strong enough for vigorous action" (Coleman, 2006, p. 6).

1. **Identify**: _____

2. **Validate**: _____

3. **Admire**: _____

Sadness Continuum

1	2	3	4	5	6	7	8	9	10

Down~Blue~Disappointed~Gloomy~Hurt~Sad~Devastated~Depressed~Despair

Sadness is your healing emotion. With sadness, you pull inward, isolate, and stay close to home. Sadness produces heaviness, which encourages you to rest to heal the psyche. "This introspective withdrawal creates the opportunity to mourn a loss or frustrated hope, grasp its consequences on one's life, and, as energy returns, plan new beginnings. This loss of energy may well have kept saddened—and vulnerable—early humans close to home, where they were safer" (Coleman, 206, p. 7).

1. **Identify**: _____

2. **Validate**: _____

3. **Admire**: _____

Fear Continuum

1	2	3	4	5	6	7	8	9	10

Edgy~Jumpy~Concerned~Worried~Stressed~Anxious~Fearful~Panic~Terrified

Fear is one of your primary survival emotions. "Circuits in the brain's emotional centers trigger a flood of hormones that put the body on general alert, making it edgy and ready for action, and attention fixates on the threat at hand, the better to evaluate what response to make" (Coleman, 2006, p. 6). With fear, the body temporarily freezes to assess your best action. At the same time, your blood flows to your large skeletal muscles to prepare to flee (Coleman, 2006).

1. **Identify**: _____

2. **Validate**: _____

3. **Admire**: _____

Chapter 13
Building Emotional Intelligence

Many of life's failures are people who didn't realize how
close they were to success when they gave up.

~ Thomas Edison

Remember that sometimes not getting what you want
is a wonderful stroke of luck.

~ Dalai Lama

Your anger? It's telling you where you feel powerless. Your anxiety? It's telling
you our life is off balance. Your fear? It's telling you what you care about. Your
apathy? It's telling you where you're overextended and burnt out. Your feelings
aren't random, they are messengers. And if you want to get anywhere, you need
to be able to let them speak to you, and tell you what you really need.

~ Briana Wiest

❖   Reframing Emotion

❖   **STAR** Triangle

❖   Mind-Body Connection

TED Talk: **Kelly McGonigal: How to Make Stress Your Friend** (14:28)

"This study tracked thirty thousand adults in the United States for eight years, and they started by asking people, 'How much stress have you had in the past year?' They also asked, 'Do you believe that stress is harmful for your health?' And they used public death records to find out who died... Some bad news first: People who experienced a lot of stress the previous year had a 43 percent increased risk of dying. But that was only true for the people who also believed that stress is harmful for your health. People who experienced a lot of stress but did not view stress as harmful were no more likely to die. In fact, they had the lowest risk of dying of anyone in the study, including people who had relatively little stress. Now the researchers estimated that over the eight years they were tracking deaths, 182,000 <u>Americans died prematurely, not from stress, but from the belief that stress is bad for you</u>. So this study got me wondering: <u>Can changing how you think about stress make you healthier</u>? <u>And the science says yes. When you change your mind about stress, you can change your body's response to stress. In a study conducted at Harvard University, participants were taught to rethink their stress response as helpful</u>. That pounding heart is preparing you for action. If you're breathing faster, it's no problem; it's getting more oxygen to your brain. Participants who learned to view the stress response as helpful for their performance, well, they're less stressed out, less anxious, more confident, but the most fascinating finding to me was how their physical stress response changed. <u>When participants viewed their stress response as helpful, their blood vessels stayed relaxed</u>. Their heart was still pounding, but this is a much healthier cardiovascular profile. It actually looks a lot like what happens in moments of joy and courage." K. McGonigal (September 2013). Adapted from "Kelly McGonigal: How to Make Stress Your Friend." TED Talks. https://youtu.be/RcGyVTAoXEU.

Reframing Emotions

McGonigal shares research that highlights the power of the mind. The story we tell ourselves about stress impacts how our body responds to it. People who viewed stress as helpful had a physiological response similar to courage. *Reframing* is a powerful tool used to regulate emotions. <u>Choose an emotion and identify the core value below</u>.

Uncomfortable Emotions	Core Value Reframe
1. <u>heartbroken</u>, <u>empty</u>, <u>devastated</u> by a breakup	1. Sadness means I have the courage to love.
2. <u>worried</u> about my child	2. Worry means I am a devoted, loving parent.
3. <u>guilt</u>, <u>remorse</u>, <u>regret</u> by my poor judgment	3. Remorse means I'm empathic and accountable.
4.	4.
5.	5.
6.	6.

Short Story

"Imagine you are walking in the woods, and you see a small dog sitting by a tree. As you approach, it suddenly lunges at you, teeth bared. You feel frightened and angry. But then you notice that one of its legs is caught in a trap. Immediately, your mood shifts from anger to concern. You see that the dog's aggression is coming from a place of vulnerability and pain. This applies to all of us. When we behave in hurtful ways, it is because we are caught in some kind of trap. The more we look through the eyes of wisdom at ourselves and one another, the more we cultivate a compassionate heart." ~ *Tara Brach*

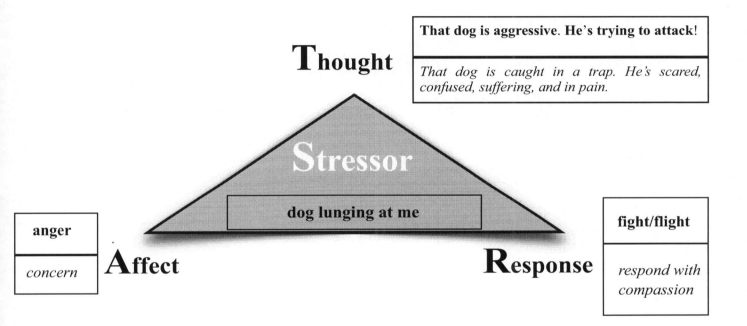

STAR Triangle

The STAR Triangle illustrates the connection between our thoughts, feelings, and behaviors. <u>Each point of the triangle is equally influential. If you change one point, it will have a ripple effect on the other two points.</u> The center of the triangle shows the environmental stressor. In the story example above, notice how the stressor stays the same, but the emotional and behavioral responses change with your thinking.

In the short story, it was easy to change your thinking when you realized the assumption was inaccurate. Your view of the dog switch from "he's aggressive" to "he's in pain." <u>What if you could correct your thinking without needing the facts of the situation to change? This is the power of the mind.</u> You can change the story you tell yourself. What if you chose to interpret anger differently? How would your response to anger change if you choose to view anger as pain, hurt, or fear? Viewing anger as pain allows you to respond with compassion. **Practice**: <u>Create a personal STAR Triangle on the next page.</u>

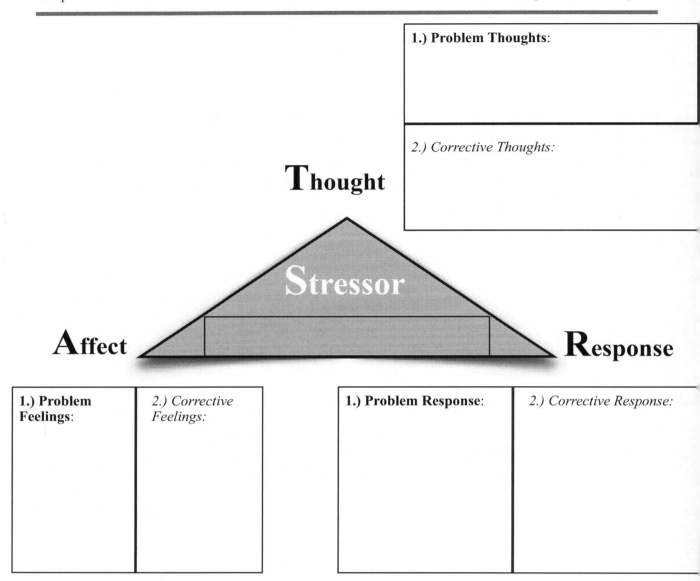

1.) **Problem Thoughts**:

2.) *Corrective Thoughts*:

Thought

Stressor

Affect

Response

1.) **Problem Feelings**:	2.) *Corrective Feelings*:

1.) **Problem Response**:	2.) *Corrective Response*:

STAR Triangle Practice

A helpful way to view the triangle is to think of yourself as a host to an unwanted houseguest. Let's say your unwanted guest is *anger*. For anger to remain in your home, the host has to create an environment where the guest feels welcome. If you stop feeding it, the guest will move on. <u>How do you feed emotional houseguests?</u> <u>Emotions are fed through your thoughts and your behaviors</u>. When anger is unwanted, you must look at what feeds it. Anger thrives on rigid, judgmental, condemning thoughts. Anger loves aggressive and rejecting behaviors. In order to stop feeding anger, you must shift your thinking as well as your behavior. Once you remove the welcome mat, your guest will pack their bags and move on.

Practice: <u>Choose a personal stressor, and complete the STAR Triangle above.</u>

1.) Pick a recent stressor and fill in the triangle's points.

2.) Catch the problem thought and correct it. Notice the ripple effect with the reframe.

Video: TED (2018): "Lisa Feldman Barrett: You Aren't at the Mercy of Your Emotions - Your Brain Creates Them."
https://youtu.be/0gks6ceq4eQ (18:28)

Discussion: Barrett discusses, "It may feel like your emotions are hardwired, and they just happen to you, but they don't. What are emotions? <u>Emotions are guesses, and you have more control over those guesses than you might imagine.</u> Predictions are basically the way your brain works. <u>Predictions link the simple sensations in your body with what's going on around you in the world, so you know what to do...</u> It's your construction of the physical sensation that leads to meaning. <u>You can turn down the dial on emotional suffering by interpreting your physical experiences differently.</u> We are responsible for our emotions because we are the only ones who can change them."

1.) Your brain makes predictions about your physical sensations. If you tell yourself a different story, your experience will change. *Example*: Your boss harshly criticizes your performance, and you notice your heart racing and stomach-turning. How will you choose to view this experience?

- <u>How will you respond if you view your racing heart as fear of failure or job insecurity?</u>

- <u>How will you respond if you view your racing heart as excitement because the criticism means you are a valuable employee?</u>

STAR Outline

You can use the **STAR** outline to increase your level of emotional intelligence. Low-EQ individuals tend to believe that their thoughts and feelings are reality-based; they don't realize that thoughts are distorted stories we tell ourselves. *Example*: Bill is someone with low EQ. While driving, the person in front of him cuts him off. Bill feels a rush of anger in response to the perceived violation, and he doesn't realize that he is producing his anger response.

The **STAR** concept is essential for emotional regulation because if you think the stressor is causing your feelings, you will view yourself as a victim. <u>For the low-EQ person, the stressor holds all the power. High-EQ people still have to deal with the same complex events, but the high-EQ individual feels grounded and empowered through accountability.</u>

(S) Stressor: Driver cuts Bill off. (*fact*)
(T) Thought: "That driver is trying to piss me off!" (*fiction*)
(A) Affect: ANGER
(R) Response: Road rage/Aggressive driving

Low EQ: **Stressor ——> Affect**   "That driver pissed me off!"
High EQ: **Stressor —> THOUGHT —> Affect**   "My *thoughts* about that driver are pissing me off."

Avoidance

Let's say that you are afraid to fly on an airplane. Your brain associates airplanes with fear. What is a typical response to a fear of flying? Most people cope with fear using *avoidance*. If you're afraid to fly, you will likely avoid flying. What would you do if you had to fly? Most likely, you would use avoidance tools like prescribed medications or excessive alcohol in order to numb the fear. Individuals who chronically abuse substances typically have low emotional intelligence and tend to use avoidance as one of their primary coping strategies. **The problem with avoidance is that no change will occur.** _Avoidance_ is a coping strategy that provides temporary relief from emotional discomfort. What happens to your fear of flying if your solution to the problem is to avoid flying? The fear stays. _Avoidance_ is a coping strategy that does not resolve problems.

Share a personal example of **avoidance**. What is the long-term impact of the behavior?

Low-EQ people often believe that they will be happy once things around them change. You may hear a low-EQ person say, "I'll be happy when there's a reason to be happy," or "I'll stop complaining when life stops handing me so many things to complain about." The low-EQ person remains passive, waiting for life to improve.

Practice - Create low EQ and high EQ thoughts for the fear of flying example:

Low EQ: S ——> A _____

High EQ: S —> THOUGHT —> A _____

Curious Stance

A curious stance is one of the best ways to increase your emotional intelligence because curiosity encourages you to pause rather than avoid or react. Slowing down reduces impulsive actions that lead to regret. When you fail to pause, you will live in a state of reactivity and give your power over to others. Read the example below, and practice:

Example 1: You arrive home late, and your family has already eaten dinner. Your partner sarcastically states, "So nice of you to join us."

Reactive Low EQ: "Some of us have to work around here to pay the bills." (_blame, defensive, hostile_)

Curious High EQ: "You must be disappointed that I missed dinner. I would be upset, too." (_compassion_)

Practice: You attend a party with your partner, and they notice you talking to a recently divorced person. While driving home, your partner states, "Why do you drool all over other people in front of me? You look like such a fool."

Reactive Low EQ:

Curious High EQ:

Notice how curiosity encourages you to search for clues beneath the surface. Reactive responses are sarcastic and defensive. To avoid reactivity, the goal is to look beneath the anger for the pain. When you consider anger is a shield used to protect vulnerability, you allow yourself to soften your response. Notice that curious responses include accountability through "I" statements. Accountability is a critical component in relationship stability. **Practice**: Think about the last time you felt angry. What was the vulnerable emotion under anger? _____ Anger is used as a shield to protect your fragile core self. The more fragile your core, the more likely you will use anger as a defense. You may view others who are aggressive as emotionless, but in reality, their hostile shield is a sign of fear.

Quiz: Which thoughts are **Low EQ** (*S—A*) and which thoughts are **High EQ** (*S—THOUGHT—A*)

1. "I'm tired because I have to do everything around here."   Low EQ   High EQ
2. "My boss is stressing me out."   Low EQ   High EQ
3. "I'm freaking myself out. I need to slow down."   Low EQ   High EQ
4. "They're pushing my buttons. They're pissing me off."   Low EQ   High EQ
5. "I'm feeling stressed out because I'm worried about tomorrow."   Low EQ   High EQ
6. "If people weren't so ridiculous, I wouldn't be annoyed."   Low EQ   High EQ
7. "I've taken too much on. I'm feeling overwhelmed."   Low EQ   High EQ
8. "I'm feeling frustrated because I want you to see it my way."   Low EQ   High EQ
9. "If I could just catch a break for once, I would be happy."   Low EQ   High EQ
10. "I lost control of my anger. I regret what I said."   Low EQ   High EQ
11. "If you would just listen to me, I wouldn't have to yell."   Low EQ   High EQ
12. "People are so stupid; I'd rather just stay home."   Low EQ   High EQ

Visualization

It can be helpful to imagine the weather when thinking about emotions. At times, we experience devastating storms that catch us off-guard. Some storms are intense but fleeting, and others linger, unrelentingly wearing us down.

When you're overwhelmed by an intense storm, you often remind yourself that the clouds will eventually part and the sun will shine again. Normalizing is a healthy coping strategy that increases your tolerance. All emotions are temporary. Emotions vary in intensity and duration, but they are temporary. When under the influence of uncomfortable emotions, picture a storm with dark skies, pounding rain, and crashing lightning. Imagine the storm blowing in fiercely, and it dissipates just as quickly. Embrace the emotional storm as a natural part of life.

Whether you recognize your emotions or not, they will have a powerful influence. Denying emotion is like standing in the rain without an umbrella and pretending it's not raining.

Whether you acknowledge the rain or not, you will get wet. Emotions distort reality and motivate behavior. Imagine trying to see through a thick, low-lying fog when thinking about how emotions distort reality. The fog naturally and unavoidably impairs your view. If you're driving your car through a thick fog, you need to accept that your view is impaired and slow down to prevent an accident. You are responsible for the damage if you ignore or deny the fog and crash. Blaming the fog doesn't change the reality or the consequences of your error. To increase your emotional intelligence, knowing which emotion you are experiencing at any given moment and the potential impact of each emotion is essential.

Mind-Body Connection

Every time you have an angry, sad, or unkind thought, your brain releases chemicals that are distributed to every cell in your body, and you will physically feel every thought you have (Amen, 2015). The brain uses emotion to motivate behavior. Fear is a physically uncomfortable emotion because your brain wants you to act. *Example*: If my rent is due and I don't have the money, I will likely feel anxious (*nervous stomach, tight chest, rapid heart, shortness of breath*). The anxiety is physically uncomfortable, and it pushes me to solve my problem. If anxiety wasn't uncomfortable, I may ignore the motivator and end up being evicted. One of the best ways to increase your emotional intelligence is to gain awareness of the physical responses produced by each feeling. **Practice**: Circle three feeling words below and write them in the spaces provided. Start with the first feeling word, and take a moment to repeat it to yourself several times. Pay attention to how each feeling affects your body. Every feeling produces a physical response, and the physical response pushes you to act. One of the best ways to elevate your emotional intelligence is to gain awareness of the physical sensations tied to each emotion.

Feeling List - Circle three of the feeling words below that catch your attention:

excited	sensitive	anxious	compassionate	shocked	exhausted	worried
relieved	lonely	happy	cautious	grateful	jealous	hopeful	hurt
scared	furious	mad	overwhelmed	loving	peaceful	sad	resentful
depressed	irritated	relaxed	joyful	hopeless	timid	edgy	content

Feeling   **Physical Response**

1._____ >>>>>>>> _____

2._____ >>>>>>>> _____

3._____ >>>>>>>> _____

Mind-Body Example

Imagine you are walking alone down the street, and suddenly, a stranger with a weapon steps in front of you. With this threat, your brain's natural survival response will automatically engage. This survival response is called fight, flight, or freeze. While your emotional response may be automatic, your behavioral response is your choice. People often say, "I had no other choice. They gave me no option." Usually, this statement of blame is used to cope with regret or shame. Your actions are your free will. Can you think of a time when you felt like you had no choice but to act the way you did? If you were the unarmed individual walking down the street in the example, do you believe you have a choice in how you would respond to the threat? What would you do in that situation? _____

Automatic Response

In most life-threatening situations, your brain automatically initiates the fight-or-flight response: your heart will beat faster, your muscles will tense, your breathing will become rapid, your eyes will dilate, your mucous membranes will dry up, and the blood vessels leading to your skin will constrict. This response allows you to fight harder, run faster, see better, breathe easier, and reduce blood loss in case of injury. *Example*: Have you ever been really nervous during public speaking? During the event, did you experience cottonmouth or cold hands? That is your fear response drying up your mucous membranes and constricting the blood vessels to your skin. The survival response also produces tunnel vision. Your brain wants you to focus only on surviving the threat. You may notice the tunnel vision effect when you try to stop thinking about a stressful situation, but it's all you can think about.

Behavioral Response

In any life-threatening situation, your brain will assess the threat in a fraction of a second to help you determine your best course of action. This is where an individual's free will comes into play. In the example, do you think 100 percent of people will respond to the stranger with the weapon the same way? Can the stranger make you fight? Can the stranger make you run? Can the stranger make you freeze? You may choose to run or fight or freeze because you decide it's your best chance of survival, but the stranger cannot make you do anything. You will assess the threat and determine your course of action. **Practice** - Circle the feeling and behavioral responses below that follow each thought:

Thought #1: "He picked the wrong one to mess with; he will regret this."

Emotion:	Angry	Hopeless	Afraid
Behavior:	Freeze	Run	Fight

Thought #2: "This is not a good situation. My family really needs me; I need to get out of here."

Emotion:	Angry	Hopeless	Afraid
Behavior:	Freeze	Run	Fight

Thought #3: "There's no way out. If I move, I'm dead."

Emotion:	Angry	Hopeless	Afraid
Behavior:	Freeze	Run	Fight

Homework - Emotions are messengers highlighting our core values. <u>Embracing uncomfortable emotions is one of the best tools to defeat resistance. Every uncomfortable emotion is telling you something beautiful about yourself.</u> *Example*: If you feel angry that your child was bullied at school, the anger is a reminder that you love your child and you don't want them to suffer. **Practice** - <u>Reframe uncomfortable emotions this week to uncover one of your core values, and complete the STAR Triangle below:</u>

Uncomfortable Emotions	Core Value Reframe
1.	1.
2.	2.

1.) Problem Thoughts:

2.) Corrective Thoughts:

Thought

Stressor

Affect

Response

1.) Problem Feelings:	*2.) Corrective Feelings:*

1.) Problem Response:	*2.) Corrective Response:*

Chapter 14
Mindful Breathing and Relaxation

Be the silent watcher of your thoughts and behavior. You are beneath
the thinker. You are the stillness beneath the mental noise.
You are the love and joy beneath the pain.
~ Eckhart Tolle

Once you know who you really are, being is enough. You feel neither superior
to anyone, nor inferior to anyone and you have no need for approval
because you've awakened to your own infinite worth.
~ Deepak Chopra

Leave your front door and your back door open. Allow your
thoughts to come and go. Just don't serve them tea.
~ Shunryu Suzuki

The best remedy for those who are afraid, lonely, or unhappy is to go outside.
~ Anne Frank

❖   Mindful Meditation Practice

❖   Visualization Exercise

TED Talk   Andy Poddicombe: All It Takes Is 10 Mindful Minutes (9:24)

"I guess we all deal with stress in different ways. My own way of dealing with it was to become a monk. So I quit my degree, headed off to the Himalayas, and studied meditation. People often ask me what I learned from that time… It gave me a greater appreciation and understanding for the present moment. By that, I mean not being lost in thought, not being distracted, not being overwhelmed by difficult emotions, but instead, learning how to be in the here and now, how to be mindful, and how to be present.

"There was a research paper that came out of Harvard just recently that said, <u>on average, our minds are lost in thought almost forty-seven percent of the time. At the same time, this sort of constant mind wandering is almost a direct cause of unhappiness</u>. Now we're not here for that long anyway, but to spend almost half of our life lost in thought and potentially quite unhappy. It just seems tragic, especially when there's something we can do about it. A positive, practical, achievable, scientifically proven technique that allows our minds to be more healthy. The beauty of it is that even though it only takes about ten minutes a day, it impacts our entire life. <u>That's what meditation is. It's familiarizing ourselves with the present moment. Most people assume that meditation is about stopping thoughts, getting rid of emotion, and controlling the mind, but actually, it's quite different from that.</u> **It's more about stepping back**, **sort of seeing the thought clearly**, **witnessing it coming and going**, **witnessing emotions coming and going without judgment**, **but with a relaxed, focused mind**. And it's only in learning to watch the mind in this way that we can start to let go of those storylines and patterns of the mind. <u>We can't change every little thing that happens to us in life, but we can change the way we experience it</u>."
A. Poddicombe (January 2013). Adapted from *"Andy Poddicombe: All It Takes Is 10 Mindful Minutes."* TED Talks. https://youtu.be/qzR62JJCMBQ.

Video Discussion: Poddicombe states, "We can't change every little thing that happens to us in life, but we can change how we experience it." Mindful meditation is one of the most powerful tools in our toolbox.

1.) What is mindful meditation?

2.) How can you incorporate meditation into your life?

Video: Headspace (2020): "Andy Puddicombe: Guided Meditation in Himalayan Forest." https://youtu.be/BR6yH4S1UMU (12:25)
Discussion: After the meditation, share your experience:

Video: Headspace (2012): "Andy Puddicombe: Guided 10-Minute Meditation." https://youtu.be/oVzTnS_IONU (10:59)
Discussion: Following the group meditation, share your experience.

> *Once you know who you really are, being is enough. You feel neither superior to anyone, nor inferior to anyone and you have no need for approval because you've awakened to your own infinite worth.*
>
> *~ Deepak Chopra*

Mindful Meditation Practice

What does it mean when you hear people say they're stressed out? Feeling stressed is a fear response. Resistance tends to be one of the most destructive coping strategies used with fear. With resistance, suffering is prolonged because avoidance blocks healing. <u>Acceptance is the antidote to resistance</u>. <u>Mindfulness is observing and accepting your thoughts and feeling without judgment</u>. Personal strength comes from learning to embrace your most uncomfortable emotions. Mindfulness will not eliminate discomfort but will increase your ability to tolerate and move through each emotion. When you resist an emotion, you use unhealthy coping strategies, such as control or avoidance.

What does it mean to take a nonjudgmental observer stance and embrace an emotion with acceptance? **Mindfulness is the practice of watching the function of the mind**. With mindfulness, you observe the fine details of the present moment without trying to alter or evaluate them. Mindfulness requires focusing on *facts* rather than *fiction*.

Grounding Breath

To center yourself and relax, the mind needs a present-moment focal point. The breath is an ideal focal point for the mind because it's always available. Focusing on breathing grounds you in the here and now. For many people, social situations produce anxiety. Imagine that you are attending a gathering, and you find yourself feeling anxious. In this situation, social anxiety often encourages avoidant behaviors. Avoidance can contribute to decisions like skipping the event, leaving early, or heading straight for the alcohol. Substance abuse is a form of avoidance frequently used to numb uncomfortable emotions. Now, imagine that the social gathering has a focal point. For example, let's say that everyone at the party is standing around a large bonfire or watching a band perform. With these present-moment objects, your anxiety is reduced because your mind has found a focal point. **The breath is a present-moment focal point you carry with you at all times**.

Visualization Exercise

Let's orient ourselves with the here and now. Place both of your feet flat on the ground. Hold yourself upright in a comfortable position. Gently close your eyes and take a moment to feel what it's like to sit in the room with your eyes closed. What do you hear? Do you notice the clock ticking or the beating of your heart? Take a slow, deep breath into your stomach. Feel your stomach expand as you inhale. Focus all your attention on the feeling of your lungs expanding with your breath. As you exhale, relax your shoulders.

Picture yourself comfortably walking on a path through a beautiful forest of tall trees. The temperature is pleasant, and you enjoy the filtered sunlight. You smell the clean air of the forest floor, and you take in the natural scent of the fresh leaves. As you walk, you notice a clearing at the end of the path that leads to a sandy beach. The beach is inviting, and you wander down the path. You remove your shoes as you step onto the soft, warm sand. The ocean smells fresh, and you enjoy the cool, gentle breeze combined with the warm sun. You sit on the sand to watch the waves meet the shore. You are comfortable and relaxed as you listen to the calling of distant seabirds. As you look out to the ocean, you notice the detail of each wave as it approaches the shore. In the distance, the wave builds out of the flat surface. As it approaches, it becomes steeper until it crests into a breaker. When the wave reaches the shore, it forms into whitewater and disappears as it is drawn back to sea.

The pattern of the waves approaching the shore is soothing. As you watch the process, you realize that the ocean's rise and fall reflect your feelings. Sitting on the beach, you are in the position of an observer. Rather than being engulfed by the wave, you watch the process from the safety of the shore. Next, you visualize yourself gently floating on the surface of the water. While floating, you are safe, dry, and peaceful. On the surface, you can feel the power of the deep water beneath you. The ocean holds all your emotions, and you feel the energy constantly moving below. Floating on the surface, you are unaffected by the emotional energy. As you notice an emotion, you simply imagine placing it back into the water beneath you. The process repeats with each emotional wave. The emotional wave rises, but you release it in the vast body of water below. The emotion rises like a wave, and you release it back into the ocean. Resisting an emotion is like trying to stop a wave from reaching the shore. Instead of resisting, you channel the emotional energy into the sea. You feel serenity wash over you as you find empowerment from this new perspective. Take a slow, deep breath into your stomach. Feel your stomach expand, exhale, and relax your shoulders.

Video Homework: Brett Larkin Yoga (2020): "20-Minute Guided Meditation for Higher-Self (for beginners)." https://youtu.be/f4qUbICmhBk (20:33)

Discussion: Note the messages or wisdom you receive from your child, highest, and oldest self.

Homework - To be a curious observer, follow these steps:

1. **Collect data with curiosity**: Stay with the *facts* rather than *fiction*. Don't judge, resist, or assume. Share an example:

2. **Follow your feelings to your thinking**: If my body is in fight-or-flight mode, my thoughts must encourage anger or fear. What am I thinking right now? Share an example:

3. **What is the emotion encouraging you to say or do**? While the emotion pushes you in a specific direction, you decide what you say and do. Don't let the emotion lead you. Share an example:

4. **Stay in the present moment**: Notice the natural process of breathing. You tend to ride emotional rollercoasters when focusing on the future or past. Share an example:

Chapter 15
Gaining Self-Esteem
through Accountability

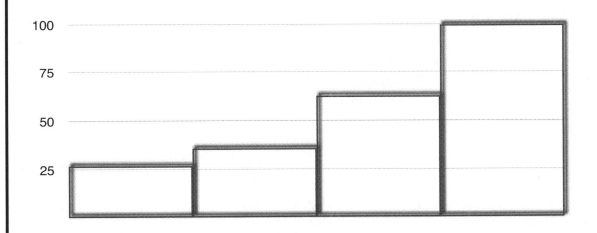

Accountability Meter

Group Exercise

Use the accountability meter above to shade in the bar representing the percentage you believe you are responsible for the incident that led to your enrollment in this program. Aside from yourself, is there anyone else whom you hold accountable for your behavior? Please indicate on the accountability meter anyone who shares responsibility and their percentage of accountability.

Short Story

Two brothers were once convicted of stealing sheep and were branded on the forehead with the letters **S T**, which stood for "Sheep Thief." Unable to bear the shame, one brother fled to a foreign land, where he still had to explain his brand. <u>He wandered from land to land, hoping to escape his guilt, but he died in bitterness, buried in a forgotten grave.</u>

The other brother repented of his crime. He did not flee. <u>Instead, he bore his shame, acknowledged his guilt, and resolved to make amends.</u> He stayed with his people, determined to win back their respect. As years passed, he gained a reputation for great honesty and kindness.

One day, a stranger came to town and saw the old man with **S T** branded on his forehead. The stranger asked someone what the letters meant. A villager said, "It happened long ago, and I have forgotten the details, but I think the letters are an abbreviation for 'Saint.'"

Such is the choice for us. We can run and hide. We can deny and dispute, but we cannot escape. <u>The only way to heal is to surrender and face the facts.</u> When we repent and make amends, we turn toward the light of truth and health. <u>No power is stronger on earth than the courage to face our past.</u> We are not called to spectacular sainthood but to truth, forgiveness, and a new life today. ~ *A. Philip Parham*

Story Discussion: Parham's short story reminds us that we cannot change the past and outrun shame. Both brothers experienced shame in the story, but their coping strategy was the defining difference in their lives. The natural response to shame is to go into hiding, but at what cost? Hiding from shame leads to escape coping strategies like addiction, blame, anger, depression, abandonment, and self-sabotage.

1.) <u>What did the brother who stayed have that the other brother lacked?</u>

2.) Share a personal example of when you had the courage to "surrender and face the facts." <u>What was the result of your vulnerability and accountability</u>?

Video: TEDx (2013): "Shaka Senghor: Writing My Wrongs." https://youtu.be/IV_uAL9ADBU (12:25)
Discussion: Senghor states, "I realized that prison isn't always a physical space. Sometimes, prison is the mental limitations we put on ourselves. Sometimes, you have to make the best of a very bad situation. If you educate yourself, you will always be free... Hurt people, hurt people. That's how the cycle repeats itself over and over... One of the most important things you can do is look at the child in everyone you encounter. When you can see the child in them, it's easy to be empathetic. Hope is one of the most important tools at our disposal." Senghor is a vulnerable, high-accountability person.

1.) <u>Share a personal example of "seeing the child" in someone and responding with empathy</u>:

Low Accountability = Low Self-Worth

How does accountability increase your self-worth? Imagine that each of us has two circles. The size of the outer circle (*protective shield*) is fixed; its circumference does not change. Unlike the protective shield, the size of the inner circle (*core self*) is variable depending upon your level of self-esteem. The Low Accountability Diagram below shows a smaller, more fragile core self. The outer protective shield is filled with your defenses and distortions, which are problem-coping strategies during times of insecurity. The smaller or more fragile your core self (*inner circle*), the larger or more protective your shield (*outer circle*). In other words, the lower your self-worth, the greater your need for protection.

Low Accountability Diagram
Low Self-Worth
Rigid, Defensive, Guarded Stance

Notice the insecurity and uncertainty of the core self in the Low Accountability Diagram. Individuals with low accountability tend to feel uncomfortable in their skin and have rigid thinking patterns. These unhealthy thought processes are an attempt to protect their fragile core. These coping strategies make the low-accountability individual feel lonely, victimized, and powerless. Low-accountability people often struggle with anxiety, depression, and anger. They generally feel like life is chaotic and out of control or chronically disappointing and unfair. Their internal emotional state depends upon the external environment: "If things go my way, I feel okay. If things don't go my way, I'm miserable." An individual with an insecure core self struggles to maintain feelings of safety, which is why the defensive shield is so protective. Low-accountability individuals tend to believe, "Deep down, there is something very wrong with me." The only way out of living in this unstable state is to strengthen your core self and reduce your protective shield defenses. The most effective strengthening tactic is shifting your thought processes toward personal accountability.

High Accountability = High Self-Worth

Take a look at the High Accountability Diagram below. <u>With a high level of accountability, the core self (*inner circle*) increases in size until it nearly fills the outer circle.</u> What does this mean? <u>With a high level of self-worth, you don't need much self-protection.</u> You generally feel confident and comfortable. You are able to embrace and acknowledge your strengths as well as your weaknesses. You don't need to seek approval from others because you provide yourself with compassion and acceptance. You also don't need to be right, and you can tolerate when others disagree. You are generally comfortable with relationships and intimacy. <u>You can genuinely care about others because you authentically care about yourself.</u>

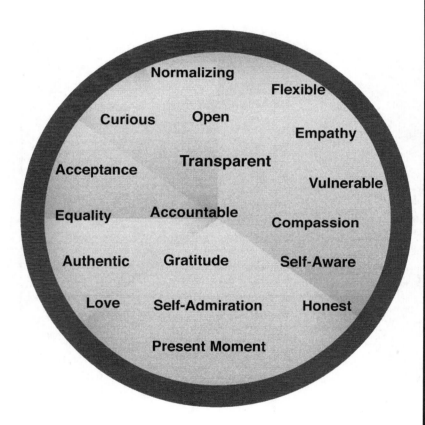

High Accountability Diagram
High Self-Worth
Grounded, Authentic, Curious Stance

Notice the characteristics that make up the core self in the High Accountability Diagram. <u>The more of these characteristics you hold, the stronger your sense of self-worth. Individuals with high self-worth have flexible thinking patterns and tend to be likable.</u> High-accountability people feel comfortable with themselves and generally don't seek attention or approval from others. They also don't feel the need to keep others at a distance. <u>Individuals with a strong core need very little self-protection, but that doesn't mean they don't get hurt. These individuals are not immune to life's hardships, but they are better equipped to tolerate and adapt to disappointment.</u> High-accountability individuals tend to believe, "I'm far from perfect, but I like who I am." <u>Holding yourself accountable strengthens your self-esteem because you don't need to hide anything about yourself. Accountability sends messages of self-acceptance.</u> When you deny, distort, blame, or minimize, you send messages of shame to yourself.

Example Accountability Diagram

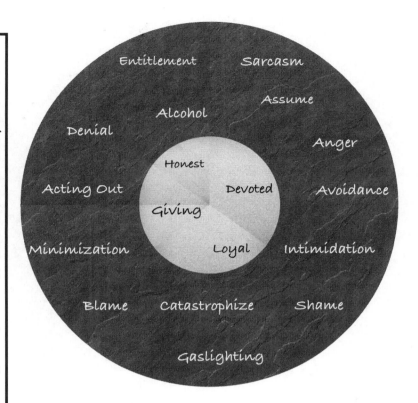

Protective Shield:

My protective shield goes up when I feel insecure or not good enough. I carry trust issues and abandonment fears from my childhood. My walls of protection are triggered when I feel rejected or inadequate. The rejection can be as simple as someone not texting me back, disagreeing with me, or not listening. I immediately go into fight-or-flight mode and begin thinking, "I don't need them. I don't like them."

- I use **sarcasm** to keep people away when I'm afraid I'll get hurt
- I use **shame** to get others to feel the same insecurity I'm feeling
- I use **intimidation/gaslighting** to try to control others when I'm feeling out of control
- I use **assuming/catastrophizing** to prevent feelings of disappointment
- I use **blame** to try to get others to feel sorry for me and to avoid feeling guilty
- I use **denial** so I can blame
- I use **anger** to keep people at a safe distance
- I use **minimization** to reduce my feelings of regret
- I use **alcohol** to get out of my head and escape my thoughts
- I use **avoidance** when the other tactics of control fail
- I use **acting out** to distract others from the truth of the situation
- I use **entitlement** to make others feel inadequate

Core Self:

I have access to my best self when I'm feeling secure and confident. Usually, I feel good enough when I receive positive feedback from others. This security tends to be short-lived because my confidence wears off when I'm not appreciated. Then, I start feeling not good enough again. Because I need positive feedback to feel adequate, I quickly blame others when I feel insecure. An example is when I get angry at my kids for not being thankful enough. I want to learn to feel good about myself without needing external validation. Right now, my core strengths include the following:

- I'm **honest**
- I'm **generous** and **giving**
- I'm **loyal**
- I'm **devoted** to my family

Personal Accountability Diagram

Create your accountability diagram below. Each of us has a *core self* and a *protective shield*. <u>This exercise requires insight, self-awareness, and vulnerability</u>. Own your strengths and weaknesses, and fill in the elements below. The protective shield (*outer circle*) includes character deficits, imperfections, distortions, and unhealthy coping. During this program, you will actively strengthen your core self and defeat your protective shield.

My Protective Shield:

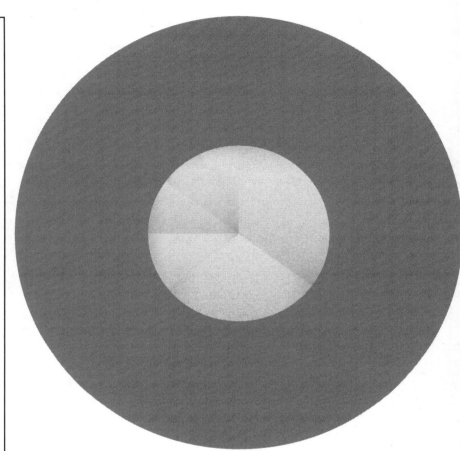

Personal Accountability Diagram
my current protective shield/core self

My Core Self:

Catch/Correct Practice - To strengthen your core self and defeat the protective shield, use the three steps of *Catch/Correct*. Read the examples below, and create your own:

1. **Protective Shield**: Identify the problem trait and describe why you use it.
2. **Catch**: Provide personal examples of the distortion/defense.
3. **Correct**: Describe the steps you will take to defeat it.

Example #1
1. **Protective Shield**: "I use *blame* to avoid guilt and to get empathy from others."
2. **Catch**: "I told you to stop, but you didn't." "You're way too sensitive." "You're never happy."
3. **Correct**: Switch the "you" statement to an accountable "I" statement: "I chose to lose it." "I hurt your feelings." "I want you to be happy, and I'm worried I don't make you happy."

Example #2
1. **Protective Shield**: "I use *minimization* to avoid problems and feeling regret."
2. **Catch**: "I *barely* touched you." "I was *just* trying to get you off me." "I was *only* defending myself."
3. **Correct**: Remove minimizers: "I put my hands on you." "I pushed you." "I was violent with you."

Example #3
1. **Protective Shield**: "I use *denial* to avoid feeling guilty when I *blame*."
2. **Catch**: "I'm confused because that *never* happened." "It's all in your head; you're crazy."
3. **Correct**: OYOS: "You're right; I did hurt you." "I don't want it to be true, but it is."

Practice #1
1. **Protective Shield**:

2. **Catch**:

3. **Correct**:

Practice #2
1. **Protective Shield**:

2. **Catch**:

3. **Correct**:

Practice #3
1. **Protective Shield**:

2. **Catch**:

3. **Correct**:

> *Fight for the things you care about, but do it in a way that will lead others to join you.*
> *~ Ruth Bader Ginsburg*

Accountability Practice: Switch each low-accountability statement below into a high-accountability statement. *Hint*: High-accountability statements place 100 percent of the responsibility upon the self.

1. "I wouldn't be controlling if you were trustworthy."

2. "If you didn't call the cops, I wouldn't have been arrested."

3. "If you didn't block the door, I wouldn't have touched you. I was just trying to leave."

4. "If you don't want me in your face, show me respect."

5. "If you don't want me to get mad, don't make me mad."

6. "I told you to stop, but you wouldn't stop. You knew what was coming."

Video: TEDx (2018): "Jahan Kalantar: A Perfect Apology in Three Steps." https://youtu.be/Pwl5PExezeg (7:05)

Discussion: Kalantar states, "We never learn to say sorry properly, and we are anxious about doing so. Being vulnerable is terrifying, but through vulnerability, we can access our authentic voice. What goes into a good apology? There is a framework you can use: 1.) *Why…* 2.) *Because…* 3.) *And…* When you say sorry, look people in the eye and use the framework. Don't be afraid to be vulnerable and authentic because the power of any message is how honest a place it starts its journey."

Example: 1.) "I'm sorry I yelled at you…"

              2.) "because it hurt and scared you…"

              3.) "and I do not want you to feel hurt or scared."

Homework - Practice vulnerability and accountability by using the apology formula:

Describe the situation: _____

Step 1.)

Step 2.)

Step 3.)

Chapter 16
Accountability Letter

The more perfect a person is on the outside, the more
demons they have on the inside.
~ Sigmund Freud

You know how blame is described in the research?
A way to discharge pain and discomfort.
~ Brene Brown

Healing comes from taking responsibility: to realize that it is you, and no
one else, who creates your thoughts, your feelings, and your actions.
~ Peter Shepherd

Take accountability, blame is the water in which many
dreams and relationships drown.
~ Steve Maraboli

Enlightenment is when a wave realizes it is the ocean.
~ Thich Nhat Hanh

❖   Accountability Reframes

❖   Defeat Minimization, Denial, and Blame

Video: TEDx (2019): "Darryll Stinson: Overcoming Rejection, When People Hurt You and Life isn't Fair." https://youtu.be/8yBfAeadqjI (13:07)

Discussion: Stinson shares stories of traumatic experiences during his childhood. He uses accountability reframes to empower himself and heal. What are the reframes he uses to defeat blame and victim stance? Create reframes you can use to free yourself from stagnation and victim stance:

Video: TEDx (2017): "Billy Johnson: Rediscovering Hope Through Self-Forgiveness." https://youtu.be/voXQ5iBNllk (9:43)

Discussion: Johnson quotes Norman Cousins, "Death is not the greatest tragedy in life. The greatest tragedy is what dies inside us while we live." Johnson shares his story of defeating shame through forgiveness and compassion. Johnson states, "Never look down on anyone unless you're helping them up." Share how you can use self-forgiveness and compassion to heal:

Accountability Exercise

Brene Brown said, "Courage starts with showing up and letting ourselves be seen." People often hold onto blame as if it were a security blanket. Accountability requires the courage to let go of blame. Protective shield defenses work like hammers chipping away at your self-worth. When you deny, minimize, or blame, you send messages to yourself that your truth is shameful. Accountability is a source of personal empowerment because it moves you toward self-acceptance. Before you begin your letter, read the examples and complete the sentences below:

I struggle with accountability when I'm under the influence of (*emotion*) _____

This emotion encourages negative thoughts like _____

_____

These thoughts come from some of my past experiences, including _____

_____

A statement of **self-acceptance** sounds like _____

_____

A statement of **self-compassion** sounds like _____

_____

A statement of **self-admiration** sounds like _____

_____

Example Letter of Accountability 1

When I first started this program, I told a very different story. It wasn't that I wanted to lie; I was deep in denial and didn't even know it. Over time, we believe the lies we tell ourselves until we don't even know the truth anymore. The way I first told this story went like this: "My partner was abusing alcohol for years. He forced us to ride emotional rollercoasters, and I walked on eggshells. The kids were upstairs, and my partner threatened to hurt himself again. I tried to calm him down, but he was drunk and inconsolable. I told him the marriage was over, and he ran to the kitchen to grab a knife. I didn't want him to hurt anyone; I had to knock the knife out of his hands. I was afraid to get too close, so I grabbed a chair and used it to protect myself. When the police came, he told them I had attacked him, and they arrested me. How does someone get arrested for a domestic assault while trying to prevent a suicide?"

That was my story when I started the program, and it was a victim story. I felt powerless in my toxic marriage, and I was passively waiting for him to change. I thought he *made* us ride those emotional rollercoasters, and I had no idea that I was the one who had to change. So, here's my story today, and it's a story of accountability:

I grew up in an abusive home, but I didn't know it; I just thought I was unlovable. Fast forward to my marriage, I became the abuser. I married a very sweet, kind, and unstable person. He is a people-pleaser, and I think I married him because he reminded me of myself as a kid. I always sought approval, and my parents used that against me. Growing up, I hated that about myself. It turns out, I've done the same thing to my partner.

On rare occasions when he would feel good about himself, I'd find a subtle way to destabilize him. I would casually insert self-doubt while pretending to be loving. For example, he came home from work one day and excitedly told me he was getting a raise. I pretended to look happy, but deep down; I felt insecure. That insecurity quickly turned to anger. Then, I smiled while reminding him of the raise he received at the old job just before they laid him off. He was fragile and unstable because I did this to him ALL THE TIME. After I'd casually put him down, I would see his insecurity return and I'd feel comfortable again. I realize now that his confidence scared me, and I didn't want to be alone in my inadequacies, so I did everything I could to keep him unstable with me.

That day, I wasn't trying to prevent a suicide; I was abusing him. I used every tactic I knew to push him past his limit. As a child, I desperately wanted to escape my life. When he reached the breaking point, I told him that only bad people would consider ending their lives. He was in the depths of despair, and I shamed him. I felt relief when he grabbed the knife because I wanted to hit him. It's horrible to admit, but I was an expert at victim blaming, just like my parents. It was always my fault when they abused me. I didn't have to hit the knife out of his hands; I wanted to hit him. I pretended to feel afraid of him, so I could justify picking up the chair. When I swung it at him, he didn't even try to stop me or protect himself. It was as if he felt like he deserved it. The pain in his eyes when I pretended to be scared was greater than any emotion I'd ever seen. I wanted him to feel worthless because I've felt worthless my whole life, and I was transferring my pain to him. I'd broken him down so much; he was lifeless.

My heart breaks when I realize what I've done. <u>I've been in denial because I was too afraid to accept it, but I will never heal if I don't speak the truth</u>. This story makes me sound horrible, and I have done terrible things, but I'm a good person who has felt lost for a long time. Instead of recovering from my childhood, I've been recreating it in my marriage. I don't know if my partner will ever forgive me, but I must focus on myself right now. I need to heal so I can trust myself. I'm thankful for the arrest because it changed me. I won't need to transfer my pain to others anymore because now I can lean into the pain. I've finally found self-acceptance, and I'm letting the old baggage go.

Example Letter of Accountability 2

I felt like everything was against me in my life. Each minute that went by seemed to get darker and darker. I didn't know what I was feeling, and I didn't know what to do with it. Was it anger, depression, anxiety, sadness, or maybe all at once? I didn't have the insight back then. I used to think that bad feelings were automatic; I didn't know that my feelings were coming from my thoughts. At times, I felt lost and alone because I never knew myself. I didn't know who I was until I came to this program. I've been walking through my life as a stranger until now. My children always asked me what was wrong, and I had no words to answer that question. I wanted to be understood and someone to help me feel better. I gave all my power away, thinking that others *made* me feel bad. I had no idea I was in the driver's seat. I have been a passenger this whole time, passively waiting for things to get better and blaming everyone else. I feel sorry for the person I used to be. I was hopeless, lost, scared, and very out of control. I was a ticking time bomb, and I feel so sad that my family had to live in that dark place with me. I blamed them for absolutely EVERYTHING all the time.

I've made many mistakes, but the biggest was getting to that very dark place. I felt like I was never good enough. Everyone was my enemy, including myself. I felt extremely resentful when my partner constantly reminded me of what I was doing wrong. The negative thoughts in my head made me feel like I was endlessly treading water, trying not to drown. With each complaint, it felt like my partner was shoving my head beneath the water. It was like I was literally drowning, but I kept being pushed deeper. The complaints were a plea to connect; instead, I felt like a failure. And sure enough, the ticking time bomb stopped ticking...

That day, I became a monster without control over any of my words or actions. The week leading up to it was very stressful, and I set myself up to explode. I worked long hours with people I didn't like, but I was too stubborn and insecure about looking for another job. I basically had a pity party in my head all week, and I felt very justified in my resentments. I'd come home each day and bark orders at everyone. It was like I was on a power trip; I was totally entitled. Finally, by the end of the week, my family had enough of my anger.

On Friday, I came home and did all the same abusive stuff. I was spreading misery and secretly hoping they'd take the bait so I could go off. I knew I was wrong, but it felt good to be mean for some reason. I was suffering inside, but I didn't know it. All I knew was that I was angry. I didn't know how to be vulnerable and share my feelings, so I put up my wall and attacked. My oldest child finally took the bait that day and went off on me. That's all I needed... I threw a glass across the kitchen, yelling horrible things and threatening to kill everyone. I told my child they were the reason I was miserable. I think my goal was to play the victim to get everyone to rally around me. I really just needed support, but I didn't know how to ask for it. I didn't know how to make myself feel better at that time. I threw a huge fit, and the kids were terrified and crying. As soon as my kid got in my face to calm me down, I could justify the violence as self-defense. The next thing I knew, my oldest was on the ground, and I stood there raging over a helpless body. I was totally spinning out of control. Thankfully, my little girl started crying, and her screams snapped me out of it. I didn't know it at the time, but getting arrested was the best thing to have happened because I'm learning to love myself. I have been transferring my self-loathing to my children, and they deserve to grow up in a home where they are safe and loved every day. Instead of blaming, I now recognize my feelings and work through them. This has been a tough pill to swallow, but I'm growing into a better person, parent, and partner. Greatness comes from a lot of hard work, and I'm doing the work. I'm not giving up, and I still have a long way to go.

Accountability Letter

Steve Maraboli said, "Take accountability; blame is the water in which many relationships drown." Write a personal letter of accountability to share with the group. Use as much detail as possible to describe your thoughts, feelings, and behaviors during the incident that led you to this program. While you may feel tempted to describe your behaviors as defensive, your self-esteem comes directly from your accountability. Remember that no one can make you feel, think, or do anything. Use "I" statements such as: "I chose…I felt…I thought…" **The goal of this exercise is personal empowerment**. Do not judge yourself during this process. You behaved the way you did because it made sense to you at that time. Turn toward yourself with acceptance and compassion, and allow yourself to have the courage to be vulnerable. Most participants write several drafts of this letter before sharing it with the group. If you choose, you may use a separate sheet.

Accountability Letter

Chapter 17
Effects on Children

The tragic reality of children growing up in domestic violence is that they end up with mental health problems at a rate higher than children who are actually the direct victims of physical abuse.

~ Bruce D. Perry

We're all just walking each other home.

~ Ram Dass

The beauty of the human brain is that it's a mirror to the child's developmental experience. If you want your child to be kind, then you have to be kind to your child. If you want your child to be good at self-regulation and not lose their temper, then you have to not lose your temper.

~ Bruce D. Perry

❖   Effects of Domestic Violence Exposure

❖   Problem Parenting

❖   Parenting Styles

❖   Healthy Parenting

Video: California Department of Justice, Office of the Attorney General (2008)
First Impressions…Exposure to Violence and A Child's Developing Brain (14:44)

Bruce D. Perry, MD, PhD, senior fellow, ChildTrauma Academy: "Unlike other organs, the brain is undeveloped at birth, and it is waiting for experiences to shape how it will develop. The amazing thing about the human brain is that the younger you are, the more spongelike your brain is. But the very same biological sponginess that allows us to rapidly acquire language is also the same sponginess that makes younger children more vulnerable to trauma than older children. Most people think that young children don't really understand what's going on and that they are resilient, but the fact is that if anybody is impacted more severely, it's the younger child. Repeated exposure to violence impacts brain development. Children exposed to domestic violence literally are experiencing a state of fear, and it changes the brain of these children."

Linda Chamberlain, PhD, MPH founding director, Alaska Family Violence Prevention Project: "When kids are chronically stressed, one of the problems we see is difficulty in attachment and bonding because they're so focused on survival. A lot of these kids get labeled as bad, difficult, and defiant, but this is a very natural response given their circumstances. What the child is doing is a survival strategy, but it creates behaviors that are very difficult in the classroom. When they are in crisis mode, they can't learn. Your children are going to learn how to deal with stress from you. The biggest thing that helps children who have been exposed to violence is to get them to talk about their feelings and receive those critical messages that it's not their fault. One of the great things about brain science that we've learned is that until the day you die, you have the ability to add new neurons in your brain. The brain can rewire and heal itself."

California Department of Justice, Office of the Attorney General, Edmund G. Brown, Jr. (2008). *First Impressions…Exposure to Violence and A Child's Developing Brain.* Iron Mountain Films, Inc. https://youtu.be/brVOYtNMmKk.

Video Discussion:

1.) Perry stated, "The tragic reality of children growing up in domestic violence is that they end up with mental health problems at a rate *higher* than children who are the direct victims of physical abuse." Why do you think children who witness domestic abuse struggle with higher rates of mental illness?

2.) Perry stated, "The beauty of the human brain is that it's a mirror to the child's developmental experience. If you want your child to be kind, you have to be kind to your child. If you want your child to be good at self-regulation and not lose their temper, then you have to not lose your temper." Share a personal example of how the brain is a mirror to experiences:

Childhood Domestic Violence Association (February 21, 2014):

* Five million children witness domestic violence each year in the United States.

* Domestic violence in childhood is directly correlated with learning difficulties, problems with attention and memory, and lower IQ scores.

* Children who grow up with violence are six times more likely to commit suicide, fifty percent more likely to abuse drugs and alcohol, and 74 percent more likely to commit violent crimes.

114

Domestic Violence Exposure

What causes pathology in young people? "It's the exposure (*witnessing*) or personal victimization of young people to domestic violence: physical or sexual abuse or neglect" (Hovel, 2015, p. 14). "Boys who observe domestic violence are six times more likely to commit similar acts as adults; girls who witness domestic violence are much more likely to become abusive themselves or to find partners who are abusive" (Wexler, 2013, p. 191). Research has shown that using physical punishment as a form of discipline negatively impacts the developing brain of children. Studies found that frequent spanking of three-year-old children was associated with higher levels of aggression at five years old, including temper tantrums and aggression toward animals (Taylor et al., 2010). Frequent physical punishment before adolescence is correlated with a child's acts of abuse toward animals (Flynn, 1999). "Animal cruelty is linked directly or indirectly with every violent crime and even with most nonviolent crime" (Hovel, 2015).

Symptoms - Children who suffer domestic violence exhibit common symptoms:

1. **Delinquency**: sexual acting out, substance abuse, alcohol abuse, impulse control problems

2. **Poor Social Skills**: bullying, isolation, frequent fighting, low self-esteem, poor eye contact

3. **Hypervigilance**: memory and concentration problems, inability to learn, misdiagnosed with ADHD

4. **Chronic Fear**: crying spells, nightmares, clinging behaviors, panic attacks

5. **Controlling Behavior**: dependency issues, poor boundaries, eating disorders, abusive friendships

6. **Violent Behavior**: violence toward siblings, self-harm, suicidal ideation, animal abuse

7. **Sleep Disturbance**: nightmares, afraid of going to sleep, difficulty sleeping through the night

8. **Emotional Dysregulation**: temper tantrums, emotional rollercoaster, crying, emotionally numb

9. **Depression**: isolation, low motivation, aches and pains, frequent illness, stomachaches

---

Video: Sprouts (2021): "UK Trauma Council: Childhood Trauma and the Brain." https://youtu.be/xYBUY1kZpf8 (5:10)

Discussion: UK Trauma Council states, "A brain that has adapted to survive in a threatening or unpredictable world may not work so well in an ordinary environment. This creates latent vulnerability where early abusive or neglectful experiences puts children at greater risk of developing mental health problems in the future. Too much focus on threat cues can lead to missing out on positive social cues. Over time, this can cause social thinning. All children need care and stimulation from adults who value them. When children experience abuse and neglect, their brain adapts to help them cope."

1.) This video highlights changes in three brain systems: the **reward system** (*misreading social cues*), **memory system** (*increase in negative memories/decrease in detail recall*), and **threat system** (*increased hypervigilance which leads to problems in learning/development*). Share your thoughts about the video and your experience with adapting to childhood trauma:

Problem Parenting

Your child's brain is like a sponge soaking up the environment and forming beliefs about the world. As a parent, you are your child's primary source of information. Children learn about their self-worth, coping with stress, and how to treat others by watching your behavior. Childhood is the time when we develop core beliefs. Core beliefs form the lens through which we see and interpret information. Your view of your child will become their self-view. If you devalue or reject your child, they will develop a sense of worthlessness. Self-worth is a critical component in our decision-making process. Children who grow up in violent, chaotic, or unsafe homes carry the effects with them for the rest of their lives.

In all relationships, *intent* does not hold the same weight as *consequence*. *Example*: I'm cleaning my gun in the living room, and it accidentally discharges. While I didn't *intend* to shoot you, you still got shot. Even when the intent is innocuous, consequences can be devastating. Many adults raised in emotionally abusive homes will say, "My parents did the best they could." Unfortunately, acknowledging good intent does not eliminate suffering.

Parenting Styles

There are four standard styles of parenting. When learning about these styles, it's helpful to visualize life as an ocean. At birth, your child cannot swim, and their survival is based on your care. Imagine that you've been carrying your child safely on your back, but they've grown, and you can no longer stay above water holding the weight. If your child doesn't learn to swim, you will both drown. You reach the point where you can no longer stay above water, and gently, you let go. You swim a short distance away where you wait and watch. This is the natural process of life: All children must let go of their parents and learn to swim to survive, but we each have our own process. As you swim away, your child begins to panic and flail in the water, screaming for you to return. How you handle this emotional challenge will tell you a lot about your parenting style. Generally, there are four responses:

Shame Parenting

The first common response is authoritarian (*shame)* parenting. With shame parenting, you use rejection, aggression, and degrading to force your child to behave the way they're "supposed" to behave. When a shame parent swims away, they might say, "What's wrong with you?! Everyone swims; you don't see anyone else throwing a fit. Knock that off, and act your age!" This parent is likely using the same treatment they received during childhood. Children who grow up with shame parenting will learn how to swim, but in the process, they develop a critical internal dialogue and harden with self-loathing. Their view of others becomes cynical, and they quickly realize that vulnerability leads to pain. Frequently, these children struggle through life, feeling lost and alone. They are at higher risk for **co-dependency**, **aggression**, **social problems**, **academic problems**, **bullying**, **isolation**, **mental health problems**, **substance abuse**, **impulsivity**, **delinquency**, and **self-harm**. Life becomes scary, and they learn to be aggressive, manipulative, or defensive to survive. The chronic message of shame parenting: "There's something wrong with you. You're not good enough."

Share a personal example of **shame** parenting:

Helicopter Parenting

The second standard response is over-involved (*helicopter*) parenting. As a helicopter parent, you notice your child's discomfort and want to protect them from distress. You quickly return to rescue without providing the time needed to figure out how to swim. This is only a temporary fix because your child is too heavy for you to hold. This process repeats over and over as you are forced to let go. Each time you return to "save" your child from their struggle, you're enabling a dependent state and weakening their self-esteem. <u>You are sending a message that your child cannot succeed without you. The result is that the helicopter parent feels valuable, and the child feels incompetent.</u> These children are at higher risk for **oppositional/defiant behavior, poor self-control, poor emotional regulation, egocentric/narcissistic tendencies, low self-esteem,** and **social problems.** The chronic message of helicopter parenting: "You can't succeed without me; don't even try."

Share a personal example of **helicopter** parenting:

Neglectful Parenting

The third typical response is *neglectful* parenting. These parents do not set firm boundaries or high standards. <u>They tend to be indifferent to their child's feelings, wants, and needs.</u> A neglectful parent will not notice their child's distress in the water. They'll swim away, and they won't look back. These parents are uninvolved to an extreme level and generally lack interest in their children. Neglectful parents often struggle with mental health issues, trauma, or addiction. They often live in survival mode, which blocks their ability to focus on their children. These children struggle with **impulsivity, delinquency, mental health problems, suicidal ideation, self-harm, low self-esteem,** and **substance abuse.** The chronic message of neglectful parenting: "You don't matter. You're worthless."

Share a personal example of **neglectful** parenting:

Authoritative Parenting

The fourth common parenting style is *authoritative* parenting. These parents effectively set healthy limits while maintaining a nurturing stance. With authoritative parenting, you notice your child struggle to swim, but you do not rush back to rescue them. Instead, you keep a healthy distance while sending supportive, encouraging messages. When the child is panicking in the water and calling for help, this parent responds calmly: "You can do this. Learning to swim is very scary. I was scared, too. Take a deep breath and believe in yourself. I'm right here." Notice how the healthy parent accepts the struggle and does not judge the child's process. This parent knows that empowerment and healthy boundaries will lead to success. <u>The healthy parent</u>

supports the child through life's stresses while viewing challenges as an opportunity for growth. Children who receive authoritative parenting grow up with **healthy self-esteem**. **They are independent**, **likable**, **socially accepted**, **academically successful**, and **generally well-behaved**. They are less likely to engage in antisocial or deviant behaviors and courageously take on new challenges because they are not afraid to fail. The general message of positive parenting: "You are valuable. You are worthy of love."

1.) Share a personal example of **authoritative** parenting:

2.) Which parenting styles were present in your childhood home? What was the impact on you?

3.) As a parent, which parenting style(s) do you gravitate toward most often? Share an example:

Video: Sprouts (2021): "Five Parenting Styles and Their Effects on Life." https://youtu.be/fyO8pvpnTdE (7:32)
Discussion: Sprouts states, "*Authoritarian* parents are controlling and demand obedience without considering the child's point of view. *Permissive* parents are loving, but they don't exert any control. *Authoritative* parents are firm but loving and encourage independence within limits. *Neglecting* parents are uninvolved and often uninterested in their own child. *Over-involved* parents are known as '*snowplows*' removing obstacles or '*helicopter*' parents who hover and micromanage every aspect of their child's life. Since they don't let their children do anything alone, they can't learn to overcome challenges."
1.) Which parenting style in the video is most familiar to you? Share your experience:

Deconstructing Shame Parenting

Many good-intentioned parents fall into the habit of using shame. The intent is to teach, but the child's interpretation is, "I'm not good enough. There's something wrong with me." Many anxious parents shame their children into compliance. *Example*: A mother worries that her son's lack of motivation to clean his room is a sign that he won't succeed. She uses shame to motivate him, "If you keep being such a lazy slob, you'll be a loser in life." Beliefs are formed through repeat exposure. Children who repeatedly absorb messages like, "You're not good enough" or "You can't do anything right" begin to believe the messages to be truths about themselves. The messages may have been used as motivators by desperate parents, but unfortunately, they become the child's self-view. Once you hold a belief about yourself, it can turn into a self-fulfilling prophecy. What is the behavior of a child who believes they're a 'lazy slob'? Usually, they continue to be disorganized and unmotivated.

Defeat Shame:
- no *should statements*
- no *why questions*
- no *supposed to*
- no *comparing*
- no *negative labels*
- no *eye rolling*
- no *mocking*
- no *revenge*
- no *good/bad*
- no *right/wrong*
- no *always/never*

Remove all negative labels to defeat shame. Using the example of a messy room, keep the negative label out of the message. Use factual statements like, "Your room needs to be cleaned before you do anything else." Parenting without shame requires **empathy**, **normalizing**, and **healthy boundaries**. **Practice**: Read the examples, and create your own.

Empathy: A simple formula for empathy is "Me, too." Why would a teenager fail to clean their room? Empathy from a parent in this situation may sound like: "Sometimes I dread cleaning, too."
1.) Use *empathy* to correct shame parenting: "You're getting bullied because you're being a wimp. Stand up for yourself!"

Normalizing increases tolerance and reduces emotional flooding. In this example, normalizing may sound like: "Keeping a clean room is a low priority for every teenager."
2.) Use *normalizing* to correct shame parenting: "Act your age; stop whining! You're not going to that party!"

Healthy boundaries require you to remove yourself from the equation. I'm *personalizing* if I think, "He didn't clean because he's disrespecting me." A healthy boundary sounds like: "It's up to you when you clean your room, but there will be no electronics until it's done."
3.) Use *healthy boundaries* to correct shame parenting: "Can't you be nice for once? Help your sister with her homework!"

Deconstructing Helicopter Parenting

Many good-intentioned parents will helicopter to shield their kids from distress. The problem is that emotional suffering is a natural part of life, and resilience is developed during childhood. Over-involved parents are raising their children in an unrealistic world that does not exist. These kids are not allowed to regulate emotions or self-soothe, which leads to dependency issues and low self-esteem. Young adults raised by helicopter parents frequently fail at independence and return to the safety of their parent's home.

The sad truth is that most helicopter parents have wonderful intentions and don't realize that their child's level of functioning is tied to their ability to tolerate and regulate emotions. Rather than eliminating challenges or struggles, it is essential to help your child cope with the harsh realities of life by nurturing, empathizing, and showing compassion. *Example*: If your daughter is afraid to audition for the play because she doesn't think she'll get selected, don't discourage her from trying. If rejected, she can learn how to manage disappointment in the safety of a loving home. A child who is comfortable with failure is a child who does not use avoidance as a coping strategy. Children will work toward goals when they aren't afraid to fail. The message we want to teach our children is, "<u>Sometimes we get what we want, and sometimes we don't</u>. <u>Failure means you had the courage to try.</u>"

Catch/Correct Practice - Identify the parenting style for each, and create an authoritative response:

Example 1: Your adolescent sadly tells you they got in trouble at school.

1.) "That's not my problem. I don't want to hear it." _____

2.) "I'm calling the school right now. You did nothing wrong." _____

3.) "You're an embarrassment. Why can't you ever behave?" _____

4.) Create an *authoritative* response: _____

_____

Example 2: Your young child throws a temper tantrum at bedtime.

1.) "You are ridiculous. Stop being such a whiny baby!" _____

2.) "Do whatever you want. I don't care if you're tired tomorrow." _____

3.) "Okay, you can stay up. I'll drive you in late tomorrow." _____

4.) Create an *authoritative* response: _____

_____

Example 3: Your teen comes home upset because they were fired from their summer job.

1.) "Let's drive back there right now so we can talk to your manager about this." _____

2.) "Wow, you must be so embarrassed. Only a loser would get fired from such a basic job." _____

3.) "I'm not sure what you expect me to do. It's your life, not mine." _____

4.) Create an *authoritative* response: _____

_____

Example 4: Your kids continue wrestling after you've told them to stop, and one gets injured.

1.) "Don't come crying to me. I told you to stop." _____

2.) "It's all my fault you got hurt. I'm so sorry! I should have protected you." _____

3.) "Are you deaf? You never listen! Fools like you deserve to get hurt." _____

4.) Create an *authoritative* response: _____

Chapter 18
Effective Parenting Skills Training

Native American Legends
Two Wolves — A Cherokee Legend
An old Cherokee is teaching his grandson about life.
"A fight is going on inside me," he said to the boy. "It's a terrible
fight, and it is between two wolves. One is evil—he is anger, envy, sorrow,
regret, greed, arrogance, self-pity, guilt, resentment, inferiority, lies, false pride, superiority,
and ego." He continued, "The other is good—he is joy, peace, love, hope, serenity, humility,
kindness, benevolence, empathy, generosity, truth, compassion, and faith. The same fight is
going on inside you - and inside every other person, too." The grandson thought about
it for a minute and then asked his grandfather, "Which wolf will win?"
The old Cherokee simply replied, "The one you feed."
Source: www.firstpeople.us

❖   Positive Parenting

❖   Natural / Logical Consequences

❖   Defeat Power Struggles

❖   Pick Your Battles / Shaping / Modeling / Consistency

Positive Parenting

Authoritative (*positive*) parents are masterful at working with their children instead of against them. They consistently use creativity, empathy, affection, clear limits, and healthy boundaries to guide their children toward success. Research shows that children who receive positive parenting function at higher levels academically, psychologically, and socially. The Gottman Institute's five-step emotional coaching program promotes healthy intellectual and psychosocial growth. Gottman's (2019) five steps include 1.) awareness of emotion, 2.) connecting with your child, 3.) listening to your child, 4.) naming emotions, and 5.) finding solutions.

Video: TEDx (2020): "Lael Stone: How to Raise Emotionally Intelligent Children." https://youtu.be/6fL09e8Tm9c (12:11)

Discussion: Stone states, "How did the adults in your life respond to you? If you were lucky, the adults in your life would have given you lots of space to express how you feel without trying to fix what was going on. Our current mental health landscape sees a steady increase in psychological distress. There are three ways kids deal with emotions. 1.) **Repression**: You learned it wasn't safe to express your feelings. Perhaps you were given a look that made you draw everything inside, and you learned to push the emotions down deep. The impact is that those feelings stay there, and then, as adults, those feelings can turn up again when life throws us a curveball with similar themes. Repression mechanisms look like another glass of wine, hours mindlessly scrolling, or making yourself so busy at work that you don't have time to feel. 2.) **Aggression**: As a child, we felt really powerless. We grew up in an authoritarian environment where we didn't have a voice; we couldn't say how we felt, and those feelings would come out in aggression or rage. 3.) **Expression**: As a child, we grew up in an environment where all feelings are welcome. As adults, when things are hard, we write in our journals, call a friend, run, do yoga, speak to our therapist, and we find a way to lean into the feelings, and then we let them go. As humans, we need a safe place to unpack all of who we are. Instead of trying to fix my kids' problems or make them happy all the time, I just said, 'Tell me all about it.' I just listened."

Questions: As a child, did you cope using *repression, aggression,* or *expression*? What coping style are you promoting for your children? Share your childhood and adult experiences:

Power Struggles

Power struggles are like quicksand. The more you struggle, the faster you sink. Imagine a game of tug-of-war over a pool of quicksand. You and your child are on opposite ends of the rope, pulling as hard as possible. The goal is to overpower your opponent, but what happens to the relationship when someone finally wins? Usually, you both feel exhausted, disconnected, and resentful, and the relationship sinks. How can you avoid quicksand? Drop the rope and walk away from the edge. What does dropping the rope look like? Choose to disengage by setting clear limits and implementing consequences. Use helpful parenting tools, such as: *picking your battles, shaping behavior, modeling,* and *consistency.*

Video: Sprouts (2018): "Attachment Theory: How Childhood Affects Life." https://youtu.be/WjOowWxOXCg (7:35)
Discussion: <u>Can you identify your attachment style from childhood? How can we raise securely attached children? Share your thoughts</u>:

Consequences

Parenting is one of life's most challenging jobs. Parenting responsibly requires implementing consequences rather than punishment. Punishment means intentionally harming or inflicting pain, and consequences are results from our actions that encourage learning.

Punishment Examples: Using shame, humiliation, intimidation, violence, or force. If a child doesn't complete their homework, the punishment is a spanking. A child doesn't turn off the TV, and the punishment is yelling. A child refuses to brush teeth, and the punishment is a threat. A teen doesn't do the laundry; the punishment is wearing pajamas to school.

Consequence Examples: When implementing a consequence, avoid any messages of disgust, sarcasm, contempt, or disappointment. If a teen is texting during dinner, the logical consequence may be losing the phone. A child refuses to eat dinner, and the natural consequence is being hungry. If kids don't complete their chores, they do not earn an allowance.

Natural Consequences

Natural consequences occur without any intervention by the parent. *Example*: If a child leaves the house without a coat in the winter, the natural consequence is being cold. The parent doesn't have to do anything to create the consequence; it naturally occurs. **Learning from natural consequences is an essential part of developing personal agency**. <u>As adults, we experience natural consequences all the time</u>. If you don't show up for work, the consequence is termination. If you fail to pay rent, the consequence is eviction. The landlord doesn't need to use shame to gain compliance; eviction is all adults need to pay on time. **Natural consequences are beneficial for parent-child bonding**. <u>Rather than being the enforcer, the parent can be an empathic teammate</u>. In our winter coat example, when the child comes home and tells you they weren't allowed to go outside for recess without a coat, the parent can empathize, "Oh no, that's awful! You love recess. Do you think you want to bring your coat tomorrow?" This example is beneficial on several levels: First, the message to the child is that they're very important to you, and you don't want them to suffer. Second, by asking how they'd like to solve the problem, you're sending a message of value, which directly boosts your child's self-esteem. Unless there is a risk of danger to the child, parents can take a healthy step back and allow the world to teach them naturally.

Share an example of a **natural consequence**:

Logical Consequences

When the natural consequence is unsafe or takes too long to produce desired change, the best alternative is a logical consequence. **Logical consequences allow children to connect the dots between their behavior and the consequence**. <u>When choosing logical consequences, pick something directly related to the problem behavior</u>. If a child is playing video games instead of doing homework, a logical consequence is removing electronics until the homework is completed. If a child does not eat vegetables at dinner, a logical consequence is losing dessert. **It's important to keep consequences as brief as possible and use the one-day-at-a-time rule**. If consequences are excessive in length, it often produces hopelessness and can lead to deviant behaviors such as lying, blame, manipulation, and deception. Logical consequences work best when the child knows ahead of time what the consequence will be for any given issue. *Example*: If a teen isn't doing their chores, you can gently remind them that there is no free time (computer, TV, friends, etc.) until the chores are completed.

Share an example of implementing a **logical consequence**:

Natural/Logical Consequence Practice

1. Your child forgets to study for a test.

   Natural: _____

   Logical: _____

2. Your adolescent misses the bus.

   Natural: _____

   Logical: _____

3. Your teen does not come home on-time for dinner.

   Natural: _____

   Logical: _____

Pick Your Battles

Set your child up for success rather than failure. When setting limits, it's essential to pick your battles carefully. Parents with good intentions can micromanage and end up in chronic power struggles. Before setting a limit, ask yourself how important the issue is and if **a natural consequence can effectively motivate your child**, **then back away and allow them to learn without your interference**. A natural consequence for a teen who misses the bus may be walking to school and receiving a tardy. The next day, they will likely choose to get out the door in time to catch the bus. In this example, the teen was allowed to learn how the world works without fighting with a parent. Anytime you can join your child's team, instead of working against them, choose to play on the same team. Instead of telling my child to stop jumping on the furniture, I guide them with the challenge of hopping around the living room on one foot. If your child dreads the bedtime routine, you may want to guide them by creating a game of racing to get their pajamas on. You can also motivate your child by saying, "I hope we have time to read two books; brush your teeth, so we have time!" Be an ally by remaining empathic. Your child isn't resisting bedtime because they're a bad kid; they're resisting because they're human. Empathy means reminding myself, "Sometimes I drag my feet, too."

Sometimes, a parent will not be able to wait for the natural consequence to produce the desired change. In the case of a child who maintains consistently failing grades, it's clear that the grades are not a motivator. In this circumstance, the parent will need to intervene with a logical consequence. Before implementing a consequence, you must first assess the situation. If a learning issue affects your child's ability to succeed, it's crucial to provide the necessary resources. If you determine that your child's social life or technology is interfering, then applying limits can be an effective motivator.

Share examples of being an ally to your loved one by **picking your battles**:

Shaping Behavior

Any behavior that receives attention is reinforced. In other words, **anytime you call attention to something your child is doing, the child is more likely to repeat the behavior**. For many parents, when their children are happy and quiet, the parent disengages, but with conflict, the parent becomes active. *Example*: If a child screams because they can't solve a problem, and the parent immediately fixes it, the screaming is reinforced. Alternatively, the complaining is reinforced if a child whines for another cookie and the parent gives it to them. Anything that receives attention will be reinforced. Reinforcement is like watering a flower. If you water the flower, it will grow; if you stop watering the flower, it will die. It's important to know what you water. Are you watering the flowers or the weeds?

You can't stop watering the weeds entirely by ignoring all negative behaviors. If a child hits another child or breaks a toy, the child receives a natural or logical consequence. When delivering the consequence, it's essential to do so with a matter-of-fact tone. Children misbehave because they're human and learning how to function in the world. If a child hits another child, a logical consequence is a statement of apology and/or ending the play date early. If a child breaks a toy, a logical consequence may be a time-out or loss of the toy. It's essential that parents set clear, consistent limits without the use of shame, criticism, or disgust.

Water the flowers by catching your child doing things you like, **and warmly comment on the behavior**. *Examples*: You notice your son sitting still during dinner and reinforce the behavior, "I really like eating dinner with you." You find your daughter quietly drawing, encouraging her by saying, "It looks like you love to draw." <u>When making statements with the intent to reinforce desirable behaviors, avoid seeking a response.</u> Your child doesn't need to respond. **The goal is to water the flowers by calling attention to the desirable behavior.** <u>It's important to note that reinforcement works in all relationships.</u> Consider watering the flowers with your partner, roommates, family, or employees.

Share examples of <u>reinforcing positive behavior</u> by **watering the flowers**:

Modeling

Another effective positive parenting tool is modeling. All of your actions influence your children. They're watching you very closely, and you are teaching them how to behave in the world. This is why the saying, "Do as I say, not as I do," is unrealistic. A parent who smokes cigarettes is raising a child who is likely to smoke, even if the parent endlessly tells the child, "Don't ever smoke; it'll kill you." Parents who discipline with corporal punishment are teaching their children violence. Imagine how confusing it is for a child when a parent hits them while simultaneously saying, "We don't hit!" *Example*: A parent finds the milk left out all night and asks the kids who did it. One honest child confesses, and the parent angrily shames that child. This parent just taught their children to avoid vulnerability in the future. The children will likely use denial or blame with the next mistake to avoid accountability.

Our children naturally want to admire and respect us. The best way to encourage respect is to show respect. If you want your children to be kind and loving, show them kindness and love. If you want your children to be honest, show them honesty. <u>If you want your children to take responsibility for themselves, you must hold yourself accountable for all of your behaviors.</u> **One of the greatest gifts to your children is to teach vulnerability by acknowledging when you are wrong.** *Example*: "I was really angry, and I yelled at you. It's not okay that I treated you that way, and I'm very sorry." <u>If you want your children to use blame and anger to cope, show them blame and anger.</u> *Example*: "If you weren't so difficult, I wouldn't have to yell!" You are your child's greatest teacher.

Anytime life throws you a curveball, you can strengthen your coping skills. Try to avoid rescuing your children from some of life's painful realities. *Example*: If your son comes home upset because he didn't make the basketball team, a great response would be, "Sadly, sometimes we work really hard, and things just don't go our way. What's important is that you tried for something you wanted, and maybe it will be your turn to get it next time." <u>This response validates their feelings, and at the same time, it encourages acceptance and hope.</u> A **problematic response** in the scenario would be, "Coaches pick favorites; you never had a chance. You were the best out there, but the coach already had the team picked." <u>In this response, the parent is trying to help the teen feel better, but they are modeling blame, denial, and anger to cope.</u> It's important to model the reality that we don't always get what we want, and sometimes life doesn't seem fair because life isn't fair. To encourage resilience, validate your child's pain, normalize the experience, and encourage them to try again.

Share examples of <u>guiding</u> your loved one using **modeling**:

Consistency

Your children will develop frustration tolerance, self-esteem, and the ability to cope with the harsh realities of life during their childhood years. The reality is that life is filled with disappointment. Parents who try to protect their children from emotional discomfort are doing their children a disservice. *Example*: If a child is frustrated because they can't figure out the math homework and a parent completes the homework, the parent is taking away this child's opportunity to cope with frustration. If a child asks for candy in a store and the parent says, "No, not today," it's essential that the parent sticks with the no. If the child throws a fit and the parent gives in, that parent just reinforced the temper tantrum. That child will now use the tantrum to get what they want in the future. Is the child using the tantrum because they're a bad kid? No! The child is using it because it works. Who taught the child that the temper tantrum is an effective strategy for getting what they want? You! Thinking before you set a limit is critical because consistency is key.

<u>In order to promote consistency and compliance, set a reasonable length of time for each consequence</u>. <u>The younger the child, the shorter the length</u>. It's important to note that it is not the length of the consequence that determines its effectiveness. **Try to set a consequence as close to the infraction as possible and keep it as brief as possible**. Removing a toy from a child for the day is usually plenty of time to have an impact. A compelling motivation for a teen can be losing the phone for an evening. A consequence rarely needs to be implemented for longer than a few hours to a few days.

Share examples of <u>setting healthy limits and following through</u> with **consistency**:

Video: Dr. Gabor Mate. "How Not to Screw Up Your Kids." https://www.youtube.com/
Discussion: Dr. Mate states, "The child's brain can't handle the attachment void when there is no attachment figure. Without the parent or nurturing adult, the child will fill that void with the peer group and become far more attached to the peer group than is healthy for them. Discipline is the very opposite of punishment. Anything you do that undermines your relationship with the child will actually undermine the child's development because it makes the child insecure." <u>Share your thoughts about the video</u>:

Video: TED (2021): "Molly Wright: How Every Child Can Thrive by Five." https://youtu.be/aISXCw0Pi94 (7:42)

Discussion: Molly Wright states, "Our brain develops faster in our early years than at any other time in our lives. It can create up to one million neural connections every second. But we need your help. Our healthy development needs these top five things: 1.) Connecting; 2.) Talking; 3.) Playing; 4.) A healthy home; and 5.) Community. All of this helps us reach our full potential. So, what's something you can do that can really make a difference? Scientists call it serve and return: Connect, talk, and play with us. Copycat games build imagination and empathy. Naming games build vocabulary and attention. Games like peekaboo build memory and trust. Each time you talk to us, play with us, and make us laugh, it not only strengthens our relationships and mental health, it actually teaches us some of the most important life skills. Interactions early and often matter." What are you already doing as a parent to promote healthy brain development? What areas do you need to work on? Share your thoughts about the video:

Video: TEDx (2020): "Shaka Senghor and Ebony Roberts: Co-Parenting as Allies, Not Adversaries." https://youtu.be/nRFA1C9spko (14:15)

Discussion: Senghor and Roberts discuss navigating divorce while protecting children from trauma. Roberts states, "We made a choice, in the beginning, to co-parent as allies, not adversaries. We chose to break the toxic pattern we see play out over and over again when parents lose focus on what's most important: the children." Senghor shares his ritual of using positive affirmations with his child every night. Share your thoughts about the video:

Homework - Over the week, practice the following effective parenting skills.

1. **Shaping Behavior**: Catch your child doing something you like and reinforce it. Share an example:

2. **Natural Consequences**: Share an example of allowing your child to experience a natural consequence:

3. **Logical Consequences**: Share an example of implementing a logical consequence:

4. **Modeling**: Describe a time when you guided your child by example through your behavior rather than telling your child what to do:

5. **Consistency**: Share an example of when you successfully set a reasonable limit and followed through, showing consistency:

Chapter 19
Assertiveness Training

Your problem isn't the problem, your reaction is the problem.
~ Buddha

Assertiveness is not what you do, it's who you are.
~ Shakti Gawain

Nobody can make you feel inferior without your consent.
~ Eleanor Roosevelt

When we avoid difficult conversations, we trade short-term discomfort for long-term disfunction.
~ Peter Bromberg

When you don't expect anything from anyone,
you experience true peace.
~ Sangeeta Rana

❖ Deconstructing Communication Styles

❖ Healthy Boundaries

❖ Defeat Personalizing

❖ Accept/Assert Rule

Communication Styles

There are three communication styles when confronted with a problem or conflict: **passive**, **aggressive**, and **assertive**. Many people identify with using different styles in different settings. *Example*: "I'm assertive at work but passive at home." In previous chapters, we've discussed problem-coping strategies, such as *avoidance* and *control*. The passive communication style is an avoidant coping strategy, and aggression is a form of control. When you notice yourself using a problem-coping strategy, it's generally a sign of insecurity. An individual who is assertive at work feels confident and secure. If that same individual is passive or aggressive at home, it indicates a lack of security in that setting.

Passive Style

On the surface, *passive* people can appear to be unaffected by the world around them, but the reality is that internal discomfort runs high. The passive person feels trapped in an internal battle. They often struggle with low self-worth and fear of rejection. They tend to overvalue what other people think and undervalue themselves. When you choose passivity, you are likely to feel as if other people are taking advantage of you, and you will remain silent rather than express your wants and needs. Often when passive people try to set limits, they do so by using passive-aggressive sarcasm. **Passive people may successfully avoid many relationship conflicts**, **but their internal conflict runs high**. Passive individuals frequently ruminate about the wrongdoings of others, as well as how they feel bulldozed, manipulated, or mistreated by them. **The passive stance leads to victim thinking**. Rumination also focuses on themes of disgust at one's own failure to assert, which further destroys their self-esteem.

It's helpful to imagine the passive person as a boiling pot of water. With each failure to assert, the boiling water becomes more rapid and threatens to spill over. The passive individual does everything they can to suppress their emotions and keep the lid on the raging pot. **Passive people walk around dissecting and analyzing themselves and others**, **leading to chronic anger and resentment**. The goal of passivity is to avoid conflict and rejection, but eventually, the individual has stuffed so much anger and hurt that they can no longer keep the lid on the pot, and they explode. **A passive person feels like a prisoner of their thoughts**. If you struggle with passivity, apply the **Accept/Assert Rule** whenever you find yourself stuck ruminating. When you feel trapped by overthinking, the first step is *accepting* the situation without trying to change it. Then, you can choose to *assert* directly or let it go. Accept/Assert defeats harmful rumination and overthinking.

> ### Passive Beliefs
> *It's best not to create any waves.*
> *People won't like me if I disagree.*
> *It's my job to make others happy.*
> *If you don't have something nice to say, don't say anything.*

Passive Example - Share an example of when you have responded with passivity. What was your internal dialogue? Did you find yourself ruminating? Please share your experience:

Aggressive Style

Similar to passive people, the *aggressive* coping person struggles with chronic internal discomfort. Aggressive people fear rejection and frequently feel taken advantage of and victimized. **Unlike the passive individual who believes safety comes from remaining silent, the aggressive person believes safety comes from remaining in the attack position.** Aggressive individuals experience chronic power struggles. While some may describe the passive person as indifferent, people often describe the aggressive person as challenging, oppositional, or hostile. Aggressive people are working from a framework of justified anger, and they spend much time in their heads feeding their resentment, hostility, and intolerance.

Like passive people, aggressive individuals struggle with insecurity and low self-esteem. While the passive person attempts to protect their self-worth by seeking approval, the aggressive person attempts to elevate self-esteem by devaluing others. The power struggle for the aggressive person tends to result from the false assumption that "Life is a battle, and there is no such thing as a win-win." Essentially, the aggressive person attempts to heal their fractured ego by controlling the competition. The aggressive individual does not realize that devaluing others diminishes one's own self-worth. Like the passive person, the aggressive person has a strong need for external validation, but the aggressive individual demands or intimidates others to get it. If you struggle with aggression, apply the **Accept/Assert Rule** whenever you feel angry, bitter, or resentful. First, *accept* the situation without trying to change or control it. Then, you can choose to let it go or *assert* without aggression.

> ### Aggressive Beliefs
> *You can't trust anyone.*
> *Others will take advantage of me if I let them.*
> *Showing emotion is a sign of weakness.*
> *If we disagree, we have a problem.*
> *Admitting failure is not an option.*
> *I have the right to demand respect.*
> *I have the right to speak my mind.*
> *People should be told when they're wrong.*
> *I need to fight for what is right.*

Aggressive Example - Share an example of when you have responded with aggression. What was your internal dialogue? Did you find yourself ruminating? Please share your experience:

Assertive Style

Assertiveness is characterized by the belief that everyone has the right to express their thoughts and feelings equally. Assertive people allow themselves to set limits, share their thoughts, and express their needs without expecting or demanding approval from others. At the same time, they allow others to freely express their thoughts, feelings, and needs without judgment. **For the assertive person, approval is provided by the self, which allows for healthy boundaries and easy communication.** These individuals do not need to overpower others (*aggressive*) or receive approval (*passive*) to feel comfortable with themselves. Setting limits is done with a tone of respect. Assertive people are high in personal agency and have healthy boundaries, allowing them to remain comfortable even during conflict.

The internal state of the assertive person is relatively peaceful because they naturally apply the **Accept/Assert Rule**. If they want to express their thoughts or feelings, they're free to do so. If they choose to remain silent, that's okay, too. <u>Unlike passive and aggressive individuals, assertive people view themselves and others through a lens of acceptance and rarely feel trapped by overthinking.</u>

> **Assertive Beliefs**
>
> *We don't always agree, and that's okay.*
> *We are all of equal value.*
> *Others do not define me; I define myself.*
> *I only have control over myself.*
> *We are all far from perfect.*
> *Everyone has a right to their thoughts and feelings.*
> *I don't need to be right to feel okay about myself.*
> *If I make a mistake, it's a reminder that I'm human.*
> *It's okay if others don't like me; I like myself.*
> *If it's not mine, I need to stay in my lane.*

Assertive Example - Share an example of when you have responded with assertiveness. What was your internal dialogue? <u>Please share your experience</u>:

> *Your problem isn't the problem, your reaction is the problem. ~ Buddha*

Communication Styles Example

Dara has plans with her friend Page. Page wants to go to their usual hangout, but Dara recently broke up with her partner, and she knows they will probably be there. Dara tells Page that she does not want to run into her ex, but Page keeps pushing. Page tells Dara that they'll leave if things get uncomfortable. Dara concedes, and when they arrive, she almost immediately sees her ex. What she does next depends upon her coping style:

Passive Style: Dara will avoid her ex and passively say to Page, "They're here, so I think maybe we should get going." Page responds, "It's no big deal, just give it a minute. Maybe they'll leave." <u>Dara continues to look at her watch as time passes, feeling increasingly uncomfortable and trapped in the situation</u>. Dara will **struggle with an internal battle**: "It's not fair to make her leave when we just got here. What's wrong with me? I can't avoid this forever. I just need to chill out." Dara feels her stomach tighten as she nervously paces. Dara will **feel victimized** as she finds herself trapped by her commitment to her friend. Dara will silently feel anger and resentment toward herself and Page. Dara may also use the **passive-aggressive tactic of sighing**. <u>The loud sigh is often used to reduce your anxiety while passively encouraging others around you to solve your problems.</u>

Aggressive Style: Dara will say, "I'm out of here! You knew I didn't want to be here. I'm not going to deal with this just so you can have a good time." <u>Notice the use of personalizing; she views herself as a victim and justifies her anger.</u> **The aggressive person uses victim stance to justify the attack.**

Assertive Style: Dara will evaluate the situation with healthy boundaries. She will independently decide if she is ready for the discomfort. If she chooses to give it a chance, she will likely tell Page, "I'm going to see how this goes, but I might be leaving in a minute." If she decides to leave immediately, she'll say, "I'm just not up for this tonight. Sorry, but I'm going to head out." <u>Notice how the assertive person's decision-making process does not involve blame.</u> **The assertive person has healthy boundaries, maintains an internal locus of control, and does not play the victim.** Assertive people set limits without aggression.

Discussion:

1.) <u>In this scenario, which Dara would you be? Why?</u>

2.) <u>Apply the Accept/Assert Rule for Dara:</u>

3.) <u>What similarities do you notice between passive and aggressive thinking</u>?

Practice - Use the following example to practice each communication style.

Example: Ty has car trouble, so she asks Jacy for a ride to work. The following day, Jacy leaves early to allow extra time to grab her friend, but Ty isn't ready when she arrives. As she waits, Jacy worries that she will be late for work. <u>Create responses below for Jacy using each style:</u>

Passive Style: _____

_____

Aggressive Style: _____

_____

Assertive Style: _____

_____

Nobody can make you feel inferior without your consent. ~ Eleanor Roosevelt

Video: TEDx (2020): "Frederik Imbo: How Not to Take Things Personally?" https://youtu.be/LnJwH_PZXnM (17:36)

Discussion: Why do we take things personally, and what happens to us emotionally when we personalize? Imbo talks about how we personalize when our ego gets in the way. He asks, "Do you want to be right, or do you want to be happy?" He describes two tools to defeat personalizing:

1.) **It's not about me**: This first step requires healthy boundaries. Share an example using this tool:

2.) **It is about me**: Apply this second step if the first step doesn't work. This tool requires insight and self-awareness. Share an example using this tool:

Healthy Boundaries

Healthy boundaries are essential to achieve assertiveness. Personalizing is a fiction that creates poor boundaries because you define yourself by others. **When you personalize, you give your power away and ride emotional rollercoasters**. With an observer stance, you maintain healthy boundaries by staying with the facts. To remain in an observer position, remind yourself, "It's not about me," and ask yourself, "What does their behavior say about them?"

Healthy Boundaries Practice

1. Your friend tells you they are too tired to go out, so you make other plans. Later that night, you see them out with another group of friends.
Personalizing: "They lied to me because they don't like me."
Observer Stance: "I guess they changed their mind and decided to go out."

2. You give your partner a gift. Instead of gratitude, they tell you they wish you were more thoughtful.

Personalizing: _____

Observer Stance: _____

3. You're worried your financial support is the only reason your partner is in the relationship.

Personalizing: _____

Observer Stance: _____

4. After working overtime for weeks, your boss tells you to focus more on the job.

Personalizing: _____

Observer Stance: _____

Accept/Assert Rule

Imagine a relationship conflict as a tug-of-war. You pull on one end of the rope with all your strength, but you are not gaining any ground. Then, you notice that the other end of the rope is tied to a brick wall. When you realize your efforts are in vain, you drop the rope. **Accept/Assert Rule** teaches us how to drop the rope and let go of power struggles. Power struggles are internal (*rumination*) and external (*interpersonal conflicts*). How does it work?

Accept: Step one: Stabilize emotionally using acceptance. Acceptance requires healthy boundaries. Boundaries remind you that other people's behavior defines them, not you. A helpful guide to achieving acceptance: "Sometimes...me, too." *Example*: Your child throws a fit publicly because he doesn't want to leave the park. *Personalizing* sounds like: "My son is throwing a fit because he's trying to embarrass me." *Healthy boundaries* sound like: "My child is expressing frustration because he's feeling disappointed." *Acceptance* sounds like: "Sometimes, when things don't go my way, I get frustrated, too."

Assert: Step two: Once you have stabilized emotionally, you are ready to assert. With assertiveness, you do not manipulate, intimidate, or attempt to change others; instead, you state the facts and validate their perspective. In the example above, *assertiveness* sounds like: "Disappointment is frustrating, and it's okay to feel that way. Time to go, but we'll come back."

Accept/Assert Example: You do not like your mother-in-law, and she is visiting for a week. Each day, she takes subtle jabs at your parenting. Your anger grows as she criticizes you and provides unsolicited advice. You think, "I don't even want her here; she's such a nightmare." You angrily ruminate about the injustice of the situation, and your goal is to get through the week without exploding.

Accept: "Her behavior is a reflection of her, not me. What is her behavior telling me about her? Maybe getting older is scary, and she's criticizing because she feels less valuable. Maybe she's sad that her time as a parent is over. When I feel insecure, I can be difficult, too." (boundaries, normalize, me too…)

Assert: "Thank you for your feedback. It sounds like you would handle things differently. We all have our own parenting styles. You did things your way, and we're doing things ours." (state facts, boundary reminder, set limits…)

Practice 1: You have been working the same job for five years and hoping for a promotion. You're about to go home after a long shift when your boss says, "I need you to close up tonight." You begin to resist, and your boss reminds you, "Loyalty pays off." You feel manipulated and angry.

Accept: (boundaries, normalize, me too…)

Assert: (state facts, boundary reminder, set limits…)

Practice 2: Your mother agreed to loan you money to help pay your rent. Your rent is due, and your mother says she's no longer willing to help. You feel disappointed and betrayed.

Accept: (boundaries, normalize, me too…)

Assert: (state facts, boundary reminder, set limits…)

Practice 3: Your partner agrees to go to a work event with you but cancels at the last minute.

Accept: (boundaries, normalize, me too…)

Assert: (state facts, boundary reminder, set limits…)

Practice 4: You supported your friend through their emotional divorce, and now you are in crisis, but they are too busy.

Accept: (boundaries, normalize, me too…)

Assert: (state facts, boundary reminder, set limits…)

Homework - Use a personal stressor this week and create your own Accept/Assert example:

Stressor:

Accept: (boundaries, normalize, me too…)

Assert: (state facts, boundary reminder, set limits…)

Chapter 20
Effective Communication Skills Training

When you talk, you are only repeating what you already know.
But if you listen, you may learn something new.
~ Dalai Lama

The only thing I know is that I know nothing.
~ Socrates

First seek to understand, then to be understood.
~ Stephen Covey

In the end, what will hurt the most is not the
words of our enemies but the silence of our friends.
~ Martin Luther King

❖   Healthy Boundaries

❖   "I" Messages

❖   Feelings *Before* Fix

TED Talk - Celeste Headlee: 10 Ways to Have a Better Conversation (11:44)

"I have ten basic rules. I'm going to walk you through all of them, but honestly, if you just choose one and master it, you'll already enjoy better conversations. **Number one**: Don't multitask. If you want to get out of the conversation, then get out, but don't be half in it. **Number two**: Don't pontificate. You need to enter every conversation assuming that you have something to learn. The famed therapist M. Scott Peck said true listening requires a setting aside of oneself, and sometimes that means setting aside your personal opinion. **Number three**: Use open-ended questions. Try asking them things like 'What was that like?' 'How did that feel?' **Number four**: Go with the flow. That means thoughts will come into your mind, and you need to let them go out of your mind. **Number five**: If you don't know, say you don't know. **Number six**: Don't equate your experience with theirs; it's not about you. **Number seven**: Try not to repeat yourself. It's condescending, and it's really boring. **Number eight**: Stay out of the weeds. Frankly, people don't care about the years, the names, or the dates. **Number nine**: Listen. I cannot tell you how many really important people have said that listening is perhaps the most important skill you could develop. And Calvin Coolidge said, 'No man ever listened his way out of a job.' Why do we not listen to each other? Number one, we'd rather talk. When I'm talking, I'm in control. But there's another reason: We get distracted. The average person talks about 225 words per minute, but we can listen to five hundred words per minute. So our minds are filling in these other 275 words. Stephen Covey said it very beautifully. He said, 'Most of us don't listen with the intent to understand. We listen with the intent to reply.' **Number 10**: Be brief. All of this boils down to the same basic concept: be interested in other people." C. Headlee (2016). Adapted from "Celeste Headlee: 10 Ways to Have a Better Conversation." TED Talks. https://youtu.be/R1vskiVDwl4

Discussion: Headlee outlines ten basic rules for better communication. Which of these are you already mastering and which do you need to improve?

Personal Agency

With every interaction, you are sending and receiving messages. Effective communication requires listening to another person even when you disagree. Personal agency is a critical component of effective communication because it leads to managing your emotions, tone of voice, body language, and facial expressions.

The Dalai Lama said, "When you talk, you are only repeating what you already know. But if you listen, you may learn something new." *Example*: My son made a decision I didn't like, but it was his decision. I want him to change, and I provide subtle consistent pressure. As I'm persuading him to rethink things, he finally says, "I know, you think I'm a loser." A **reactive** parent may immediately become defensive: "I never called you a loser. Don't talk back to me; I'm just trying to help!" A **nonreactive**, **high-accountability** parent who listens will see this child's response as valuable feedback. If I did not call my child a "loser," I must have been sending him messages of shame. My child's comment tells me that he feels as if he's "not good enough." When I listen, I will realize my parenting mistake, and I can respond effectively. **Accountability** may sound like, "I didn't realize it, but I guess I've been pressuring you to change your decision. I'm sorry I did that to you. Thank you for telling me how you feel." Anger does not exist without judgmental thoughts, and disappointment does not exist without expectations. If I hold myself accountable, I'll feel empowered rather than victimized. "People don't disappointment me; my expectations lead to my disappointment."

Healthy Boundaries

We often run into conflicts because people do not do what we want: control issues. This is a reminder that healthy boundaries are essential for assertive communication. If you find yourself wanting to be right, wanting to be liked, or wanting to be respected, you are seeking external validation. Seeking approval or validation from others can chip away at your self-esteem, create conflicts, and lead to feelings of disappointment. Don't be a seeker! When you find yourself wanting validation, stop and ask yourself, "Am I providing myself with validation?" If I want others to like me, I need to ask myself, "Do I like myself?" If I want others to respect me, I must ask, "Do I respect myself?" If I want others to think I'm right, I need to ask myself, "Is it okay if I'm wrong?" The following communication tools decrease conflict and promote healthy relationships: **"I" Messages** and **Mirroring**: feelings *before* fix.

"I" Messages

Using the **language of accountability** is one of the most effective ways to communicate because it elevates your likability and encourages other people to listen. Blame encourages others to consider how they will defend themselves and prove you wrong. Keep in mind that your feelings come from your thinking. When you own your feelings, you draw others toward you. Anytime you use an "I" message, you are increasing the chance that your message will be heard. When formulating an "I" message, it is most effective if you **choose an emotion that does not fall on the anger meter**. If you feel frustrated, take a moment to ask yourself, "What feelings are under my frustration?" Look for feelings of fear, hurt, rejection, sadness, and insecurity, and share those vulnerable emotions instead. There are four parts to formulating the "I" message, but a simple formula is switching: **"You" —> "I"**

```
        "You" Message ————————————————> "I" Message

"You are stressing me out." ————————————> "I'm feeling overwhelmed."

"You are making me look bad." ———————————> "I'm feeling embarrassed."

"You don't love me." ————————————————————> "I'm feeling insecure."
```

"You" Message Example:

1. "You always walk away from me when I try to talk to you. You are a self-centered narcissist, and I deserve so much better!"

* How would you respond to this example?

"I" Message Example:

1. **I Feel**: "I felt rejected…"
2. **When**: "when you walked away from me…"
3. **Because**: "because I am trying to talk to you."
4. **Request**: "Will you please listen for a minute?"

* How would you respond to this example?

Practice "I" Messages - Read each example below and create a response.

1. You attend a party with your partner; they disappear with friends, leaving you alone.

I feel _____

when _____

because _____

Request: _____

2. You get a midday call from the school that your daughter is absent. You quickly call home and discover she missed the bus.

I feel _____

when _____

because _____

Request: _____

3. Your partner told you they were heading to work. Later, you find out they spent the day with friends.

I feel _____

when _____

because _____

Request: _____

4. You race home early to cook dinner for your partner, but they come home two hours late without calling.

I feel _____

when _____

because _____

Request: _____

Video: Academy of Social Competency (2018): "Communication Skills: Empathic Listening - Inside Out 2015." https://youtu.be/t685WM5R6aM (1:44)

Discussion: This clip from the movie *Inside Out* shows the power of **mirroring emotion**. The first character, Joy, is trying to *fix* the problem by attempting to pull the person away from their uncomfortable emotion. The second character, Sadness, sits with emotion and validates. Notice how leaning into the *feeling* aids in emotional regulation. With validation, the character can process the feeling and let it go.

1.) Share a personal example of leaning into the *feeling* before attempting to *fix* the problem:

Mirroring: Feelings *Before* Fix

Mirroring is one of the most effective ways to improve your relationships. This empathic technique requires you to imagine that you are a mirror. The mirror listens and reflects the other person's emotions. Validating emotions does not mean agreeing; it simply conveys that you understand the other person. In order to reflect the feelings of others, it is essential to put your feelings aside temporarily. After you reflect their feelings, then you can share your own view. When mirroring, your tone of voice is critically important. Mirroring will fail every time if your tone is hostile, condescending, or sarcastic. If someone's behavior is not making sense to you, it simply means you do not understand their context. Take a moment to place yourself in their shoes and look at the situation from their perspective. Don't let questions trick you into skipping over the mirroring technique! Read the examples below, and then practice:

Example 1: "I'm so sick of my job! Today was the worst day!"

Problem Response: "You should just quit your job; you're always complaining about it."

~ Why is this response a problem? _____

Feelings *before* Fix: "It sounds like you've had a long and frustrating day."

Example 2: "When you yell at the kids, they feel afraid. I don't want our kids to be afraid of you."

Problem Response: "You're the one who's always yelling around here, not me."

~ Why is this response a problem? _____

Feelings *before* Fix: "It sounds like you're worried that the kids feel afraid when I yell."

1. "The kids have been a nightmare all day!"

Feelings *before* Fix:

2. "We're always fighting; I don't know what else to do. We can't continue like this."

Feelings *before* Fix:

3. "I don't care what you think. You're always judging me. Just leave me alone!"

Feelings *before* Fix:

4. "You know you're going to lose your job, don't you? How are we going to pay the bills? Why am I the only adult in this relationship?"

Feelings *before* Fix:

5. "I don't know what else to do. I've tried everything, but he won't listen, and he's going to ruin his future. I feel like I'm failing as a parent."

Feelings *before* Fix:

6. "Do you even like me anymore? If you liked me, you wouldn't treat me like this. Why are we together?"

Feelings *before* Fix:

7. "When you drink, you're out of control! When are you going to get it together and grow up?"

Feelings *before* Fix:

8. "Most parents spend time with their kids. I feel sorry for our kids; you're never there for them."

Feelings *before* Fix:

Homework - Practice switching blaming "**You**" statements into accountable "**I**" **feel** statements:

1. "You never listen!" _____

2. "You're doing this just to piss me off." _____

3. "You don't respect me!" _____

4. "You only care about yourself!" _____

5. "You're always late." _____

6. "You're so rude to everyone." _____

Chapter 21
Defining Healthy Relationships

High-conflict marriage, without much affection, turns out to be very bad for our health, perhaps worse than getting divorced.
~ *Robert Waldinger*

Having close ties with others is vital to every aspect of our health—mental, emotional, and physical.
~ *Sue Johnson*

As you heal, your attractions change, too. Toxicity stops looking like excitement and peace stops looking like boredom.
~ *Unknown*

❖ Healthy vs. Unhealthy Love

❖ Healthy Boundaries vs. Violations

❖ Cake Equations - Relationship Balance

❖ How to Stay in Your Lane

Video: TED (2019): "Katie Hood: The Difference Between Healthy and Unhealthy Love." https://youtu.be/ON4iy8hq2hM (12:13)

Discussion: Hood states, "One hundred percent of us will be on the receiving end of unhealthy relationship behaviors, and one hundred percent of us will do unhealthy things. It's part of being human. One in three women and one in four men will experience this in their lifetime. The first marker of unhealthy love is *intensity*. Abusive relationships do not start abusive; they start out exhilarating. Over time, these feelings shift from exciting to overwhelming or suffocating. A second marker is *isolation*. Isolation creeps in when they start pulling you away from your friends and family. Healthy love includes independence. A third marker is *extreme jealousy*. Your partner might become more demanding, needing to know where you are and who you are with. They might start following you everywhere, online and off. A fourth marker is *belittling*. In unhealthy love, words are used as weapons. In healthy relationships, your partner's words build you up, not break you down. Finally, a fifth marker is *volatility*. Unhealthy relationships are roller coasters with high highs and low lows." While watching the video, identify personal examples of the five markers:

1.) Intensity: _____

2.) Isolation: _____

3.) Extreme Jealousy: _____

4.) Belittling: _____

5.) Volatility: _____

Characteristics of a *Healthy* Relationship

1. **Value/Empathy**: Nonjudgmental listening and respecting each other's independent opinions and interests. It is not about agreeing; it's about valuing your partner and approaching them with interest and curiosity. "Sounds like you must be exhausted. Thank you for sharing that."

2. **Authenticity**: No people-pleasing, manipulation, expectations, or demands. Honoring differences and not withholding to avoid conflicts, openly sharing without fear of judgment. "I haven't thought about it that way; that's interesting. Let me think about that."

3. **Accountability**: Accepting responsibility and eliminating the use of blame. Accountability leads to trust and safety. Admitting when you're wrong, acknowledging past inappropriate behaviors, and vulnerable communication. "I had a really stressful day and took it out on you. That was mean, and I'm so sorry I did that to you."

4. **Equality/Teamwork**: Making group decisions, financial transparency, and equal distribution of work. Focusing on mutually satisfying resolutions and dividing parental responsibilities. Being positive, united role models for the children. "You drove her yesterday; I'll take her tonight." "How about one of us cooks, and the other does the dishes? What are your thoughts?" "Are you comfortable with letting the kids stay up late tonight?"

5. **Safety**: Partners feel comfortable expressing their thoughts, feelings, and opinions. Both partners feel safe engaging in independent activities. During unresolvable conflict, partners respectfully agree to disagree. Connection, support, and safety are constant in the relationship. Relationship stability does not require agreement. "I wasn't aware you felt that way. I see it differently, but I appreciate your feedback. Thank you for sharing that with me."

<u>Which of these *healthy* relationship characteristics are you already mastering</u>? <u>Provide a personal example</u>:

Characteristics of an *Unhealthy* Relationship

1. **Intimidation**, **Violence**, **Threats**: Intimidating looks or gestures, destroying property, punching walls, displaying weapons, abusing pets, yelling, slamming doors, blocking the exit, silent treatment, threatening to hurt yourself in order to manipulate, locking your partner out, threatening to hurt anyone who talks to your partner, driving recklessly to scare your partner, or interrogating the children or threatening to take them away.

2. **Emotional Abuse**: Degrading comments, name-calling, humiliating, gaslighting, or blaming. Making your partner do something degrading. Embarrassing or talking down to your partner.

3. **Isolation**: Controlling what your partner does or where they go. Limiting their activities outside the home or requiring your partner to ask permission. Justify your controlling behavior. Discouraging contact with friends/family. Violating their privacy, checking their phone, or reading their emails. Controlling the money or limiting access to transportation.

4. **Psychological Abuse**: Minimizing the abuse, denying, accusing, or blaming your partner.

5. **Entitlement**: Acting like you are more important or your time is more valuable. Treating your partner like a child or servant. Telling your partner what to do, how to dress, and how to behave. Believing you have the right to make demands or set expectations. Acting as a dictator or telling your partner that you are the head of the household.

6. **Control**: Refusing to allow your partner to work or sabotaging an existing job. Giving your partner an allowance, controlling the finances, demanding their paycheck, not allowing your partner to have a credit card, and claiming it's your partner's fault because they don't know how to manage money. Limiting your partner's activities, demanding they check in throughout the day, or stalking your partner by phone or in person.

<u>Which of these *unhealthy* relationship characteristics have you used most frequently</u>? <u>Share a personal example</u>:

Healthy Boundary Beliefs	Boundary Violations
You have your thoughts; I have mine.	You have to see it my way.
You have your feelings; I have mine.	You're making me feel the way I do.
You have your interests; I have mine.	We should have the same interests.
You have your needs; I have mine.	We should have the same wants and needs.
It's okay if we disagree.	You should agree with me.
I don't need your approval or permission.	We need to ask each other for permission.
I decide for me; you decide for you.	I get to tell you what to do in this relationship.
What's right for me may not be right for you.	If it's right for me, then it's right for you.
We have our own beliefs and views.	Expectations and demands are natural.
We don't have control over each other.	We need to be on the same path at all times.
Our thoughts and feelings are equally valuable.	My wants outweigh your wants.
Our wants and needs are equally valuable.	I get to decide for both of us.
We don't tell each other what to do.	You have to be happy with me.

Healthy Boundaries: Stay in Your Lane

Boundaries are healthy limits you set between yourself and others. To maintain healthy boundaries, knowing that you only have control over yourself is essential. Attempting to change, control, or please others leads to boundary violations. Poor boundary people often view themselves as victims; they struggle with chronic relationship conflicts and are often described as controlling, demanding, manipulative, or aggressive. It is helpful to view a person who violates boundaries as a tornado. Poor boundary people tend to spin out of control, creating chaos. If you choose to step toward the tornado, you will spin with them. Step back and disengage to maintain a safe, healthy boundary.

Boundary Violation Example: Imagine standing in front of someone, and they step on your toes. With this boundary violation, you begin to feel awkward and annoyed. Your emotional distress will push you to act if they do not step back. Most people respond to boundary violations with anger or avoidance, which is why poor boundary people often feel like victims; they chronically experience aggression or rejection from others without realizing they are causing the conflict. Poor boundary people do not realize they are stepping on toes. How would you feel and respond if someone held their foot on your toe? _____

Video: Prince Ea (2015): "Love Yourself Before You Get into a Relationship. Please." https://youtu.be/ip_FehKz5LE. (3:05)

Discussion: Prince EA states, "What's the most important thing to remember in a relationship? It's you! You have to figure out who you are before you enter a relationship. Your partner never made you feel anything, ever: It was your interpretation of your partner that made you feel how you felt. It's all you. All this time, you thought you were in love with another person, but all this time, you were in love with your own interpretations. You were in love with yourself. I don't know about you, but my relationships never worked out when I put too much force into trying to please the other person. Being someone I was not, I lost who I was. I was focused on being compatible with another person rather than being the best me I could be. The funny thing is that when two people are working on being the best versions of themselves, cultivating their own happiness and compassion, they are most compatible." Do you have a healthy relationship with yourself? Share your thoughts:

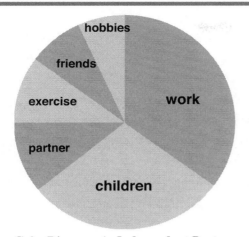

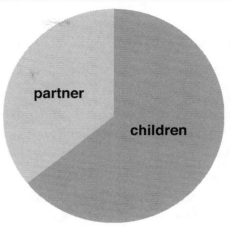

Cake Diagram A: Independent Partner   **Cake Diagram B: Co-Dependent Partner**

Cake Equation: Balanced or Imbalanced?

The *Cake Diagrams* above represent two partners in a love relationship. Imagine that every person is a whole cake, but each of us is divided differently. Some cakes have many slices, while others have only a few. The number of pieces is based on each individual's interests. The *Independent* partner above divides their cake into six different parts. Individuals with many slices tend to be self-sufficient in love relationships rather than pressuring their partners to meet their needs. The *Co-Dependent* partner above only has two sources of interest, which places a heavy burden on their partner. An imbalanced pairing ends in chronic boundary violations.

Example: "Co-Dependent" is frustrated with the kids, so they look to their partner for support, but "Independent" is not available because they are focused on a different piece of their cake (work, exercise). This lack of availability leaves Co-Dependent feeling hurt, bitter, and resentful. Co-Dependent does not have any other pieces to lean on, so their partner is their only outlet. In this equation, Independent will feel chronically overwhelmed and guilted, while Co-Dependent will feel insecure and rejected. The imbalanced equation above will lead to a volatile pursue-withdrawal cycle as both partners attempt to meet their own needs. If Independent begins to remove pieces of their cake to please their partner, they will eventually feel resentful, and the relationship will ultimately fail. In secure, satisfying relationships, both partners divide their energy similarly. **Practice** - Use the diagrams below to create your cake and your partner's cake:

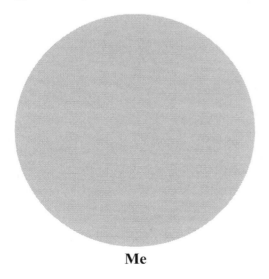

Me   **Partner**

How to Stay in Your Lane

1. **Self-Worth**: You cannot set good boundaries if you are unsure of yourself. Take time to identify your limits, and consider what makes you uncomfortable. You are your problem, and you are your solution. Look to yourself to solve your discomfort.

2. **Identify Your Feelings**: Feeling resentment indicates you are allowing others to violate your boundaries. In *nonabusive* relationships, people do not take advantage of you unless you enable them. Hold yourself accountable to regulate your emotions.

3. **Assertiveness**: Communicate directly what you want and need. If you are thinking something, find an appropriate way to say it. Get out of your head and communicate authentically. It is unrealistic to expect you will want to do the same things simultaneously. Provide yourselves the freedom to make independent decisions.

4. **Self-Awareness**: Failure to honor your needs leads to poor boundaries. Do not expect people to read your mind. Communicate clearly, with vulnerability and no expectations.

5. **Self-Care**: Permit yourself to put yourself first sometimes. Be sure that if you sacrifice for others, it is not because you were manipulated.

Practice - Rewrite the following poor boundary statements into healthy boundary statements:
1. "I'm not going without you tonight, so you'd better start getting ready."

2. "You're the reason we're drowning in debt. I'm canceling your credit cards."

3. "If you loved me, you would stay home with me."

4. "You need to change your mood, or you're going to ruin the weekend."

5. "Because of you, I have all these court fees. You'd better get a job."

Poor Boundary Quiz - Mark any statement that reflects your relationship history:
1. I feel good as long as you approve of me. _____
2. I cannot be happy unless you are happy. _____
3. My attention is focused on solving your problems and caring for your needs. _____
4. As a couple, we need to do everything together. _____
5. We must meet each other's approval on how we look and dress. _____
6. I feel embarrassed by your actions. _____
7. I don't know who I am without you. _____
8. I feel like I am walking on eggshells around you. _____
9. I am afraid to disappoint you. _____
10. We only get along when we agree. _____

Chapter 22
Divorce Predictors

I've found 94 percent of the time that couples who put a positive spin on their marriage's history are likely to have a happy future as well.
~ *John Gottman*

What we do everyday matters more than what we do once in a while.
~ *The Gottman Institute*

The simple truth is that happy marriages are based on a deep friendship. By this, I mean a mutual respect for and enjoyment of each other's company.
~ *John Gottman*

What is love? Love is the absence of judgement.
~ *Dalai Lama*

❖   Four Horsemen

❖   Harsh Start-Up / Repair Attempts

❖   Strategies to Improve Relationships

Video: The Gottman Institute (2014): "Four Horsemen of the Apocalypse." https://youtu.be/1o30Ps-_8is (2:12)
Discussion: The Gottman Institute states, "Dr. John Gottman calls these negative communication patterns 'The Four Horsemen of the Apocalypse' because they will lead to the end of your relationship. In fact, he can predict relationship failure with over 90% accuracy if the behavior is not changed. *Criticism* attacks the recipient's character instead of focusing on a specific behavior. The antidote to criticism is to talk about your feelings using 'I' statements. *Contempt* is an expression of superiority that comes out as sarcasm, cynicism, name-calling, eye-rolling, sneering, mockery, and hostile humor. The antidote to contempt is to treat one another with respect. *Defensiveness* is self-protection through righteous indignation or playing the victim. The antidote to defensiveness is to accept responsibility. *Stonewalling* occurs when the listener withdraws from the conversation without resolving anything. The antidote to stonewalling is to break for at least twenty minutes, calm down, and then return to the conversation."
1.) Share your experience with the Four Horsemen. Which one have you struggled with the most, and how has it affected your relationships?

Four Horsemen of the Apocalypse*

Gottman's research identifies the differences between "Masters" and "Disasters." This chapter will focus on Gottman's divorce predictors, principles for making a marriage work, and key strategies to improve your relationships. Gottman's Four Horsemen of the Apocalypse are negative communication styles that are lethal in relationships: *criticism*, *defensiveness*, *contempt*, and *stonewalling*. Research shows three of the Four Horsemen can be in every marriage, but contempt is the number one divorce predictor. According to Gottman (1999), if all Four Horsemen are present, divorce can be predicted with an 82 percent accuracy rate.

Horseman #1: *Criticism* is an attack on a person's character, usually with blame. According to Gottman, assertively voicing complaints can be one of the healthiest actions in a marriage, but criticism is destructive. A constructive complaint begins with "I," while a criticism begins with "You." Criticism includes negative labels and words such as *never* or *always*. Most of us do not realize when we criticize. If you frequently use criticism, your partner will be defensive. You will likely receive feedback such as: "Nothing I do is ever good enough for you," "You are never happy with me," "Why is everything always my fault?" or "You are always so negative."

Criticism Example: "You're always doing this to me. Why do you have to be so selfish?"
Practice - Remove *criticism* from the example by using accountability and direct communication:

Have you been in a relationship with someone who frequently criticizes? What was it like to be in that relationship? Share a personal example of **criticism**:

Horseman #2: *Defensiveness* increases relationship insecurity because it prevents emotional connection and effective communication. Defensiveness places a wall between you and your partner. Gottman describes it as blaming your partner, playing the victim, denying responsibility, and making excuses. If you are frequently defensive, you will likely receive feedback such as: "I cannot even talk to you," "You never listen," "You don't care," or "Why is it always my fault?"

Defensiveness Example: "You're the one who is always starting the fights, not me."
Practice - Use an "I" statement to eliminate blame and remove the *defensive wall* from the example:

Have you been in a relationship with someone who is chronically defensive? What was it like to be in that relationship? Share a personal example of **defensiveness** in your relationships:

Horseman #3: *Contempt* is the number one predictor of divorce. "The amount of contempt in stable, happy marriages is essentially zero"(Gottman, 1999, p. 47). Contempt is characterized by eye-rolling, name-calling, hostile humor, insults, and mockery. If you frequently use contempt, you will likely hear questions such as: "Why do you hate me so much?" or "Why are we together?"

Contempt Example: "You are just like your miserable father. I wish I never met you."
Practice - Share your vulnerable emotions to remove *contempt* from the example:

Have you been in a relationship with someone who uses contempt? What was it like to be in that relationship? Share a personal example of **contempt**:

Horseman #4: *Stonewalling* removes oneself from an argument by disengaging and acting like a stone wall. The message sent by a stonewaller is disapproval, abandonment, or rejection. People often stonewall when they become emotionally flooded, which leads to feeling overwhelmed, defenseless, and frozen One of the most damaging components of flooding is that it will encourage you to ignore the positives about your partner. Instead, you will focus on your partner's negative attributes. If you frequently stonewall in your relationships, you will likely receive feedback such as: "You don't care about me," "You never communicate," "I never know what you are thinking," or "Why don't I matter to you?"

Share an example of **stonewalling** in your relationship history. Did you stonewall because you were emotionally flooded, or was it an act of revenge? What impact has stonewalling had on your relationships?

Harsh Start-Up*

A conversation that begins with sarcasm, hostility, or criticism is considered a *harsh start-up*. **Gottman's research shows that when a discussion begins with a harsh start-up, it will end in a negative outcome 96 percent of the time**. Softening your approach with your partner is critical in reducing relationship conflict. Softening your approach comes from accountability, healthy boundaries, a warm tone of voice, empathy, and curiosity. Let go of the old baggage and approach your partner in the present moment. Present moment means using the words "right now" rather than "always" or "never." People who use harsh start-ups struggle with relationship anxiety and low self-esteem, and the aggression becomes part of their protective shield, which keeps others at a distance. If you frequently use harsh start-ups, your partner will be chronically defensive, and you will likely receive feedback such as: "Why are you always attacking me?" "Leave me alone," "I don't care what you think," or "You're never on my side."

Harsh Start-Up Exercise - Soften the statements below using vulnerable, direct communication:

1. "What is your problem today?"

2. "Here we go again. You always do this."

3. "You really screwed that up."

Repair Attempts*

Harsh start-ups occur in every relationship, and a *repair attempt* is the best recovery tool. According to Gottman, repair attempts are the glue of happy marriages because they de-escalate tension during arguments. <u>Repair attempts protect your partner's ego by placing the burden upon yourself with humor, accountability, or empathy</u>. Gottman's research shows that a couple's ability to reframe negative attributes improves tolerance and shortens recovery time.

Repair Attempt Examples - Read the examples below, and share an example of your own:

1. "I was being very passive-aggressive and insensitive. Can I have a redo?" (accountability)

2. "You're right; I was being dismissive and rejecting. I'm sorry I hurt you." (accountability/empathy)

3. "I was picking on you because I'm feeling anxious. Please forgive me." (accountability/vulnerability)

4. "I was having a narcissistic moment. Can we please try again?" (accountability/vulnerability)

5. "Sometimes I'm a disaster. Let me refocus and be present." (humor/vulnerability)

Practice - <u>Share a personal example of a repair attempt</u>:

Repair Attempt Practice - Create repair attempts for the examples below using accountability, humor, empathy, and vulnerability:

1. You belittled your partner in front of friends.

2. You continued looking at your phone while your partner tried to talk to you.

3. You said cruel things about your partner's mother.

4. You accused your partner of doing something that you did.

5. You called your partner a bad parent.

Bad Memories*

In failing marriages, history is rewritten in a negative light. People who divorce look back on the early days of their marriage with confusion, ambivalence, and uncertainty. In contrast, happy couples remember the highlights with fondness. "I've found 94 percent of the time that couples who put a positive spin on their marriage's history are likely to have a happy future as well" (Gottman & Silver, 1999, p. 64). Assess the health of your marriage by discussing the early days, and if you notice your memory is negative, the current prognosis of your relationship is poor.

Example: "It was a disaster from the very beginning. As soon as I met her mother, I should have run."
Practice - Think back to the beginning of your relationship, and share your earliest memory:

Video: Gottman Institute (2018): "The Easiest Way to Improve Your Relationship." https://youtu.be/ib7Ain2aVR0 (2:09)
Discussion: The Gottman Institute states, "The choices you make while interacting with your partner could, over time, make or break your relationship. *Bids for connection* can be small or big, verbal or nonverbal. We can turn toward our partner in these moments and accept their bid or turn away and ignore them. What separates relationship Masters from Disasters? In these moments, Masters turn toward each other 86% of the time. Disasters turn toward each other only 33% of the time. A tendency to turn toward your partner forms the basis of trust, emotional connection, passion, and a satisfying sex life. When couples break up, it is usually not because of big issues like conflict or infidelity. Most often, it's a result of the resentment and distance that builds up over time when partners continually turn away from bids for connection." Think about your relationship history; how often do you respond by turning toward your partner? Share an example of a *bid for connection* within your relationship history:

Nurture Your Fondness and Admiration*

According to Gottman, fondness and admiration are two of the most critical elements in a long-lasting relationship. "If a couple still has a functioning fondness and admiration system, their marriage is salvageable"(Gottman & Silver, 1999, p. 63). A couple's level of fondness and admiration is evaluated by the couple's expressed amount of mutual respect.

Choose one of the qualities that frustrate you the most about your partner, and embrace it.
Practice - Reframe the trait so you can appreciate, admire, or respect it:

Four Strategies to Improve Your Marriage* - "Master these fundamentals, and I think you'll be at least 75 percent of the way toward maximizing your marital happiness" (p. 174).

Strategy 1: **Calm Down**: Call a time-out and check your heart rate. Use self-soothing activities to shift your internal dialogue. Emotions are contagious! Don't spread emotional discomfort.

Strategy 2: **Speak Nondefensively**: A positive mindset about your partner will defeat defensiveness. Accept your own imperfections to increase your tolerance and humility.

Practice vulnerability by sharing one of your **imperfections**. How does this imperfection negatively affect your relationships?

Strategy 3: **Validation**: Allow yourself to be wrong, and hold yourself accountable. Develop empathy by placing yourself in your partner's shoes and defeating blame.

Strategy 4: **Overlearning**: Practice forming healthy habits. Focus on yourself, and don't let the response from your partner discourage you from making changes. Fake it till you make it!

Video: The School of Life (2017): "Why You Will Marry the Wrong Person." https://youtu.be/-EvvPZFdjyk (22:19)
Discussion: The School of Life states, "Hope drives rage, so I must learn to remove all expectations. If we can turn rage into grief, we have made psychological progress. We become addicted to distractions and technology to avoid being with ourselves, which is a disaster for our capacity to have a relationship with another person. Until you know yourself, you can't properly relate to another person. We choose the wrong person because we follow our instincts and our heart. We think we are out to find a partner who makes us happy, but really, we are on a quest to suffer in a way that is familiar to us. We seek the familiarity of our childhood experiences."
1.) Take notes as you watch, and share your thoughts about the video:

Chapter 23
Attachment Security

The best thing we can do with the failures of the past is let them be history.
~ *Gary Chapman*

Courage doesn't always roar. Sometimes courage is the quiet voice
at the end of the day, saying, "I will try again tomorrow."
~ *Mary Ann Radmacher*

We must be willing to learn our partner's primary love language
if we are to be effective communicators of love.
~ *Gary Chapman*

We accept the love we think we deserve.
~ *Stephen Chbosky*

Most people are only as needy as their unmet needs.
~ *Amir Levine*

❖   Identify Your Attachment Style

❖   Gottman's Emotional Bank Account

❖   Chapman's Five Love Languages

Attachment Styles

There are two branches of attachment: *secure* and *insecure*. Secure attachment leads to healthy relationships, while insecure attachment is marked by conflict and instability. Most of what you have learned about relationships is formed during your early interactions with caregivers. Your first experiences heavily influence your attachment style. Infants and young children with consistent, loving caregivers tend to grow up as confident and independent adults who can comfortably connect with others. When your caregivers respond with empathy, you learn to define yourself as worthy of love. For the securely attached child, close relationships are generally a safe source of support. On the other hand, if your early relationships are inconsistent, unpredictable, manipulative, or abusive, you tend to adapt by becoming anxious or guarded. For the insecurely attached child, close relationships can be high-risk. There are three categories of insecure attachment: *avoidant, anxious,* and *disorganized*.

Video: Psych2Go (2018): "The Four Attachment Styles of Love." https://youtu.be/23ePqRkOKtg (7:17)
Discussion: Psych2Go states, "It's important to note that your attachment style can change. **1.)** Secure: they tend to have honest, open, and equal relationships where both partners can thrive and grow together. They have higher emotional intelligence, which helps them communicate their feelings effectively. **2.)** Anxious (preoccupied): they romanticize love and are often attracted to partners they can save or who can save them. They can be demanding, obsessive, and clingy. They are prone to overanalyze situations, have mood swings, and often mistake turbulent relationships for passion. **3.)** Avoidant (dismissive): They tend to be emotionally distant, come across as self-sufficient and independent, and can avoid true intimacy. If their partner threatens to leave them, they have the ability to shut their emotions down and pretend they don't care. **4.)** Fearful/ Avoidant (disorganized): They fear being too close or distant. They can be unpredictable, and they're often overwhelmed by their own emotions. They face a lot of inner conflict between wanting intimacy and resisting it." Which style(s) are most familiar to you? Can you identify your attachment style and that of your partner? How has your style affected your relationships?

Cave Attachment Style

The *avoidant* style of insecure attachment can be described as a **cave response**. During times of distress, avoidant individuals will withdraw for protection. They may physically walk away from a conversation or silently shut down. Cave people avoid vulnerability using walls of protection. These walls may help keep them emotionally safe, but they lead to attachment insecurity, increasing conflict. Partners of cave people will describe feelings of *loneliness*, *rejection*, and *abandonment*. If you choose a relationship with a cave person, reframe their retreat as *protection* rather than *rejection*. Keep in mind that a bear does not hibernate to hurt or reject winter; the bear hibernates to survive. For the cave person, avoidance is a survival response.

Share an example of the **cave** coping style in your relationships:

Tornado Attachment Style

The *anxious* style of insecure attachment can be described as a **tornado response**. During times of distress, anxious individuals will begin to spin. <u>The initial spinning is often the calm before the storm because it goes unnoticed by others.</u> Early storm warning signs appear in rumination, hyperfocus, and obsessive thoughts. While survival for the cave person is to hide, survival for the tornado is contact. When subtle attempts to connect are missed, the spinning accelerates. <u>As the tornado gains momentum, it begins to pull others toward it.</u> Partners of tornado people will describe feeling *baited* or *pulled into the ring*. If you are in a relationship with a tornado, it is essential to see their pursuit as a bid for *connection* rather than *aggression*. <u>These individuals are desperate to attach, and their pursuit can be through attention-seeking, aggression, people-pleasing, or controlling behaviors.</u>

Share an example of the **tornado** coping style in your relationships:

Rollercoaster Attachment Style

The *disorganized* style of insecure attachment can be described as a **rollercoaster response**. This style usually develops when an individual is traumatized by an attachment figure during childhood. <u>Rollercoaster people cycle between demanding and distancing behaviors as they seek connection, but at the same time, they experience tremendous fear within relationships.</u> They vacillate between longing for closeness and fear of intimacy. Partners of rollercoaster people will describe feeling like they are living in *lose-lose situations, chronic conflict,* or *chaos*. If you are in a relationship with a rollercoaster, it is crucial to see the conflict as *confusion* rather than *manipulation*. <u>Under distress, the rollercoaster person does not know how to exit the ride.</u>

Share an example of the **rollercoaster** coping style in your relationships:

Anchor Attachment Style

The *securely* attached person can be described as an **anchor**. These are grounded individuals whose stability does not depend upon their relationship status. They are highly tolerant, give others the benefit of the doubt, and are forgiving. They are curious, resilient, and flexible people who focus more on adapting than digging in their heels.

<u>Through your early childhood experiences, your brain becomes wired with an attachment style, but you can rewire your brain.</u> "The ancient practice of mindfulness meditation, as it turns out, produces real, measurable changes in the brain in key places so that deeper connections, better love, and healthier relationships can really take hold. In as little as 20 minutes a day. We can, in fact, not only cause the neurons in our brains to change and to grow new connections and pathways, but we can produce new neurons throughout our entire lives" (Lucas, 2012, p. xv).

Three Elements of Secure Attachment:

1. **Connection**: Knowing that you are available when I need you. Knowing that I can count on your warmth and support. Knowing that I am a priority to you.

2. **Empathy**: Knowing that you will respond to me with empathy and compassion. Knowing that even if we disagree, we will remain connected.

3. **Transparency**: Knowing I can be vulnerable in the relationship without fear of rejection or judgment. Knowing that I can be authentic.

Share an example of responding with the **anchor** coping style in your relationships:

Video: TEDx (2022): "Ashley Harvey: Put on Your Attachment Hat and Change Your Romantic Attachment Style." https://youtu.be/jHpdf4ekrXM (18:09)

Discussion: Harvey states, "You need to know **five principles** to put on your attachment hat: **1**: Attachment is intertwined with fear and distress. The Beckes and Coan distress-relief dynamic: 'I'm in *distress* —> You give me *support* —> I feel *relief* —> *Repeat*.' **2**: Childhood affects adult attachment. We all create internal working models of ourselves and others during childhood, and we all struggle in some way with basic attachment fears: 'Am I good enough?' 'Am I lovable?' 'Can I count on you?' We carry these fears into our current relationships; sometimes, they become self-fulfilling prophecies. **3**: Our attachment styles can vary. When we are in distress and our attachment needs are not met, we have two choices: we can amp up (*anxiety*) or tamp down (*avoid*). **4**: Attachment underlies conflict. Sue Johnson helps us understand the pursue/withdraw pattern: As soon as one person minimizes, the other maximizes. **5**: Attachment is key to connection. Once we name the pattern, we can begin to change it." Share an example of the common pursue/withdraw pattern in your relationship history:

Why Attachment Style Matters

One of the most common partnerships is when a *tornado* pairs with a *cave*. The cave person frequently shuts down, which triggers the tornado's insecurity. When the tornado feels rejected, they begin to spin with anxiety. The cave retreats deeper when the tornado spins out of control. One attachment style triggers the other, and the cycle repeats.

What happens when an *anchor* pairs with an insecure attachment style? The anchor does not follow the bear into the *cave*. Instead, the anchor gives the partner plenty of time and space to exit the cave independently. Anchors do not become storm chasers. Instead, they stay grounded and wait for the *tornado* to run its course. They do not jump on the ride when an anchor is paired with a *rollercoaster*. Instead, they remain grounded while their partner rides the chaos. When two anchors are together, the relationship is generally stable, even during distress, as one partner grounds the other. When one partner falls, the other partner helps them back up, and neither partner will kick the other when they are down.

Attachment style is the foundation for every relationship problem pattern you experience. Personal agency is critical for security. If you choose a partner with an insecure attachment style, personal agency means you'll focus on how YOU behave when your partner retreats to the cave, starts to spin, or rides the rollercoaster. You will not focus on how your partner should change. Healthy relationships require accepting your partner as is and focusing on adapting rather than controlling. Fear is at the base of each insecure attachment style (*Am I good enough? Do I matter? Am I worthy?*). If you've heard your partner say something like, "I wish you loved me the way you love the children," you likely have a *secure* attachment style as a parent but an *insecure* attachment style as a partner. Most people will say things like, "I don't have these problems with anyone other than my partner," "We never had any issues until we had kids," or "Our problems started when I lost my job." Attachment insecurities are triggered during times of distress. Children, financial problems, and life transitions tend to be stress-inducing experiences.

Video: School of Life (2018): "What is Your Attachment Style?" https://youtu.be/2s9ACDMcpjA (6:38)

Discussion: School of Life states, "Roughly half of us are not secure in love, and we have an above average propensity to fall in love with someone from the other damaged side, thereby aggravating our insecurities." Think about your current or most recent relationship. How did you and your partner respond during times of distress? Describe your relationship problem pattern using the *cave, tornado, rollercoaster,* and *anchor*:

Turning Toward Your Partner

According to Gottman's research, an **emotional bank account** grows when partners make daily investments. The difference between happy and unhappy couples is how they manage their positive-to-negative ratio. You make deposits when you turn toward your partner's bid for connection. Small, consistent deposits are essential, and one negative interaction can act as a large withdrawal. A solid emotional bank account leads to high tolerance, which means you will give each other grace during sticky points. Many couples attempt to make deposits, but they do so using foreign currency. Deposits must be made in your partner's love language. With consistent, daily relationship investments, a couple can successfully reduce the insecure attachment response and defeat their problem relationship cycle.

Video: The Gottman Institute (2018): "Invest in Your Relationship/The Emotional Bank Account." https://youtu.be/QHN2EKd9tuE (2:09)

Discussion: The Gottman Institute states, "What's an emotional bank account? It represents the positive and negative balance in your relationship. The best couples maintain a high balance, and couples that break up are often in the red. You make deposits through positive interactions, and you withdraw through negative ones. What does a deposit look like? It's simply showing your partner that you care for and support them. A withdrawal is either hurtful behavior toward your partner or ignoring their invitations to connect, but withdrawals and deposits don't hold equal weight. Gottman found it takes five positive interactions to make up for one negative. Happy couples maintain at least a 5:1 ratio." Thinking about your current or most recent relationship, describe the positive-to-negative ratio: _____

Share an example of depositing into your partner's emotional bank account using their love language:

Video: Psych2Go (2020): "Five Ways to Work with Your Partner's Love Language." https://youtu.be/heww-ZuAs_c (5:08)

Discussion: Psych2Go states, "Everyone gives and receives love in different ways: **1.)** *Words of Affirmation*: Partners want to know in words how you feel about them. **2.)** *Quality Time*: To work with this love language, reserve space in your schedule to spend with your partner. **3.)** *Gifts*: It is not the expense of the gift; it's how much effort you put into it. **4.)** *Acts of Service*: This is anything that makes your partner's life easier. **5.)** *Physical Touch*: To work with this love language, intentionally touch your partner every day."

Can you identify your primary love languages? _____

Words of Affirmation	Physical Touch	Quality Time	Acts of Service	Receiving Gifts
❖ validation	❖ holding hands	❖ one-on-one time	❖ doing chores	❖ thoughtful gifts
❖ encouragement	❖ hugs	❖ weekends away	❖ caring for kids	❖ small gestures
❖ admiration	❖ affection	❖ long walks	❖ running errands	❖ cards/notes
❖ appreciation	❖ intimacy	❖ shared interests	❖ cooking	❖ small surprises
❖ empathy	❖ warm gestures	❖ watching movies	❖ cleaning	❖ serve tea/coffee
	❖ cuddling	❖ adventures	❖ offering help	❖ love note
Trigger	**Trigger**	**Trigger**	**Trigger**	**Trigger**
❖ silence	❖ pulling away	❖ not making plans	❖ not helping	❖ forgetting
❖ criticism	❖ sitting apart	❖ walking away	❖ broken promises	occasions
❖ sarcasm	❖ touching others	❖ interrupting	❖ laziness	❖ re-gifting
❖ name-calling	❖ no intimacy	❖ being distracted	❖ making messes	❖ ignore requests

Chapman's Five Love Languages*

Daily deposits in your partner's emotional bank account must be made in the correct currency. Most people attempt to show love the way they receive it, but couples often do not speak the same language. Speaking your partner's language is critical if you want the deposit to count. *Example*: "Cave" is in a love relationship with "Tornado." Cave feels loved through *Acts of Service*, and Tornado receives love through *Physical Touch*. Daily deposits using your partner's love language reduces relationship distress, but each partner continues to make deposits in the wrong currency. Cave tries to show love by cleaning the kitchen, but Tornado feels rejected because they want their partner to stop cleaning and hug them. Cave feels frustrated and confused by Tornado's lack of appreciation. This cycle repeats as each partner attempts to show love in the wrong language, leaving the other partner feeling hurt and rejected.

Daily Investment Practice - Gottman's research shows that small daily deposits hold more weight than occasional over-the-top gestures. A simple formula for success: Make one deposit daily using your partner's love language. Improve your fluency by creating specific examples for each love language below:

Words of Affirmation: _____

Physical Touch: _____

Quality Time: _____

Acts of Service: _____

Receiving Gifts: _____

*(Chapman, 1992)

Identification Practice - Uncover your partner's love language based on their complaints:

Complaint ─────────────────> **Love Language**

1. "You never spend any time with me." ──> _____

2. "I have to do everything around here." ──> _____

3. "Unless we are together, you never think about me." ──> _____

4. "Why do I always have to say 'I love you' first?" ──> _____

5. "Why don't you ever kiss me goodbye anymore?" ──> _____

Skills Practice - Respond to your partner's *bid for connection* using each love language:

1.) Your partner feels overwhelmed because they had a very stressful day.

Words of Affirmation: _____

Physical Touch: _____

Quality Time: _____

Acts of Service: _____

Receiving Gifts: _____

2.) Your partner complains that you only care about your job and friends.

Words of Affirmation: _____

Physical Touch: _____

Quality Time: _____

Acts of Service: _____

Receiving Gifts: _____

3.) Your partner is furious because you forgot your anniversary again.

Words of Affirmation: _____

Physical Touch: _____

Quality Time: _____

Acts of Service: _____

Receiving Gifts: _____

Relationship Maintenance

In the early stage, couples have communication styles that encourage bonding and connection. They ask curious questions, maintain eye contact, and physically turn toward each other. These verbal and nonverbal behaviors send messages of interest and value, but communication styles change over time. When conversations become more mechanical, transactional, and emotionless, partners begin to doubt their relationship, and problem patterns develop. Curious questions sound like: "What are your dreams?" "What's your favorite time of day?" "What scares you the most?" Mechanical questions sound more robotic or aggressive: "Who's doing the dishes?" "Are you taking out the garbage?" "How late are you working tonight?" To bring love back to life, your conversations need to change.

In the January 2015 *New York Times* article "The 36 Questions that Lead to Love," Daniel Jones discusses UC Berkley's research conducted by psychologists Arthur and Elaine Aron. This study highlights how mutual vulnerability fosters closeness and connection. The exercise is designed as a 45-minute bonding experience, but many couples benefit from asking each other one question per day. The study breaks the questions into three sets, with increasing intensity. The first set includes questions such as: "What would constitute a 'perfect' day for you?" The second set of questions includes: "What is your most terrible memory?" The final set of questions includes: "If you were to die this evening with no opportunity to communicate with anyone, what would you most regret not having told someone? Why haven't you told them yet?" **Practice**: Try this exercise with your partner, and share your experience. The 36 questions can be accessed online: https://ggia.berkeley.edu/practice/36_questions_for_increasing_closeness

Video Homework: TEDx (2019): "Maya Diamond: The Surprising Key to Building a Healthy Relationship that Lasts." https://youtu.be/Xvb-v83qJ8U (8:31)

Discussion: Diamond states, "Relationships that last have one thing in common: emotional responsiveness. According to Dr. Sue Johnson, the founder of Emotionally Focused Therapy, emotional responsiveness contains these three crucial elements: **1.) Accessibility**: You are there when I need you. **2.) Responsiveness**: You celebrate the good times with me, and you soothe me when I'm having a hard time. **3.) Engagement**: I am your priority, and you value me. Your level of emotional responsiveness can make or break your relationship. Attachment theory and neuroscience say we need each other, we are hardwired for relationships, and our ability to be responsive to each other's needs and emotions is fundamental in creating a healthy, thriving relationship. What is blocking so many of us from being emotionally responsive partners? **Block number one** is believing that your partner is an adult, so they shouldn't require emotional responsiveness. **Block number two** is feeling overwhelmed by work or stress, so you are not available or present for your partner. **Block number three** is feeling overwhelmed or invaded by one of your parents growing up, and so being there for someone else makes you want to run for the hills. **Block number four** is being overwhelmed or disconnected from your own needs, so you disregard your partner's needs or feelings just as you've been conditioned to do to yourself."

1.) Share a personal example of *accessibility, responsiveness,* and *engagement*:

2.) Share a personal example of struggling with one of the blocks:

Chapter 24
Empathy and Acceptance

Empathy is walking a mile in somebody else's moccasins.
Sympathy is being sorry their feet hurt.
~ *Rebecca O'Donnell*

If you feel pain, you're alive. If you feel other people's pain,
you're a human being.
~ *Leo Tolstoy*

We have two lives, and the second one begins
when we realize we only have one.
~ *Confucius*

Out of your vulnerabilities will come your strengths.
~ *Sigmund Freud*

Love and compassion are necessities, not luxuries.
Without them, humanity cannot survive.
~ *Dalai Lama*

❖ Leaning into Relationships

❖ Mirror Emotions - Feelings *before* Fix

❖ Practice Acceptance - Let Go of Baggage

TED Talk - Robert Waldinger: What Makes a Good Life? Lessons from the Longest Study on Happiness (12:46)

"The Harvard Study of Adult Development may be the longest study of adult life that's ever been done. For seventy-five years, we've tracked the lives of 724 men. Since 1938, we've tracked the lives of two groups of men. The first group started the study when they were sophomores at Harvard College. They all finished college during World War II, and then most went off to serve in the war. And the second group that we followed was a group of boys from Boston's poorest neighborhoods. These boys were chosen for the study specifically because they were from some of the most troubled and disadvantaged families in Boston of the 1930s. What are the lessons that come from the tens of thousands of pages of information that we've generated on these lives? Well, the lessons aren't about wealth or fame or working harder and harder. The clearest message that we get from this seventy-five-year study is this: good relationships keep us happier and healthier. Period. We have learned three big lessons about relationships. First, social connections are really good for us, and loneliness kills. It turns out that people who are more socially connected to family, friends, and community are happier, physically healthier, and live longer. The second big lesson we learned is that it's not just the number of friends you have, and it's not whether or not you're in a committed relationship, but the quality of your close relationships that matters. It turns out that living in conflict is really bad for our health. **High-conflict marriage, for example, without much affection, turns out to be very bad for our health, perhaps worse than getting divorced**. The people who were the most satisfied in their relationships at age fifty were the healthiest at age eighty. The third big lesson that we learned about relationships and our health is those good relationships don't just protect our bodies; they protect our brains. **Over and over, through these seventy-five years, our study has shown that the people who fared the best were the people who leaned into relationships with family, friends, and community**. The good life is built with good relationships." R. Waldinger (December 2015). Adapted from "Robert Waldinger: What Makes a Good Life? Lessons from the Longest Study on Happiness." https://youtu.be/8KkKuTCFvzI

Discussion: What does it mean to *lean* into relationships? Share a personal example:

Empathy Versus Sympathy

Empathy is placing yourself in someone else's shoes and seeing the world through their eyes. With empathy, you allow yourself to reflect and validate the emotions of others without personalizing. Acceptance is a critical component of empathy because judgment cements you into a rigid perspective that blocks curiosity. An empathic lifestyle can be challenging because our brain is wired to protect us from physical and emotional pain. Empathy requires us to sit with the suffering of others without trying to fix the problem. Many relationship conflicts come from failed attempts to solve problems. When seeking support from loved ones, we look to see if we matter. If you hear, "I've already tried that," "You're not listening," or "I know, but…" you're likely trying to problem-solve rather than empathizing. If you struggle with empathy for others, this indicates the need for more self-compassion. <u>Without empathy, relationship conflicts run high because humans bond through vulnerable emotions.</u>

What is the difference between sympathy and empathy? <u>Sympathy falls into the fix-it category, while empathy validates feelings.</u> To express sympathy is to make it known that you are aware of another's distress, and the goal is to make the discomfort disappear: "I'm so sorry for your loss; they lived a good life." Expressing empathy takes things a step further by showing a deeper understanding of the person's emotional experience and leaning into their feelings with validation: "Losing a loved one is unbearably painful; you must be so sad."

Empathy Example

Imagine you are trapped at the bottom of a deep, dark well. You see your friends and family waiting for you at the surface as you look up. They are calling down to you, offering words of support and encouragement: this is *sympathy*. <u>With sympathy, others want to help you out of the hole you've found yourself in, and they feel sorry for you.</u> From the edge of the well, your loved ones can provide comfort during your struggle, but it comes from a distance. Now you look to your left and see someone standing next to you. This person suffering with you can see the world from your perspective; this person has *empathy*. <u>Empathy requires feeling, imagining, and relating to the emotions of others.</u> Sympathy can lead to feelings of inferiority, loneliness, or being pitied. Empathy enables everyone to feel equal and connected.

Video: RSA (2013): "Brene Brown on Empathy." https://youtu.be/1Evwgu369Jw (2:53)
Discussion: Brown states, "What is empathy, and why is it very different than sympathy? Empathy fuels connection and sympathy drives disconnection. Theresa Wiseman came up with four qualities of empathy: perspective-taking, staying out of judgment, recognizing the emotions in other people, and then communicating that. Empathy is feeling *with* people. In order to connect with you, I have to connect with something in myself that knows that feeling. Rarely can a response make something better. What makes something better is connection." Empathy is sitting with the emotions of others without trying to fix or solve the problem. <u>Share a personal example of mirroring someone's feelings *before* trying to fix the problem</u>:

Fix-it Example: You get home after driving in traffic for several hours. When you arrive, you share your traffic nightmare with your partner. Your partner responds sarcastically, "Well, I've told you before that you need to leave the office earlier."

1. What are you thinking and feeling when you receive this *fix-it* response?

2. What messages do *fix-it* responses send?

3. What would be an empathic response in this example? Create a response you would like to receive:

Empathy Formula: Feelings *before* Fix

  A simple empathy formula is: Mirror the *feelings* before trying to *fix* the problem. "Compassion means to be with, feel with, suffer with" (Brach, 2003, p.200). Take a moment to imagine, without judgment, what the person must be feeling given the circumstances. You can ask yourself, "What would I feel in this situation?" <u>This is where acceptance is critical because if you judge, you will take a detour away from empathy</u>. *Example*: Your grieving friend tells you, "My dog got out of my yard again and was hit by a car." A judgmental *fix-it* response may sound like, "On, no! It's too bad you didn't fix the fence." Notice how the fix-it response devalues the other person and stomps on their emotions. An acceptance-based, empathic response may sound like, "That's heartbreaking. I know how much you loved your dog. You must be devastated." Practice creating empathic responses below by mirroring feelings. Mirroring statements often begin with: "You must be feeling…" or "It sounds like you're feeling…."

Video: Jason Headley (2013): "It's Not About the Nail." https://youtu.be/-4EDhdAHrOg (1:41)

Discussion: This humorous video clip depicts empathic listening using Feelings *before* Fix. In love relationships, telling your partner what to do is easy, especially when the problem is glaringly obvious, but responding with empathy requires slowing down and letting go of control. <u>What is the most challenging part of mirroring emotions for you?</u> <u>Share your strengths/weaknesses:</u>

Practice Feelings *before* Fix: Create a fix-it and an empathic response for each example below.
Example: Your partner angrily says, "Well, I didn't get the job."
Fix-it: "Maybe you weren't qualified; just apply for another job."
Mirror Feelings: "You worked really hard to prepare; you must be very *disappointed*. It's their loss."

1. Your partner says, "You don't do anything special for me anymore."

Fix-it: _____

Mirror Feelings: _____

2. Your daughter shows you that she received a low test score and said, "I'm so stupid."

Fix-it: _____

Mirror Feelings: _____

3. Your son tells you he did not make the basketball team after practicing for months.

Fix-it: _____

Mirror Feelings: _____

4. Your colleague who rarely shows up on time for work says, "I can't believe I didn't get that promotion."

Fix-it: _____

Mirror Feelings: _____

Judgment Blocks Empathy

Steve Maraboli said, "Why let go of yesterday? Because yesterday has already let go of you." Resentments are a direct reflection of a failure at acceptance. When you determine that something is *wrong,* anger is justified. Rather than accepting life in the present moment, we ruminate over how we've been mistreated. In relationships, judgment leads to baggage when we define others through their past actions. The baggage becomes a heavy weight that anchors you in a hostile place, and naturally, you will drag your partner down. What would it be like if you could live in the present moment? You would be free from the baggage that holds you back. Picture a garden filled with beautiful flowers. Now imagine that your thoughts are a watering can. Whatever you water will grow. Typically, in relationships, we focus on what we do not like and water the weeds. We complain about our partner's weaknesses, and the weeds grow. Practice staying in the present by eliminating the baggage from the statements below:

Baggage Statement ——————————> Present Moment Statement

"You never listen." ——————————> "I'd really like you to listen for a moment."

"You're so difficult all the time." ——————> "I feel like it's difficult to talk to you right now."

"You're always such a downer." ——> _____

"You'll never change." ——> _____

Notice how staying in the present moment reduces conflict. Unfortunately, we tend to follow the misguided assumption that complaining will produce change, but what happens when we chronically focus on the negative? If I believe, "My partner never listens," I will naturally filter information to support my belief. Essentially, I will ignore all the times when my partner is listening; instead, I will only notice when my partner fails to listen. Ultimately, rather than producing change, I am watering the weeds. In this scenario, my partner thinks, "There's no point in trying because I never get credit anyway." The key is to water the flowers instead of the weeds. Guide your thoughts toward what you want rather than what you don't want. Catch your partner doing something you like and comment on it. At the same time, try to ignore the things you don't like. Use acceptance to let the weeds die.

Practice Acceptance to Defeat Baggage: Train yourself to accept what you cannot change. Friedrich Nietzsche said, "To live is to suffer; to survive is to find some meaning in the suffering." The Dalai Lama said, "Remember that sometimes not getting what you want is a wonderful stroke of luck." Resisting an uncomfortable reality doesn't produce change; it simply adds emotional distress. Acceptance requires the knowledge that we all take turns suffering, and sometimes, not getting what we want is a gift.

1.) Share an example of a time in your life when you struggled or suffered, but in the end, it turned out to be a gift:

Practice Feelings *before* **Fix**: For each scenario below, respond by mirroring emotion.

    Example: Your partner tells you that their car is falling apart, and they want to trade it in for something newer. You feel frustrated that you can't afford a new car now.

    Fix-it: "You're always asking for everything; you're never satisfied."

    Mirror Feelings: "You must be so *tired* of your car with all of its problems. I would feel very *frustrated* with that car, too. Let's start putting money aside…."

---

1. Your daughter sadly states, "I feel like I have no friends." You think, "It's probably because you're rude to everyone." Instead of negatively labeling her, use **feelings** *before* **fix**:

2. Your partner complains, "We don't get along anymore; we're always fighting." You think, "We're always fighting because you're always complaining." Instead of blaming, use **feelings** *before* **fix**:

3. Your best friend sadly tells you, "I just found out my father died." You think, "You hated your father and haven't talked to him in years." Instead of judging, use **feelings** *before* **fix**:

4. You encouraged your son to study, but he resisted. Later, his grade was very disappointing. Your son states, "I guess I should have studied more." You want to respond by saying, "You should have listened to me. Every time you screw up, it's because you don't listen." Instead of shaming, use **feelings** *before* **fix**:

5. Your partner says, "I want to get married and start a family. Everyone we know is getting married." You think, "That's because everyone we know is crazy, and I'm not getting married anytime soon." Instead of sarcasm, use **feelings** *before* **fix**:

6. Your brother tells you, "I'm thinking about ending my marriage." You think, "I knew it would never last, and I told you it was a mistake to get married." Instead of shaming, use **feelings** *before* **fix**:

7. Your partner tells you, "I'm so tired of cooking and cleaning all the time. It's a never-ending, thankless job." You think, "I'd like to be the one who stays home with the kids all day." Instead of diminishing your partner's feelings, use **feelings** *before* **fix**:

Chapter 25
Empathy Essay

In the end, just three things matter: How well we have lived.
How well we have loved. How well we have learned to let go.
~ Jack Kornfield

Compassion begins with the capacity to hold your own life with a loving heart.
~ Tara Brach

How others treat me is their path; how I react is mine.
~ Wayne Dyer

The untrained mind keeps up a running commentary, labeling everything,
judging everything. Best to ignore that commentary. Don't argue or resist, just
ignore. Deprived of attention and interest, this voice gets quieter and quieter,
and eventually just shuts up.
~ Plato

You do not become good by trying to be good, but by finding the goodness that
is already within you, and allowing that goodness to emerge.
~ Eckhart Tolle

❖   Empathy Essay

❖   Defeat Minimization/Denial/Blame

Video: Goalcast (2018): "Terry Crews I Wanted to Save My Mother." https://youtu.be/L79t3fPHvlI (4:37)

Discussion: Crews states, "I would wake up to the sounds of breaking glass and people screaming; it was a nightmare. We lived a nightmare for years. He went on terrorizing us forever. So many days, I thought, I'll never be like that, but I picked up many damaging things from that trauma. A lot of things had been assimilated into my life, and I felt like it was my way or the highway." Crews shows insight and self-awareness. He acknowledges that he was a victim who later became an aggressor, and his courage to be accountable helped him heal. Notice your feelings as you listen to Terry Crews share his childhood trauma. Are you able to feel his pain? Empathy means placing ourselves in someone else's shoes and feeling *with* them. Judgment blocks empathy. Please share your thoughts about this video and how you relate to his story:

Empathy Essay

Write your *Empathy Essay* to share with the group. Empathy requires putting yourself aside and seeing the world from another person's perspective. Tell the story of the incident that led to your placement in this program through the eyes of the other person (partner, child, family member, etc.). If you asked the person to describe the incident today, they might tell a very different story, but this essay is about their view *during* the event. This is one of the most challenging exercises because it requires insight, courage, and vulnerability. If you sound like the victim, start your essay again! It's highly unlikely the other person viewed you as a victim during the conflict. You will share your essay with the group and receive feedback regarding any use of minimization, denial, or blame. Remember to write your essay in the other person's voice, from their perspective. This essay is a requirement for program completion. This essay is *not* about accuracy; it is about empathy. If needed, you can use a separate sheet. Before you begin your essay, read the examples and complete the sentences below.

I struggle with empathy when I'm under the influence of (*emotion*) _____

This emotion encourages negative thoughts like _____

_____

These thoughts come from some of my past experiences, including _____

_____

A statement of **self-acceptance** sounds like _____

_____

A statement of **self-compassion** sounds like _____

_____

A statement of **self-admiration** sounds like _____

Example Empathy Essay - written in my child's voice

Things have been really uncomfortable in my house for a while now. My parents fight a lot, and I just try to stay in my room to avoid it. That night, my mom and dad were downstairs, drinking and watching a movie. My little brother was sleeping in his room, and I was supposed to be asleep, but the yelling kept me awake. It came from the kitchen, and it wasn't like one of their usual arguments. I tried to put my pillow over my head so I didn't have to hear it, but I also wanted to know that everything was okay. I hoped my baby brother stayed asleep because I didn't ever want him to feel afraid or sad, and I didn't want him to feel the way I felt. I want him to grow up in a happy home, so I try to give him that home, even though it's a lie.

My parents kept screaming, and they were saying horrible words. It always sounds like they hate each other, and I wonder if it's our fault they stay together. I want to tell them they don't have to stay together for us, but I'm too scared to speak up. I don't want them to hate me the way they hate each other. Things started to quiet down a little, and I could hear footsteps going up and down the stairs. I thought it was over and everything was okay, but then I heard something breaking. It sounded like glass being thrown against a wall. I heard my dad yelling about not driving drunk, and my mom screamed to let her go. I kept hearing the footsteps, the banging on the walls, and the yelling. I just wanted to sleep, but I couldn't. All I could do was listen and hope that everything would be okay. I didn't want my mom to leave, but I also didn't want them to keep fighting.

The next thing I heard was someone running up the stairs, and their bedroom door slammed shut. Then, I heard more footsteps running up the stairs, and my mom started banging on their bedroom door. She was yelling at my dad to let her in and screaming horrible things at him. It sounded like the door was going to break into a million pieces. The banging was so loud that I imagined all the walls falling down, and we would have no safe place to hide. I was wide awake and terrified. I thought of my little brother; I had to get him out of the house before the walls fell. I made my way to my door, and when I thought it was safe, I quietly tiptoed down the hall as fast as I could to his room. I woke him up, and I held him while I listened. My little brother was crying, and he was holding me so tight. I told him I would protect him and that he didn't have to worry about anything. I told him I would get him out of the house before it fell.

When we thought it was clear, we ran downstairs and into the garage as fast as we could. I wanted this night to be over, so I called the police. I didn't know what else to do. I was so scared for my little brother. We were freezing in the garage, and he wanted to go back to bed, but our house wasn't safe. The garage was dark, cold, and scary, but it wasn't as scary as inside our house. When the police came, I let them in. We were walking inside when my mom met us in the hallway. I was so scared that she would be mad at me; I didn't want to do anything wrong. She just sat down and told the story. My dad came down, and the paramedics checked them. Our house was filled with strangers asking questions. They talked to my brother and me, and I told them everything. I didn't hold anything back because I always told the truth. I saw my mom stand up slowly and turn around. They put handcuffs on her, and they took her away. My brother started screaming, and I held him. I kept telling him that Mommy would be back, but we didn't see her for a few days, and my brother couldn't stop crying. We didn't want any of this to happen. I felt guilty for doing what I did. When I finally talked to my mom, I was so relieved because she told me she was proud of me for doing what was right. She told me that I was very brave for calling the police and thanked me for protecting my brother. When she hugged me, it was the first time I let myself cry. I don't know if what I did was right, but the fighting stopped. Our house feels different, but it's finally safe.

Example Empathy Essay - written in my partner's voice

The past few years have been a constant rollercoaster ride of emotions. Her anger would build each day like something was slowly taking over my partner. I started questioning why I was still in this marriage. Why does my life revolve around her emotional state? Why would she ever understand how I feel when she manipulates me? She gets into sudden moods, and there's no reaching her. I've learned not to let my guard down, and I've been living in a constant state of readiness. She carries the pain of her childhood and finds ways to spread misery because she doesn't know how to release it.

I wanted to talk to her about my mother coming to visit, but she was in such a bad mood all week. I tried to talk to her each day, but she seemed so annoyed that I couldn't get the words out. Finally, I couldn't put it off any longer. I decided to make a nice dinner and casually mentioned it when we were all eating. Usually, she doesn't freak out in front of the kids, but her face changed as soon as I started talking. She looked furious, as if she was disgusted with me. She looked at me like she wanted me to be quiet, and I could have just stopped talking, but I was so tired of tiptoeing around her all the time. My whole life revolves around not making her mad, and I live every day trying to make sure she doesn't lose it in front of the kids.

At that moment, I realized that I couldn't live like that anymore, so I kept talking even though she was trying to silence me. She told me that I was ruining dinner and told the kids that she felt sorry for them because of me. The kids were so scared they wouldn't look up from their food. Her tone sounded like she hated me. I tried to change the subject quickly, but it was too late. I knew it would get worse, so I told the kids to go to their rooms. As they started to stand, she slammed her fist on the table so hard that I thought it would snap in half. We all froze. My heart was in my throat, and no one dared to breathe. That's when she picked up her plate and threw it in the garbage can. Our youngest immediately started crying, and I knew I had to do something to stop her.

I threatened to call the cops if she didn't leave, but she just laughed at me. I ran to get my phone, but she grabbed it and threw it against the wall. She threw it so hard that my phone shattered into pieces. I told our oldest to run to the neighbors to call the police, and that's when she slapped me. I was stunned. Until that moment, all of the abuse had been verbal. I couldn't believe she slapped me; my face was burning. I was so angry; I told her I wanted a divorce and that the kids were coming with me. I turned my back on her to leave, and that's when she shoved me against the wall. My head was ringing, and I couldn't hear anything. She started kicking me and throwing things at me. I was terrified of what this was doing to the children. Tears were streaming down their faces, but she didn't care. She didn't look like my partner anymore; she was an enraged stranger. I was so devastated that I slowly slid to the floor. My kids ran over to me, sobbing uncontrollably. She didn't say a word; she just walked out of the house.

That night still haunts me, and I'm afraid I'll never feel safe with her again. I'm not even sure I've ever felt safe with her. Our kids don't deserve this life, and I'm the only one who can protect them. On that day, my children watched as their mother beat me. I will never forget the look in her eyes when I was on the floor. I was devastated, but her eyes were hollow and vacant. I saw how quickly things could spiral out of control and how quickly our lives changed forever. When she walked out, I knew I could no longer live with that constant threat. I could not risk my safety, and more importantly, I had to protect the kids. I had to make a change to escape this vicious cycle. I've loved her more than I've ever loved anyone, but this isn't love. She's always told me that she wanted our kids to grow up in a safe home, but she recreated her childhood trauma. It's time to break the cycle; I can't hold onto hope anymore.

Empathy Essay

Chapter 26
Contentment

As soon as we wish to be happier, we are no longer happy.
~ *Walter Landor*

I cried when I had no shoes, but I stopped crying
when I saw a man without legs.
~ *Shakespeare*

No amount of regret changes the past. No amount of anxiety changes
the future. Any amount of gratitude changes the present.
~ *Ann Voskamp*

New beginnings are often disguised as painful endings.
~ *Lao Tzu*

This is a wonderful day. I've never seen it before.
~ *Maya Angelou*

The happiness of your life depends upon the quality of your thoughts.
~ *Marcus Aurelius*

❖   Science of Happiness

❖   Acceptance, Gratitude, Compassion, and Present Moment

TED Talk Dan Gilbert: The Surprising Science of Happiness (21:16)

"It turns out the prefrontal cortex does lots of things, but one of the most important things it does is an experience simulator. Human beings have this marvelous adaptation that they can actually have experiences in their heads before they try them out in real life. Let's see how your experience simulators are working. Here are two different futures that I invite you to contemplate. You can try to simulate them and tell me which one you prefer. One of them is winning the lottery. This is about 314 million dollars. And the other is becoming a paraplegic. Interestingly, there are data on these two groups of people, data on how happy they are. The fact is that a year after losing the use of their legs and a year after winning the lotto, lottery winners and paraplegics are equally happy with their lives. From field studies to laboratory studies, we see that winning or losing an election, gaining or losing a romantic partner, getting or not getting a promotion, passing or not passing a college test, and on and on, have far less impact, less intensity, and much less duration than people expect them to have. A recent study showing how major life traumas affect people suggests that if it happened over three months ago, with only a few exceptions, it has no impact whatsoever on your happiness. Why? Because happiness can be synthesized. Human beings have something that we might think of as a 'psychological immune system'—a system of cognitive processes, largely nonconscious cognitive processes, that help them change their views of the world, so they can feel better about the worlds in which they find themselves. We synthesize happiness, but we think happiness is a thing to be found." D. Gilbert (February 2004). Adapted from "Dan Gilbert: The Surprising Science of Happiness." TED Talks. www.ted.com.

Discussion: Gilbert shares research that major life successes, failures, and traumas "have far less impact, less intensity, and much less duration than people expect them to have." Why don't these positive and negative life experiences affect our long-term happiness? Share your thoughts:

Synthesized Happiness

Most people enter therapy to find happiness. They describe what it felt like to be happy and want to find their way back to that feeling. Where did happiness go for all of these people? Why do we struggle with so much anxiety, depression, and anger? Why is it so difficult to feel sustained contentment? The likely answer to these questions is that the steps we are taking to achieve happiness are not the steps that lead to it. Studies show that our external environment does not control sustained contentment; it is not something that can be found or given to us. Happy people do not have better life circumstances than unhappy people; they simply have patterned ways of thinking that produce contentment. In order to achieve this baseline, your thought patterns need to change. If happiness is manufactured through our thought processes rather than our life circumstances, what thoughts produce happiness? Thoughts of *acceptance, gratitude, compassion,* and the *present moment* produce happiness. If you focus on the daily practice of these four thought patterns, you will elevate your happiness level.

Video: TED (2017): "Emily Esfahani Smith: There's more to life than being happy." https://youtu.be/y9Trdafp83U (12:18)

Discussion: Smith states, "I used to think that the whole purpose of life was pursuing happiness, but instead of feeling fulfilled, I felt anxious and adrift. The data shows that chasing happiness can make people unhappy. According to research, what predicts this despair is not a lack of happiness; it's a lack of something else: a lack of having meaning in life. What's the difference between being happy and having meaning? Studies show that people who have meaning in life are more resilient, do better in school and work, and live longer. I've found four pillars of a meaningful life: 1.) **Belonging**: being in relationships where you are valued for who you are intrinsically and where you value others. 2.) **Purpose**: the key is using your strengths to serve others. 3.) **Transcendence**: your sense of self fades away, and you feel connected to a higher reality. 4.) **Storytelling**: the story you tell yourself about yourself. We don't realize that we're the authors of our stories, and we can change how we tell them." Provide personal examples for each of the four pillars:

Belonging: **Transcendence**:

Purpose: **Storytelling**:

Acceptance

Eckhart Tolle said, "Whatever the present moment contains, accept it as if you had chosen it. Always work with it, not against it." Resisting reality does not change anything; it simply heightens your emotional distress. Acceptance is the antidote to resistance. You will naturally feel discomfort during a stressor, but resistance will add emotions to the equation. *Example*: My car has a flat tire (*fact*). Resistance sounds like: "I always have bad luck; I can never catch a break." This stressor will naturally bring feelings of frustration, but what other emotions are added with resistance? _____ In this example, acceptance may sound like: "*Sometimes* things don't go our way. I guess it's *my turn* to get a flat." Notice how acceptance allows you to experience stressors without the added emotional weight of resistance. An easy formula for acceptance is to use the words: *sometimes*, *my turn*, or *me too*. **Practice**: Defeat resistance in the examples below using: *sometimes*, *my turn*, or *me too*.

> **Acceptance Mantras**
> That's for my future self; I'll have to wait and see.
> That was a human moment.
> My past self was doing the best they could.
> I need to allow it to be if I don't have control.

Example Stressor: You discovered your partner had an affair.
Acceptance: *Sometimes,* people have poor judgment. Everyone suffers; it's *my turn*. I've made decisions that have hurt others, *too*. I've been self-centered, *too*.

Stressor: Your academically-focused teen gets caught cheating on a test.
Acceptance:

Stressor: Your company is going through layoffs, and they cut you even though you are a top performer.
Acceptance:

Stressor: Your partner feels overwhelmed, and they angrily blame you for not doing enough to help.
Acceptance:

Gratitude

David Steindl-Rast said, "It is not joy that makes us grateful; it is gratitude that makes us joyful." Practicing gratitude leads to an abundance mindset as you focus on what you *have* rather than what you lack. Robin Sharma said, "What you focus on grows, what you think about expands, and what you dwell upon determines your destiny." Practicing gratitude is the easiest way to elevate your happiness level. A simple formula to defeat overwhelm and victim stance: Switch "*have*" —> "*get*." *Examples*: "I *get* to mow the lawn because I *get* to have a lawn." "I *get* to drive the kids around because I *get* to have kids, and I *get* to have a car." "I *get* to do the dishes because we *got* to eat today." "I *get* to argue with my family because I *get* to have a family." **Practice**: Begin each morning with three personal gratitude statements.

Gratitude Challenge - Complete the sentences below.

1. A person I'm grateful for is _____ because _____

2. A place I'm grateful for is _____ because _____

3. A food I'm grateful for is _____ because _____

4. An experience I treasure is _____

5. An activity I love to do is _____

6. If today was my last day, I'm grateful for _____

7. A goal I feel good about achieving is _____

8. One thing I'm grateful for in my childhood is _____

9. One thing I'm grateful for about where I live is _____

10. A role model who inspired me is _____

11. One part of nature I'm grateful for is _____

12. I'm grateful that I am _____ because _____

13. A past struggle I'm grateful for is _____ because _____

14. The best gift I've ever received is _____

15. A person who makes me happy is _____ because _____

16. One of my very best days was _____

17. Something that makes me feel peaceful and safe is _____

18. A person who believes in me is _____

19. I'm grateful for my passion _____ because _____

20. A sound that makes me happy is _____ because _____

21. One thing I'm grateful about myself is _____

Video: TEDx (2021): "Molly Countermine: Life isn't Supposed to be Good... All the Time." https://youtu.be/5oy9LWrRPIo (13:09)

Discussion: Countermine states, "Rates of anxiety and depression worldwide have increased by almost twenty percent in the past two decades, and these numbers are even higher for teens. The human brain wasn't designed to make us happy. The brain was designed to keep us safe by responding to perceived threats and danger, but because many of us no longer have to worry about being chased by a tiger, our brains tend to focus on the threats that do seem real. The human brain was designed to adapt to new experiences. Habits like deep breathing, being in the moment, and accepting all emotions have increased happiness levels and decreased stress. I noticed something interesting was happening; I was developing a new relationship with my anxiety. When I felt it coming on, I didn't brace myself; I simply paused, took a few deep breaths, noticed what I was feeling, thought about what those feelings were telling me, and then told myself that it's okay to not be okay. You can do an arrival practice in a number of different ways, but basically, they go something like this: We get comfortable, we center ourselves by putting our feet on the ground, we sit up straight, relax our shoulders, and we begin to breathe deeply. We notice our thoughts and feelings, acknowledge and accept them for whatever they are, and then let them go. We offer ourselves some loving kindness and compassion; we extend that compassion to others and the world. Life is hard sometimes; it's painful, scary, and sad. It's also overwhelmingly beautiful and filled with joy and happiness, and love sometimes. The trick to being human is to embrace all of life because life isn't supposed to be good all the time; it's just supposed to be life." Countermine highlights how acceptance, compassion, and the present moment increase happiness levels and decrease stress. **Practice** - Accept an uncomfortable emotion by pausing, breathing, and noticing what you feel. Identify what the feelings are telling you:

Compassion

Voltaire said, "Appreciation is a wonderful thing: It makes what is excellent in others belong to us as well." Compassion is produced when you authentically care about the welfare of yourself and others. Compassion for others requires acceptance and good boundaries. Personalizing, comparing, and judging will block compassion every time. If you struggle with compassion for others, it indicates a need for more self-compassion. Change always starts with the self. **Challenge**: Create an internal thought of loving-kindness for every person you see during a 24-hour period. Thoughts of loving-kindness sound like: "May you have peace. May you have joy. May you feel good about yourself. May you be free from suffering."

Practice Compassion - Complete the sentences below:

1. It was very challenging, but I handled _____ really well.

2. One thing I respect and admire about myself is _____

3. One thing I truly love about myself is _____

4. A painful time I wish I didn't have to experience was _____

5. My heart goes out to myself when I think of _____

6. I showed compassion for _____ when I _____

Present Moment

Thich Nhat Hanh said, "<u>Waking up this morning, I smile. Twenty-four brand new hours are before me. I vow to live fully in each moment and to look at all beings with eyes of compassion.</u>" People who place their happiness in the future often never feel happy. Happiness is not waiting for us; happiness is a choice we make each moment. Mindfulness is a critical skill for emotional regulation. Many of us distance ourselves from happiness when we think things like, "I'll be happy when I'm appreciated," "I'll be happy when my kids move out," or "I'll be happy when it's Friday." This future-focused thought pattern leads to feelings of frustration and anxiety. <u>A person with a future-focused habit will continue to apply the formula even after they reach their goal.</u> *Example*: The person who thinks, "I'll be happy when I get a promotion" will eventually achieve that goal, and then they think, "Okay, now I'll be happy when I retire."

Marcus Aurelius said, "<u>Give yourself a gift: the present moment.</u>" On the other end of the spectrum, many people are past-oriented thinkers. Thought patterns focused on the past sound like, "I was happy when I was younger," "I was happy when I was ten pounds lighter," or "I was happy when I was working." The fascinating aspect of the past-oriented thinker is that when we dig, we soon discover that the individual was not happy during those times. Back when they were working, they were thinking things like, "I would be happy if I didn't have to work," "My last job was better," or "I was happier when I was still in school." <u>In order to experience happiness, we need to remember that the only moment that exists is the present moment. If I'm not happy in the present, happiness does not exist.</u> In his 2013 TEDxStanford talk, Shirzad Chamine discusses how to <u>strengthen your positive intelligence brain through the mindfulness practice of shifting your focus to physical sensations for ten seconds a few times every hour.</u>
Practice: Take a moment to orient yourself to the present and fill in personal examples for each category below.

Practice Mindful Touch (contact, breath, heartbeat): I notice the contact between my feet and the floor, between my skin and my clothes, and between my body and the chair. <u>Add your own</u>:

Practice Mindful Sight (notice fine details, patterns, colors): I notice the colors of the trees, the texture of the brick, the glossy shine on the car, the patterns in the carpet, and the shapes of the clouds. <u>Add your own</u>:

Practice Mindful Sound (notice sounds around you): I notice the sound of my shoes on the floor, the car driving by, the sound of the wind through the leaves, and the different sounds of the birds. <u>Add your own</u>:

Practice Mindful Smell (breathe deeply): I notice the aromatherapy of fresh coffee, spring flowers, the smell of freshly cut grass, the smell of dinner cooking, and the smell of toothpaste. <u>Add your own</u>:

Practice Mindful Taste (slow, mindful eating): I focus on the temperature and taste of my hot tea, the temperature and taste of ice cream, and the salty crunch of potato chips or sour oranges. <u>Add your own</u>:

Chapter 27
Core Values and Goals

To become learned, each day add something.
To become enlightened, each day drop something.
~ *Lao Tzu*

Perhaps some detours aren't detours at all. Perhaps they are the path.
~ *Katherine Wolf*

The journey of a thousand miles begins with one step.
~ *Lao Tzu*

Your core values are the deeply held beliefs that
authentically describe your soul.
~ *John C. Maxwell*

The meaning of life is to find your gift.
The purpose of life is to give it away.
~ *Pablo Picasso*

❖   Connecting Values with Goals

❖   Road Maps

Video: MercyMe (2016): "Dear Younger Me." https://youtu.be/zoO0kyPRu3M (3:19)

1.) What message would you tell your younger self? _____

2.) Are you living by that message today? If not, what changes would you like to make?

3.) What does the message reveal about your core values?

Core Values

Pablo Picasso said, "The meaning of life is to find your gift. The purpose of life is to give it away." Your core values highlight your gifts and guide your behaviors. The pathway to your best self requires keeping your core values within focus. An indication that you've acted in a way that violates a core value is when you hear yourself justifying or denying, blaming others, minimizing, or feeling ashamed. What do you value most? **Practice** - Circle the values below that are most important to you. Then, list your top five in the spaces, and provide specific examples of how you live by each core value. *Example*: My core value is health: I exercise, skip fast food, and cook healthy meals daily. You may add values to the list.

Accountability	Creativity	Generosity	Leadership	Religion
Achievement	Decency	Growth	Love	Reputation
Adventure	Decisiveness	Happiness	Loyalty	Respect
Authenticity	Dignity	Harmony	Money	Responsibility
Challenges	Enlightenment	Health	Nurturing	Safety
Commitment	Environment	Honesty	Order	Service
Community	Excitement	Independence	Parenting	Stability
Compassion	Energy	Influence	Power	Strength
Competition	Fairness	Integrity	Pride	Truth
Consistency	Freedom	Kindness	Privacy	Wisdom
Country	Fun	Knowledge	Recognition	Work

1.	**1.**
2.	**2.**
3.	**3.**
4.	**4.**
5.	**5.**

Video: Positive Hit (2020). "Mel Robbins: The Five Second Rule." https://youtu.be/2n41e9su3fM (6:46)

Discussion: Robbins states, "We want to change, live a better life, create more for our families, and be happier. The desire is there, but how do you go from knowledge to action? There were moments all day long when I knew (knowledge) what I should do, and if I didn't move within five seconds, my brain would step in and talk me out of it. Every human being has about a five-second window in which you can move from an idea to action before your brain kicks into full gear and sabotages any behavior change. Remember that your brain is wired to stop you from doing anything uncomfortable, uncertain, or scary. What the rule does is something really remarkable. When you count backward: 5, 4, 3, 2, 1, what you're actually doing is interrupting what researchers call habit loops. Your habit has been interrupted, so you've interrupted self-doubt, you've interrupted snapping at your kids, you've interrupted the desire to grab a drink, and you've interrupted procrastination. By counting backward, you've done an action. It has awakened your prefrontal cortex, which is the part of the brain that is awake when you change behavior and learn."

Questions: How can you apply the five-second rule to achieve one of your personal goals? *Example 1*: I want to exercise more and plan to hit the gym on my way home. As I'm leaving work, I hear thoughts talking me into going straight home. Instead of listening to the excuses, I count backward as I drive straight to the gym. *Example 2*: I want to be more loving in my relationship. I think about expressing gratitude to my partner, but then I quickly hear thoughts like: "My partner never appreciates me, so why should I." Before I talk myself out of it, I count backward and express my love. Practice this week, and share a personal example of breaking an unhealthy habit or defeating stagnation by using the five-second rule:

Life Goals

With your core values in mind, list your top three life goals. This list can include your dreams about the future and any short-term goals. Try to set yourself up for success by creating goals that are achievable and within your control.

Example Problem Goal	Revised Goal
1. Find the perfect partner.	1. Find peace within myself.
2. Make my parents proud.	2. Love and respect myself.
3. Be admired by my peers.	3. Appreciate my strengths.
4. Pursue a high-paying career.	4. Pursue a career that I love.

Top Life Goals

1. _____

2. _____

3. _____

Road Leading to Our Goals

Imagine navigating through a tangled web of roads to reach your goal while avoiding wrong turns and detours. Sometimes you think you're heading in the right direction, but you find that you have taken an exit ramp and you're lost. <u>What road are you driving on, and where does it lead</u>? *Example*: My goal is to be a positive parent, and I think I am driving on the road called "Positive Parenting." How will I know if I'm driving in the right direction? To safely reach your goal, identify the road signs and exit ramps. **Practice** - <u>Read the example below and then create a road map using one of your personal goals.</u>

Road Map Leading to: Positive Parenting
Road Signs Along the Way
1. I read them a bedtime story each night, and I give them positive feedback each day.
2. We have family dinners, I ask them about their highs/lows, and I listen without judgment.
3. I play with them at the park, and I smile at them when they enter a room.
4. I comfort them when they're sad, and I show them compassion when they make a mistake.
5. I hug them and tell them I love them every morning and every night.
Wrong Way! Exit Ramps and Detours
1. When I assume they're being manipulative, and I mock them while they cry.
2. When I use the silent treatment as a punishment.
3. When I compare them to each other in order to shame them.
4. When I yell at them or negatively label them.
5. When I think, "They're so spoiled and ungrateful."

Road Map Leading to:_____

Road Signs Along the Way (current thoughts/behaviors steering me *toward* my goal):

1. _____
2. _____
3. _____
4. _____
5. _____

Wrong Way! Exit Ramps and Detours (thoughts/behaviors steering me *off* course):

1. _____
2. _____
3. _____
4. _____
5. _____

Chapter 28
Self-Compassion

The curious paradox is that when I accept myself
just as I am, then I can change.
~ *Carl Rogers*

You are the universe expressing itself as a human for a little while.
~ *Eckhart Tolle*

Once we accept our limits, we go beyond them.
~ *Albert Einstein*

Only when compassion is present will people allow themselves to see the truth.
~ *A.H. Almaas*

To know even one life has breathed easier because you
have lived. This is to have succeeded.
~ *Ralph Waldo Emerson*

If you want others to be happy, practice compassion.
If you want to be happy, practice compassion.
~ *Dalai Lama*

❖   Compassionate Curiosity

❖   Letter of Self-Compassion

Compassionate Curiosity

A.H. Almaas said, "<u>Only when compassion is present will people allow themselves to see the truth</u>." Research shows that compassion produces change, while shame leads to stagnation. Compassion is one of four thought patterns that lead to human happiness; compassion creates secure attachment within relationships, compassion is a critical component for trauma recovery, and compassion is the guiding light to finding your authentic self. The Dalai Lama said, "<u>If you want others to be happy, practice compassion. If you want to be happy, practice compassion.</u>" Compassion requires the courage to live without the protective shield of anger, judgment, and shame. Carl Rogers said, "<u>The curious paradox is when I accept myself just as I am, then I can change.</u>" Approach yourself with compassion as you uncover the pain beneath your defenses.

Video: TED Talk (2019). "Lori Gottlieb: How Changing Your Story Can Change Your Life." https://youtu.be/ O_MQr4lHm0c (16:25)

Discussion - Gottlieb states, "We are unreliable narrators of our own lives. We all walk around with stories, but what happens when the stories we tell ourselves are incomplete, misleading, or wrong? Instead of providing clarity, we remain stuck. If we can change our stories, we can change our lives." Gottlieb discusses how freedom requires responsibility, "If a fight breaks out in every bar you go to, the problem might be you. We complain that we want to change, but we are truly just waiting for others to change."

1.) <u>Think of a story you are telling yourself that might not serve you well</u>. Change begins by shifting to a broader perspective. Ask yourself what the story would look like from another person's point of view. Gottlieb encourages, "Shape your obituary while you're still alive." Albert Einstein said, "Once we accept our limits, we go beyond them." **Practice**: Identify a problem story and then edit it with reframes.

Example Problem Story: "I've been telling myself the 'I'm not good enough' story my whole life. It started with my parents, and then it became my own. This story has turned me into a people-pleaser because I try to make everyone happy, and when it doesn't work, I become bitter and resentful. My story: 'I do everything to make them happy, but no one cares.' This victim story has led to chronic anger."

Example Edited Story: "I'm not a people-pleaser; I am a giver. I choose to give because that's who I am and want to be. I don't seek appreciation because I provide myself with validation. If I come home early and no one seems to care, that's okay. I came home early because that is the parent I want to be. I appreciate, admire, and respect myself, so I don't need to receive validation from others. We don't need from others what we already have."

Your Problem Story - Share one of your problem stories:

_____

_____

_____

_____

Your Edited Story - Edit your problem story:

_____

_____

_____

_____

Video: Dr. Gabor Mate. "The Most Eye Opening Ten Minutes of Your Life." https://www.youtube.com/ (10:22)

Discussion: Dr. Mate states, "There is a deep lack of meaning in people's lives. The addictions can come along and provide a false, temporary, but momentary sense of meaning. If you get triggered, that's perfectly all right, but you might want to consider what a trigger actually is. Whenever you get triggered, someone pulls that trigger, perhaps, but who's the one carrying the ammunition? Who's the one with the explosive material inside? Triggers are really great to work with if you want to get to know yourself, and if you don't want to get to know yourself, then we usually just resent whoever did the triggering, and we think they did this to us. How you handle the trigger is your call, but know that you are the one with all the explosives inside you, and you'll gain so much liberation if you find out what that ammunition is, how you got it, and whether you can really diffuse it. You can actually diffuse that ammunition inside of you by getting to know yourself, and that's where freedom actually lies. The personality is a defensive structure we develop as a way of dealing with our pain."

Question: Remember a time when you've been triggered. What does your response tell you about yourself?

Video: Lewis Howes (2019). "The Seven Day Challenge/ Dr. Joe Dispenza and Lewis Howes." https://www.youtube.com/watch?v=EjVexvICSVk (4:46)

Discussion: Dr. Dispenza states, "**Number one**: Start your day with a simple question, 'What is the greatest ideal of myself that I can be today?' Do you complain, do you blame, do you make excuses? Do you feel sorry for yourself? That's a victim consciousness. What emotions do you live by? Become conscious of those states of the mind and say, 'This is the old self.' Then say, 'What thoughts do I want to fire and wire in the brain?' Rehearse the whole thing, and install the neurological hardware in your brain. And if you keep installing it, the hardware will become a software program, and you will start thinking and acting that way. **Number two**: Take some time at the end of your day and give thanks. About twelve hundred different chemical reactions go on in the body that restore and repair the body in a state of gratitude. **Number three**: Open your awareness to the space around you, and just sense it, pay attention to it, and become more aware of it. Opening your awareness reduces stress hormones and creates more coherent brain wave states."

1.) In one word, the *greatest ideal* of myself I can be is _____

2.) A *thought* I want to have is _____

3.) A *behavior* I want to demonstrate is _____

4.) The emotions I *usually* live by include _____

5.) The emotions I *want* to live by include _____

6.) Some of my character *strengths* include _____

7.) These *strengths* impact my relationships by _____

8.) Some of my character *defects/defenses* include _____

9.) These *defenses* impact my relationships by _____

Example Letter of Self-Compassion

You learned a pattern of destructive behaviors at an early age that helped you survive each day. You learned that lying to yourself and others lessened your fear, but it turned that fear into anger. The anger made you feel stronger than you actually were. The problem eventually became that those thoughts and feelings were all a form of self-deception, and they became an excuse for hurting others to protect yourself. What you were actually feeling was **fear** - fear of being judged, fear of being ridiculed, fear of being hurt, fear of not being good enough, and fear of being rejected. Over the years, you didn't know how to set boundaries, and you always felt like people were taking advantage of you, which led to resentment. This cycle of feeling victimized repeated, and you thought others were creating this problem the whole time. Learning that you are at the center of this problem is tough to face, but it's the greatest gift because you finally have the power to change it. You've realized that your unhealthy relationships with others stem from your unhealthy relationship with yourself.

You used the internal battle during childhood as motivation, but it festered in your subconscious. It wasn't until late high school that you knew something wasn't right, and that panic really started to set in. You didn't understand the anxiety and couldn't shake it off. You couldn't imagine something was wrong with you, so you lived with the anxiety for years. It wasn't until you couldn't sit in meetings for your high-pressure job that you started to self-medicate with alcohol. At first, alcohol was the only thing that allowed you to feel normal and enjoy a moment of peace. But eventually, the anxiety cure stopped working, and the problems from drinking started to outweigh the benefits. You couldn't manage it; the expectations were too high, and the demands on you too much. Eventually, it led to a series of incidents that landed you in this program.

I'm proud of you for having the courage to be vulnerable and face your demons. You've learned that thoughts do not define or harm you unless you give them power by believing them. You've learned to acknowledge them as thoughts and let them pass. You've learned to be an observer rather than a sponge, and the intrusive thoughts no longer stick to you. I am proud of you for not avoiding your past and dealing with your traumatic experiences directly, with acceptance. You are your problem, and you are also your solution. You've defeated the fear that prevented change. Anger needs an enemy, and you are not your own enemy. No one defines you but you. You no longer fear losing control because you've learned not to give your power away to others through blame. Fear comes from looking into the future, so you focus on what is in front of you now. You turn *what-if* into *what is*. We can't change every little thing that happens to us in life, but we can change how we experience it. All of the emotions you hid for decades burst from you and manifested in a rage. That anger forced the pain you'd stowed away deep within yourself to the surface. You became that which you'd always feared, and you created the same spark that set this anguish cycle in motion. It broke you to your core until nothing was left but the pain and anger you'd stowed. And finally, you confronted it. You felt it. You learned from it. For this, I thank you.

Goodbye, old me. Thank you for your mistakes because now I can look at myself with my head held high. Today, I am finally proud of who I am. I feel sad that you had to suffer through those painful years, but I would not be where I am today without that suffering. Surviving that pain changed you, and it was an opportunity to become better on so many levels. I know that I will make many mistakes to come, but the new me will never feel ashamed because you taught me to love myself with all of my imperfections. I've learned that no one is perfect, and the goal is not perfection. And so, I challenge you: Never hide yourself again. You are worthy of love without restrictions or concessions. Love yourself for the person you are. Continue to set this example for your children. I am proud of your newly acquired parenting skills. Parenting is one of the most challenging jobs; continue to give your children a safe place to learn and grow. Set your children up for success rather than failure. Some things may not be important to you, but they are important to them. They are worthy of your love.

Continue to love yourself for both your strengths and your weaknesses. Take this time to heal yourself and remember to apply the feelings *before* fix rule. Embrace the tools given to you over the past year, and use them to create a new story – a re-story. This is your gift. Embrace it. Awareness is your light and will continue to show you the way. You have finally found the love and validation you've been searching for your whole life. That love and validation are within you. You don't have to search anymore; it's already yours. This is only the beginning, and without a doubt, there will be hardships and obstacles ahead. But, you now have the tools you need to stay on the course leading to the healthy future you are choosing to have. Thank you from the bottom of my heart for bringing me back. Goodbye old me, and thank you for the new me. I will never forget what you've given me. I love you. Every day, I want you to do three things: Forgive yourself. Thank yourself. Be yourself...

Letter of Self-Compassion

Write a personal letter of self-compassion to share with the group on your graduation day. There is no right or wrong to this exercise, and it's best to give yourself plenty of time to develop it over weeks or even months. You can write a letter of empathy to a younger version of yourself, choose a time in your history when you've struggled with emotional pain, or highlight your progress toward personal growth. Take the view of your adult self, and turn toward your younger self with acceptance and compassion.

Letter of Self-Compassion

_____

_____

_____

_____

_____

_____

_____

_____

_____

_____

_____

_____

_____

_____

_____

_____

_____

_____

_____

_____

_____

_____

_____

_____

_____

Recommended Videos by Chapter

CHAPTER 1
- Success Archive (2019). "Dr. Joe Dispenza: How Your Thoughts Are Connected To Your Future." https://youtu.be/5reo3dXOicU
- TEDx (2012). "Shawn Achor: The Happy Secret to Better Work." https://youtu.be/fLJsdqxnZb0

CHAPTER 2
- TEDx (2018). "Chiara Lisowski: Survivor Domestic Abuse Speaks Up - I Left on a Tuesday." https://youtu.be/hWlN6Jf0WzQ
- TEDx (2020). "Andrew Pain: Domestic Abuse: Not a Gender Issue." https://youtu.be/9HgPICMQLls

CHAPTER 3
- Psych2go (2020). "14 Signs of Emotional Abuse in Relationships." https://youtu.be/rFHWnAn9ULk
- Danny Gibbons (2020). "Mark'd Award Winning Emotional Abuse Short Film." https://youtu.be/EavMqZ_6UvQ
- Made by Mortals (2023). "Eggshells: A Short Film About Domestic Abuse." https://youtu.be/YlHxhmOsrHo
- WPSU (2010). "Telling Amy's Story." https://youtu.be/TsFv4DiPKFg

CHAPTER 4
- Small Voice Films (2016). "Caged In - Award Winning Domestic Violence Short Film." https://youtu.be/iiF9ays47EI
- Psych2Go (2020). "6 Differences Between Healthy and Unhealthy Love." https://youtu.be/4c5dFcC4LNY
- TEDx (2018). "Katrina Blom: You Don't Find Happiness, You Create It." https://youtu.be/9DtcSCFwDdw

CHAPTER 5
- TEDx (2015). "Kolts: Anger, Compassion, and What It Means To Be Strong." https://youtu.be/QG4Z185MBJE.
- TED (2019). "Ryan Martin: Why We Get Mad and Why it's Healthy." https://youtu.be/0rAngiiXBAc

CHAPTER 6
- TEDx (2019). "Juna Mustad: Anger is Your Ally: A Mindful Approach to Anger." https://youtu.be/sbVBsrNnBy8
- TEDx (2019). "Lucy Hone: The Three Secrets of Resilient People." https://youtu.be/NWH8N-BvhAw

CHAPTER 7
- TED (2016). "Judson Brewer: A Simple Way to Break a Bad Habit." www.ted.com
- TEDx (2018). "Lauren Weinstein: Don't believe everything you think." https://youtu.be/Xdhmgp4IUL0
- TEDx (2019). "Peter Sage: How to be Your Best When Life Gives You It's Worst." https://youtu.be/I4svF7J6MWg

CHAPTER 8
- RSA (2015). "Brene Brown on Blame." https://youtu.be/RZWf2_2L2v8
- Fearless Soul (2018). "Joe Dispenza: Learn How to Control Your Mind." https://youtu.be/v7KQsS2kLM4
- TED (2016). "Isaac Lindsky: What Reality are You Creating for Yourself?" https://youtu.be/cmpu58yv8-g

CHAPTER 9
- TEDx (2013). "Shirzad Chamine: Know Your Inner Saboteurs." https://youtu.be/-zdJ1ubvoXs

CHAPTER 10
- Daniel Beaty (2010). "Knock, Knock on Def Jam Poetry." https://youtu.be/RTZrPVqR0D8
- TED (2018). "Azim Khamisa/Ples Felix: What Comes After Tragedy? Forgiveness." https://youtu.be/85hbMtegrLc
- TEDx (2019). "Matt Brown: The Barbershop Where Men Go to Heal." https://youtu.be/4UhP3OZ9ZCEw
- TEDx (2020). "Debi Silber: Do You Have Post Betrayal Syndrome?" https://youtu.be/iyqOR69dHiU

CHAPTER 11
- TEDx (2020). "Sue Bryce: Changing Perspective from Shame to Self-Worth" https://youtu.be/5_Tq5A0m7_U
- TED (2015). "Johann Hari: Everything You Think You Know about Addiction Is Wrong." https://youtu.be/PY9DcIMGxMs

CHAPTER 12
- TEDx (2015). "Amy Morin: The Secret of Becoming Mentally Strong." https://youtu.be/TFbv757kup4
- TEDx (2016). "Joan Rosenberg: Emotional Mastery: The Gifted Wisdom of Unpleasant Feelings." https://youtu.be/EKy19WzkPxE

CHAPTER 13
- TED (2013). "Kelly McGonigal: How to Make Stress Your Friend." https://youtu.be/RcGyVTAoXEU
- TED (2018). "Lisa Feldman Barrett: You Aren't at the Mercy of Your Emotions - Your Brain Creates Them." https://youtu.be/0gks6ceq4eQ

CHAPTER 14
- TED (2013). "Andy Poddicombe: All It Takes Is 10 Mindful Minutes." https://youtu.be/qzR62JJCMBQ.
- Headspace (2020)."Andy Puddicombe: Guided Meditation in Himalayan Forest." https://youtu.be/BR6yH4S1UMU
- Headspace (2012). "Andy Puddicombe: Guided 10-Minute Meditation." https://youtu.be/oVzTnS_IONU
- Brett Larkin Yoga (2020). "20-Minute Guided Meditation for Higher-Self (for beginners)." https://youtu.be/f4qUbICmhBk

Recommended Videos by Chapter

CHAPTER 15
- TEDx (2013). "Shaka Senghor: Writing My Wrongs." https://youtu.be/IV_uAL9ADBU
- TEDx (2018). "Jahan Kalantar: A Perfect Apology in Three Steps." https://youtu.be/Pwl5PExezeg

CHAPTER 16
- TEDx (2019). "Darryll Stinson: Overcoming Rejection, When People Hurt You and Life isn't Fair." https://youtu.be/8yBfAeadqiI
- TEDx (2017). "Billy Johnson: Rediscovering Hope Through Self-Forgiveness." https://youtu.be/voXQ5iBNlIk

CHAPTER 17
- California Department of Justice, Office of the Attorney General, Edmund G. Brown, Jr. (2008). "First Impressions…Exposure to Violence and A Child's Developing Brain." Iron Mountain Films, Inc. https://youtu.be/brVOYtNMmKk.
- Sprouts (2021). "UK Trauma Council: Childhood Trauma and the Brain." https://youtu.be/xYBUY1kZpf8
- Sprouts (2021). "Five Parenting Styles and Their Effects on Life." https://youtu.be/fyO8pvpnTdE

CHAPTER 18
- TEDx (2020). "Lael Stone: How to Raise Emotionally Intelligent Children." https://youtu.be/6fL09e8Tm9c
- Sprouts (2018). "Attachment Theory: How Childhood Affects Life." https://youtu.be/WjOowWxOXCg
- Dr. Gabor Mate. "How Not to Screw Up Your Kids." https://www.youtube.com/
- TED (2021). "Molly Wright: How Every Child Can Thrive by Five." https://youtu.be/aISXCw0Pi94
- TEDx (2020). "Shaka Senghor and Ebony Roberts: Co-Parenting as Allies, Not Adversaries." https://youtu.be/nRFA1C9spko

CHAPTER 19
- TEDx (2020). "Frederik Imbo: How Not to Take Things Personally?" https://youtu.be/LnJwH_PZXnM

CHAPTER 20
- TED (2016). "Celeste Headlee: 10 Ways to Have a Better Conversation." https://youtu.be/R1vskiVDwl4.
- Academy of Social Competency (2018). "Communication Skills: Empathic Listening - Inside Out 2015." https://youtu.be/t685WM5R6aM

CHAPTER 21
- TED (2019). "Katie Hood: The Difference Between Healthy and Unhealthy Love." https://youtu.be/ON4iy8hq2hM
- Prince Ea (2015). "Love Yourself Before You Get into a Relationship. Please." https://youtu.be/ip_FehKz5LE.

CHAPTER 22
- The Gottman Institute (2014). "Four Horsemen of the Apocalypse." https://youtu.be/1o30Ps-_8is
- The Gottman Institute (2018). "The Easiest Way to Improve Your Relationship." https://youtu.be/ib7Ain2aVR0
- The School of Life (2017). "Why You Will Marry the Wrong Person." https://youtu.be/-EvvPZFdjyk

CHAPTER 23
- Psych2Go (2018). "The Four Attachment Styles of Love." https://youtu.be/23ePqRkOKtg
- TEDx (2022). "Ashley Harvey: Put on Your Attachment Hat and Change Your Romantic Attachment Style." https://youtu.be/jHpdf4ekrXM
- School of Life (2018). "What is Your Attachment Style?" https://youtu.be/2s9ACDMcpjA
- The Gottman Institute (2018). "Invest in Your Relationship/The Emotional Bank Account." https://youtu.be/QHN2EKd9tuE
- Psych2Go (2020). "Five Ways to Work with Your Partner's Love Language." https://youtu.be/heww-ZuAs_c
- TEDx (2019). "Maya Diamond: The Surprising Key to Building a Healthy Relationship that Lasts." https://youtu.be/Xvb-v83qJ8U

CHAPTER 24
- TED (2015). "Robert Waldinger: What Makes a Good Life? Lessons from the Longest Study on Happiness." www.ted.com
- RSA (2013). "Brene Brown on Empathy." https://youtu.be/1Evwgu369Jw
- Jason Headley (2013). "It's Not About the Nail." https://youtu.be/-4EDhdAHrOg

CHAPTER 25
- Goalcast (2018). "Terry Crews I Wanted to Save My Mother." https://youtu.be/L79t3fPHvlI

CHAPTER 26
- TED (2017). "Emily Esfahani Smith: There's more to life than being happy." https://youtu.be/y9Trdafp83U
- TEDx (2021). "Molly Countermine: Life isn't Supposed to be Good… All the Time." https://youtu.be/5oy9LWrRPIo

CHAPTER 27
- MercyMe (2016): "Dear Younger Me." https://youtu.be/zoO0kyPRu3M
- Positive Hit (2020). "Mel Robbins: The Five Second Rule." https://youtu.be/2n41e9su3fM

CHAPTER 28
- TED (2019). "Lori Gottlieb: How Changing Your Story Can Change Your Life." https://youtu.be/O_MQr4lHm0c
- Dr. Gabor Mate. "The Most Eye Opening Ten Minutes of Your Life." https://www.youtube.com/
- Lewis Howes (2019). "The Seven Day Challenge/ Dr. Joe Dispenza, Lewis Howes." https://www.youtube.com/watch?v=EjVexvICSVk

References

Amen, D. (2015). *Change Your Brain Change Your Life.* New York: Random House, LLC.

Brach, T. (2003). *Radical Acceptance.* New York: Random House, Inc.

Bradberry, T. (2015). "Are You Emotionally Intelligent? Here's How to Know For Sure." June 2 www.forbes.com.

Bradberry, T., & Greaves (2009). *Emotional Intelligence 2.0.* San Diego: TalentSmart.

Brown, B. (2012). *Daring Greatly: How the Courage to Be Vulnerable Transforms the Way We Live, Love, Parent, and Lead.* NY: Gotham.

Casarjian, R. (1995). *Houses of Healing: A Prisoner's Guide to Inner Power and Freedom.* Boston, MA: Lionheart Foundation.

Chapman, G. (1992). *The Five Love Languages.* Illinois: Northfield Publishing.

Childhood Domestic Violence Association (2014). "10 Startling Facts about Children of Domestic Violence." February 21. www.cdv.org.

Coleman, D. (2006). *Emotional Intelligence.* New York: Bantam Dell.

DeGue, S., & D. Delillo (2009). "Is animal cruelty a "red flag" for family violence? Investigating co-occurring violence toward children, partners, and pets." *Journal of Interpersonal Violence.* June.

Eifert, G., M. McKay, & J. Forsyth (2006). *Act on Life Not on Anger.* Oakland, CA: New Harbinger.

Fall, K., & S. Howard (2012). *Alternatives to Domestic Violence.* New York: Routledge.

Faver, C. A., & E. B. Strand (2003). "Domestic violence and animal cruelty: Untangling the web of abuse." *Journal of Social Work Education.* Vol. 39, No. 2, pp. 237-253.

Flynn, C.P. (1999). "Animal abuse in childhood and later support for interpersonal violence in families." Society and Animals. *Journal of Social Work Education.* Vol. 7, Issue 2, pp. 161-172.

Gottman, J. (1999). *The Marriage Clinic: A Scientifically Based Marital Therapy.* New York: W.W. Norton & Company, Inc.

Gottman, J. (1994). *Why Marriages Succeed or Fail.* New York: Simon & Schuster Paperback.

Gottman, J., & N. Silver (1999). *The Seven Principles for Making A Marriage Work.* London: Orion Books, Ltd.

Greenberger, D., & C. Padesky (2015). *Mind Over Mood.* New York: Guilford Publications, Inc.

Herman, J. (1997). *Trauma and Recovery.* New York: Basic Books.

Hovel, H. (2015). "The Connection Between Animal Abuse and Human Violence." New York State Humane Association. www.nyshumane.org.

Humane Society of the United States. "Animal Cruelty and Human Violence." www.humanesociety.org.

Johnson, S. (2008). *Hold Me Tight.* New York: Machete Book Group.

Katz, J. (2006). *The Macho Paradox: Why Some Men Hurt Women and How All Men Can Help.* Naperville, IL: Sourcebooks, Inc.

Lucas, M. (2012). *Rewire Your Brain for Love.* United States: Hay House, Inc.

National Domestic Violence Hotline. "Statistics." www.thehotline.org.

National Center for Victims of Crime (2005). "Lethality Risk Assessment." www.marincourt.org.

National Network to End Domestic Violence (2015). "What Is Financial Abuse and How Can We Help Victims?" www.nnedv.org.

McKay, M. & P. Rogers (2000). *The Anger Control Workbook.* Oakland, CA: New Harbinger Publications, Inc.

Perry, B. & M. Szalavitz (2006). *The Boy Who Was Raised As a Dog.* New York: Basic Books.

Siegel, R. (2010). *The Mindfulness Solution.* New York: Guilford Publications, Inc.

Sonkin, D., & M. Durphy (1997). *Learning to Live without Violence, A Handbook for Men.* Volcano, CA: Volcano Press.

Taylor, C. A., J. A. Manganello, S. J. Lee, & J. C. Rice (2010). "Mothers' Spanking of 3-Year-Old Children and Subsequent Risk of Children's Aggressive Behavior. *Pediatrics,* April.

References

US Department of Health and Human Services, Administration on Children, Youth, and Families (2013). "Child Maltreatment 2012." Washington, DC: US Government Printing Office.

US Department of Justice, Bureau of Justice Statistics (2015). "Intimate Partner Violence in the United States." November. www.bjs.gov.

US National Library of Medicine, National Institute of Health. "Health Services Research Information Central, Projects on Domestic Violence Issues." www.nim.nih.gov.

van der Kolk, B. (2015). *The Body Keeps the Score.* New York, NY: Penguin Random House, LLC.

Walker, L. (1979). *The Battered Woman.* New York: Harper and Row.

Wexler, D. (2013). *Stop Domestic Violence Program.* New York: W. W. Norton & Company, Inc.

Made in United States
Orlando, FL
14 June 2024

47717021R00111